The Art of
NATURAL BONSAI

Replicating Nature's Beauty

Dave Joyce

Sterling Publishing Co., Inc.
New York

To my dear wife, Anthea, and to our wonderful children, Mark, Craig, and Sharon,
for their love, strength, support, and inspiration, which helped me complete this book.

All royalties from the publication of this book are being donated by Anthea M. Joyce
to Cancer Research UK, registered charity number 1089464.

Library of Congress Cataloging-in-Publication Data

Joyce, David.
    The art of natural bonsai : replicating nature's beauty / Dave Joyce.
        p. cm.
    Includes index.
    ISBN 1-4027-0055-5
    1. Bonsai. I. Title.
SB433.5.J69 2003
635.9'772—dc21
                                                                    2003000851

2 4 6 8 10 9 7 5 3 1

Published by Sterling Publishing Co., Inc.
387 Park Avenue South, New York, NY 10016
© 2003 by Anthea M. Joyce
Distributed in Canada by Sterling Publishing
c/o Canadian Manda Group, One Atlantic Avenue, Suite 105
Toronto, Ontario, Canada M6K 3E7
Distributed in Great Britain by Chrysalis Books
64 Brewery Road, London N7 9NT, England
Distributed in Australia by Capricorn Link (Australia) Pty. Ltd.
P.O. Box 704, Windsor, NSW 2756, Australia

Printed in China
All rights reserved

Sterling ISBN 1-4027-0055-5

ACKNOWLEDGMENTS

❖ Dan Barton, for his wonderful bonsai encouragement, mentoring, and friendship over many joyful years. ❖ All my Classical Bonsai Circle friends, for so many "happy days" and learning experiences. ❖ Peter Adams, for his generous help and advice, especially in those early pioneering years. ❖ Gill Taylor-Duxbury, Liz Hughes, Robin Benyon, Roger Spragg, and all my other expert friends who belong to the Funkai group. ❖ John Buck, Dave Claridge, and Ron Haywood, the quiet men of bonsai, whose depth of knowledge and dry humor are beyond price. ❖ All my Midland Bonsai Society friends. ❖ Jim Steer and Frank Benson, two of the most generous bonsai buddies you will meet. ❖ Aunt Eileen Dixon, for our shared love of bonsai. ❖ Roy and Beryl Taylor, for our shared love of trees. ❖ All the audiences I have given talks and workshops to and from whom I have learned so much. ❖ David Coop, p.b.i. Home & Gardens, for his wealth of technical knowledge of pests and diseases and his enthusiasm and willingness to share it. ❖ British Agrochemical Association, for their Directory of Garden Chemicals. ❖ Kew Gardens, London; Royal Horticultural Society, Wisley; and Forestry Commission for their advice over the years. ❖ Pots by Bryan Albright, Derek Aspenall, Ian Baille, Dan Barton, Gordon Duffet, Dave Jones, and Eastern Origin.

Contents

Wisteria in bloom.

Preface

In the spring of 1996 and again in 1999, I was pleased to be invited to provide a demonstration as part of the "Joy of Bonsai" event in Bath. Among other reasons, I was pleased because the event is an expression of all that bonsai means to me. I loved working on bonsai trees with kindred spirits, exhibiting trees displaying the highest standards, and encouraging and educating visitors. Most of all, I enjoyed meeting and having fun with fellow bonsai addicts at an event that celebrates the art of bonsai.

Everyone has a different reason for growing bonsai. For me, it is a way of channeling a love of trees and of trying to make images of nature, using creativity which I have no other way of satisfying (with the possible exception of photography). All bonsai enthusiasts have one common factor. In each of us there is an inner energy and excitement that drives us to ask innumerable questions and grow innumerable bonsai trees. That spark is the "Joy of Bonsai."

In this book, I hope to share some of my joy of bonsai over the last thirty or more years. The spark has always remained. At the times when it was lowest, the friendship, encouragement, and inspiration of kindred spirits have ensured its survival. If this book helps rekindle your spark or inspire you, I am delighted.

All bonsai trees and photographs in this book are the author's unless otherwise credited.

Dave Joyce

On June 21, 1999, I took a phone call from the surgeon who had just operated on Dave, and my whole world changed. I was told that my husband had colon cancer and only months to live, at best a year.

Just twelve months earlier we had semi-retired and moved to the country, so Dave would have the time to write his bonsai book. Lying in his hospital bed, Dave announced that he would now be unable to write it. I remember standing at the bedside as my eyes opened wide in horror and my jaw dropped open in despair.

Dave wanted to commission someone else to write the book, someone who would draw on his over thirty years of hands-on experience, knowledge, extensive notes, photographs, and slides. I had to accept the fact that my husband was extremely ill, but I couldn't accept that he wouldn't fulfil his ambition to write this book. As I told the surgeon on that awful Monday, on the longest day of 1999, Dave had too much to live for to give in easily.

Over the following weeks as Dave gained strength after the operation, treatment and care was put into action by a wonderful team of dedicated people. I convinced Dave it was time he started on his book—a book only he had the knowledge to put together. Debilitating chemotherapy meant that for at least three days in fourteen he could do little but rest and, increasingly, sleep away.

Earlier, Dave had set up a consultancy business that he enjoyed enormously, keeping in contact with work colleagues, none of whom knew how ill he was. Because the business still had work, sometimes weeks would elapse when no work at all was done on the book. Other times, we were up till the early hours, writing, sorting slides, and organizing the bonsai book. Slowly, it took shape.

The last chapter was finally written around May 2000, but then came the refinements. Day after day, chapters were rearranged, and photos added. This wonderful man knew so much about so many things. By this time, Dave was unable to eat many of the foods he loved, and one of his passions in life, as all who knew him well knew, was eating. At 6' 5½" (1m 98cm), there was a lot to keep fed.

Toward the end of April, the surgeon informed us of the full extent of the cancer's metastasis. By then, the side effects of the treatment were also unbearable. In July, I begged Dave to finish the book. I breathed a sigh of relief and with much pleasure, put a sample chapter in the mail. All the encouragement and help from the family, almost bullying from me at times, had been worth it.

Dave was given enough time and strength at the end of his life to go on a wonderful pilgrimage to the Holy Land, to see our son Craig married, to see his new granddaughter Hannah for three weeks, and to write his book. He died on September 6, 2000, our 33rd wedding anniversary.

All royalties from this book will be donated to colon cancer research.

Anthea Joyce

Introduction

Scotch pine—Mother and daughter 28 years from seed (1997).

We live in a very "instant" society where quick fixes, instant meals, on-line shopping, and even the opportunity to be an instant millionaire surround us every day. Our working patterns are increasingly influenced by change and by giant issues such as the global economy, worldwide travel, telecommunications, international computer networks, and the like, leading to a faster and faster pace of life.

I hope this book helps you to call "time out" now and again to leave your fax machine, cell phone, and e-mail account behind and to escape the daily pressures we all face and be at one with nature. I'd like to help you develop your own long-term goals for your trees so you don't need to delegate this work to an expert. Your trees deserve more than an instant makeover and so do you. How satisfying it is to say, "I did that!"

I was first introduced to bonsai in 1969, thanks to a picture of a bonsai I saw in a book that was a birthday present from my dear wife. Information was hard to obtain at that time. Most of it came from pictures in one or two books that had been translated into English from Japanese. At that time, my only bonsai images were two-dimensional black-and-white pictures. My early trees were acceptable from the front, but they had no depth at all. They looked just like a flat lollipop: you turned them sideways, and they disappeared. Luckily, regional bonsai clubs started emerging in the 1970s, and my local club was formed in 1975.

The value of seeing real bonsai trees in three dimensions and of meeting other enthusiasts was a tremendous boost. The rest, as they say, is history. There was a special value, however, in trying to unravel the mysteries of bonsai growing at a time when everyone was on a learning curve and information was scarce. Taking notes was essential, and you became aware of conflicting advice and of "folklore," which had little factual basis but which had to be right because someone else had written it or said it.

I have written this book from my experiences and beliefs. I have tried to avoid repeating bonsai "folklore." The Cultivation, Care, and Winter

Protection information in Appendix I summarizes my thirty years of experience in growing and in research in Birmingham, England. However, you cannot grow bonsai by looking up the answers to all your questions in a list. Every tree is different. Generalities are very useful, but pay attention to each tree. It will let you know how it is feeling by its leaf color, texture, size, and angle; by the soil moisture, color, and smell; by the bud size and color; and by the new-shoot length, color, and thickness.

The "Overviews" give detailed information on the preferences of specific species and subspecies. They usually start with a description of the requirements of trees in their natural habitat, followed by the more specific, sometimes differing needs of the tree when grown as a bonsai.

You'll find it invigorating and illuminating to examine your trees frequently. I encourage you to take notes and photographs whenever possible and to understand your own microclimate. Be careful when reading references to the climate because what works in Birmingham, England, may not, for example, translate to Birmingham, Alabama, or to Birmingham, Michigan.

Please be sure that you follow all the necessary legal, health, and safety regulations when practicing the art of bonsai, including the safe storage, use, and disposal of tools and materials. Many hazardous chemicals are used. You must understand their usage, applicability, and disposal and you must be aware of local bans or restrictions. Careful, correct use of hand tools and power tools and the use of appropriate protective clothing are also essential.

The details in this book are correct to the best of my knowledge, but you should test the use of new chemicals, techniques, etc. carefully on a small area or a young tree before launching into your specimen bonsai. Remember, each tree behaves as an individual and, if handled carefully, will give decades of joy.

Acer palmatum—windswept style from cutting.

1

Natural Bonsai—
Definition & Goals

1–1 • Early days of a classic broom-style *Zelkova serrata* (spring 1993).

1–2 • These are three tiny toadstools under the bough of a common hawthorn bonsai.

THE TREE/BONSAI LINE

If the line between trees growing in nature and bonsai becomes blurred at times as you look at pictures in this book or if you enter a mysterious twilight zone between the two for a moment, then I have succeeded in one of my goals. Bonsai creates the illusion of a fully grown tree in a small container. You'll want to help the viewer of your bonsai cross that line.

NATURAL BONSAI

Before you start to create a bonsai, you will need a goal, an image you want to create. This may be a tree you have seen in nature or in a photograph; it may be a bonsai you particularly admired; it could be an idea generated by looking at a potential bonsai tree; or it may have come in a moment of inspiration.

At times, you are faced with a potential bonsai, and the decision-making process and options may seem complex and endless. I believe that until you can see a final design in your mind, you should not start on this tree. Instead, put it aside until you get that spark. I would like to offer a definition of natural bonsai design. I hope you will use it when considering options:

A natural bonsai has no obvious man-made elements to jar the design, such as an ugly, chopped trunk, branches, or stumps and no wire marks or sudden big changes in taper, texture, or refinement. The trunk and major branches in particular will have a pleasing taper and shape. It does not have long, straight, uninteresting branches or trunk. Rather, it has interesting curves or direction changes. It does not possess unconvincing areas of dead wood or overly large leaves or flowers. It is three dimensional, containing many areas of interest and viewing angles. Its treelike shape is pleasing, evoking images of trees in nature and allowing you to cross that tree/bonsai line.

Large, informal upright *Cotoneaster
horizontalis* (spring 1995).

A natural bonsai design may take a long time to grow because of the need to heal scars, grow a trunk and branches, or reduce branch length. However, some of the finest tree images in nature take centuries of weathering. Develop your trees on your own time scale, whether it is five, ten, twenty, or thirty years. Before you begin the process, do not forget to take photographs or you will regret it.

I have little time or interest in creating an "instant bonsai" in which a garden-center juniper is transformed into a finished bonsai in an hour or two. Another recent fashion is "logs in pots." In this instance, one searches for a trunk with a large diameter and is prepared to sacrifice all hope of a taper for the log. Although it is fashionable to believe that "size matters," in the case of bonsai, "art matters" is a better maxim.

A natural bonsai most certainly does not mean that you select a seedling or a potential bonsai and simply leave it to its own devices. The principle of laissez-faire has no place in natural bonsai. In fact, natural bonsai requires the application of all conventional bonsai growing and training techniques, such as wiring, pruning, leaf removal, and repotting; but it also involves additional development stages, requiring greater time, effort, and planning to achieve a long-term goal.

STYLIZED VS. NATURAL BONSAI

The *Cotoneaster horizontalis* illustrated here was grown from seed 28 years ago. When the seedling was about 4 inches (30 cm) long and less than ¼ inch (0.5 cm) in diameter, it was wound around a ⅝-inch (1.5 cm) garden cane in a loose spiral so that the trunk would take on the form you now see. The branches are rhythmically arranged in a rather contrived manner, giving the illusion of a pleasing, but unnatural design. I refer to this as stylized bonsai in the same manner that the pompon-styled bonsai shown (**1–3**) inside the Grand Palace grounds in Bangkok is stylized: the effects of the human hand are quite clear.

1–3 • A display on a terrace at the Royal Grand Palace in Bangkok, Thailand.

Case History

Cotoneaster *horizontalis* from Seed

1–4 • This is a summer image of a *Cotoneaster horizontalis* taken when the tree was eleven years old. The heavy branch pads are helping to thicken the trunk, but they are making the side branches too thick (1982).

1–5 • Here, the branches have been shortened and brought back into control because the trunk is thicker (late May 1990).

1–6 • How about another pad here (April 1993)?

1–7 • The new shoots are being trained (early April 1995).

1–8 • The latest image is 28 years from seed and still developing (July 1999).

Case History

Scotch Pine—Attempted *Horai* Style

Another highly stylized shape is the horai style. The horai is a grafted, neat, glaucous form of white pine (Shimofuri) trained around mulberry sticks over a period of five or six years until its shape is contorted. The first year involves the "trunk wrench," in which 8 inches (20 cm) of the black or red pine below the graft union is curved four or five times around mulberry sticks planted at odd angles in the ground and then tied with straw. In my attempt in June 1973, I used a 4-year-old ungrafted Scotch pine seedling in a pot. However, I failed to give the lower trunk any serious bending. I tried to make a better job of following the horai branching and the style of the upper trunk. The end result, 26 years later, is shown

below. Of course, this is not a horai, but it is certainly a stylized form, although the complex winding branch detail restores a small amount of natural feel to the final image.

An example of a natural bonsai style is this blue cedar (*Cedrus atlantica glauca*). Here **(1–10)**, it is 16 years old, seven years from the restyle of a 9-year-old garden-center tree (see case history in Chapter 6). A further example is the 27-year-old *Acer palmatum* **(1–11)** raised from a 4-year-old seedling (see case history in Chapter 9). Perhaps the best example is this 51-year-old common hawthorn **(1–13** and **1–14)**, a wildling owned for 23 years and nibbled on by sheep for the other 28 years (see case history in Chapter 12).

1–9 • This shows additional upper-trunk bending, but the shape of the tree is still crude (April 1988).

1–10 • The latest image (July 1999).

1–12 • This 27-year-old *Acer palmatum* was raised and trained from a 4-year-old seedling.

1–11 • I purchased this blue cedar as a 9-year-old garden-center tree. It was 6½ feet (2 m) tall. It has now been in training for seven years.

1–13 • The shade under the bough of this old hawthorn tree is inviting, but it's only 9½ inches (24 cm) high.

1–14 • A common hawthorn against a glorious Herefordshire sunset.

BEGINNING A BONSAI COLLECTION

Finding a perfectly formed wildling bonsai and being granted permission to dig or being given the best bonsai in the world ready-made would be wonderful experiences. But starting with a seed or a twig that my hands have formed into a beautiful bonsai over time gives me much greater pleasure and satisfaction. That is why less than 5 percent of my bonsai have been purchased as specimens, whereas 25 percent are garden-center stock, 60 percent started as seeds, seedlings, or cuttings, and the remaining 10 percent were wildlings.

Newcomers to bonsai may find the need to have some mature bonsai, those that look acceptably finished, in order to avoid the feeling that nothing is happening. By purchasing one or two mature bonsai or by owning some trees that have good bonsai potential, you can keep a good cross section of development in your collection while your seedlings and cuttings are growing.

TIME LINES

Do not be put off by the age of some of my trees (for example, thirty years from seed). Once fattened up, most of them have been transformed from potential bonsai to exhibition standard in five to ten years, as shown in the case histories. Remember that when I started bonsai, there was less understanding about the use of growing beds, and certainly there were no nurseries supplying grown-on bonsai as there are today. Some of my seedlings languished in small pots for several years until I saw the light.

In general, a seed, seedling, or cutting grown as discussed in Chapter 2 should reach a fattened-up size in five to ten years. This would make it suitable for transforming into an exhibition standard bonsai in the following five to ten years. Therefore, you can produce exhibition quality trees from seed or cuttings in a total of ten to twenty years. You can reduce this to five to ten years if you use a garden center, growing bed, or wildling stock.

SETTING YOUR OWN GOALS AND AGENDA

Listening to the ideas of others can be very helpful when deciding the future designs for your potential bonsai. On the other hand, do not be persuaded to develop an inferior design just because its choice permits an acceptable image today. Be prepared to use your artistic feel and ideas to develop the longer-term option. Please reread the definition of natural bonsai and see whether you can choose a natural design for the future.

My notebooks are peppered with such design drawings. Some of these do not materialize, but most of them do. Remember that it is very hard to keep an image in your head; once you have made note of it, it is safe. I can hear you saying, "but I can't draw." You are not alone. I have found drawing much simpler using the following technique.

I draw one "before" image and one or more proposed images. I begin by taking a photograph and making a slide of the potential bonsai from the expected front. This allows me to project the slide onto paper and draw around the silhouette of the main trunk, branches, and foliage masses to create a "before" image in perfect proportion. I copy this image of the tree to use as a base for redrawing proposed ideas. I always make several copies to play with. If you are like me, the first attempt may not be very good. Chapter 3 includes ideas on developing this "future" image, especially the List the Negatives section.

If you are computer literate, you can transfer your image to the computer (by film, scanner, or from a digital camera) and use a computer program to design future images with various cloning tools and the like.

Once you have drawn your image for this tree to scale, the rest is easy. All you need is patience; you have done the hardest bit. Having said that, I admit that I struggled for years, looking at my trees and not getting any inspiration or ideas on what to do next, yet alone what final image I wanted. Take heart. By taking charge and developing your own trees, this skill will come one day, almost like magic, and the design principles will crystalize. Chapter 3 will help you develop your design principles. Although you'll find my approach there, you should be a free spirit, not a clone. In this chapter, I explain all the factors that I now take into account when I look at a potential bonsai. You need to remember that I developed this strategy mainly as a result of my "hands-on" experiences. So remember, develop your trees so that you will acquire your own skills; don't delegate the job to others.

NOTEBOOKS, PHOTOGRAPHS, AND DATABASES

If your memory is as bad as mine, I strongly suggest that you make diary notes about your bonsai experiences. You'll want to include information such as what went right and wrong with your trees, when and how you planted seeds, when the seeds germinated, when and how you took cuttings, grafts, etc. You should also record when you bought a potential bonsai at a garden center or when you collected a wildling, how old it was, how much root it had, and how you treated it initially. Tips from bonsai friends, talks, or sudden observations you have about how well or how poorly your trees behaved are invaluable. For example, you'll want to remember how it responded to feeding, to shade, to pruning, etc.

I confess to keeping a computer database in which each of my bonsai has a unique number, and each of my slides has the same. I use plant labels to number my bonsai, and I use easily obtained self-adhesive numbered labels on my slides. By entering a line of essential historic information on your spreadsheet for each bonsai and each slide, you can easily build a comprehensive database.

When I give bonsai talks, I browse through my slides and select the appropriate slide numbers (for example, for junipers). My spreadsheet will then merge the historic data for each slide number. This will include the slide date, place, and description; also included will be the bonsai tree number, if appropriate, plus the bonsai type, description, age, origin, when started, and when acquired. The result will be a fully detailed juniper slide sequence to which I can add narrative sections to make a complete set of notes for the talk.

With close to 6,000 slides and more than 160 bonsai, it is a joy to use computers to keep a controlled catalog and to have the ability to merge information without duplication. A quick check tells me I have used more than 3,600 slides in over 100 club lectures in the last ten years. Believe me, having a printout in your pocket detailing dates, records, etc., is a great support when someone asks questions like, "How old is that tree?" or "When did you first style it?" If the idea of computers frightens you, at least use notebooks to record your information.

2

General Cultivation, Care & Development

INTRODUCTION

Growing healthy bonsai is not that difficult. However, the amount of conflicting advice given on such fundamental topics as soils, watering, repotting, feeding, and overwintering can intimidate the beginner.

Even for the experienced grower, separating cause and effect between many variables is a complex task. For example, a tree is sick. What is the cause? Is it the soil, the watering, the container, last winter's cold, or is it diseased? Use your notes. Eventually you'll also be able to use your years of bonsai-growing experience to help you. I hope this chapter will allow you to eliminate some mistakes, making it easier to spot why something may be wrong with your trees and how to correct the problem.

The following sections avoid many of the fundamentals. You can find information on pot shapes, colors, wiring techniques, etc. in myriad bonsai books. Instead, I've emphasized areas of special importance in bonsai welfare, presentation, and development. This book covers only outdoor bonsai. These are trees for the temperate zone, capable of surviving without artificially boosted winter temperatures. For details on growing indoor bonsai (typically tropical, subtropical, or Mediterranean trees), please consult other speciality literature.

In addition to this chapter you can find extra information, specific to each species and subspecies, in the Overviews and in the Appendix 1 summary.

2–1 ● Cloud drenched grass at Pico Arieiro, 5,900 feet (1800 m) above sea level, Madeira.

CONTAINERS

In general, bonsai containers must have at least one drainage hole in order to avoid waterlogging and, consequently, a lack of soil aeration. The larger or deeper the pot, the more drainage it will require. The inside of the pot should be unglazed below the soil level. This allows the roots to get a good grip against the textured inner clay wall and pot base.

Trident maple on rock in latter stages of training and development. It is seen here in the author's hand-cast ceramic pot after the new growth has been scissor-pruned and the new shoots have been wired.

While early books stressed the importance of using porous, earthenware bonsai pots for added drainage and grip, the reality is that unless the earthenware container is fired to the point where the clay body starts to vitrify and becomes nonporous, it will not withstand winter freeze and thaw conditions for long. Most of my ceramic pots are either stoneware (and hence fully vitrified) or highly vitrified earthenware. With the appropriate drainage holes and soil mix, these are fine.

While many pots are made of stoneware clay, I make many of my own from a combination of earthenware and stoneware clay **(2–4)**. This particular clay has no grog and is very smooth. I normally fire it toward the top of its range, but I have one pot that I didn't fire that high. As you can see from the picture, it has developed beautiful, natural lichen over the past ten years.

2–2 ● European larch in a divided pot.

This is not typical of most ceramic pots. Although not fully vitrified, this pot must have enough freeze/thaw resistance because it has been standing outside all winter for ten years. One year it was exposed to –10°F (–23°C).

Glazes vitrify the pot. However, if you are a hobby potter, why not experiment with unglazed pots, such as the lichen-covered example, using wide-firing earthenware or stoneware clay fired to the middle of the vitrification range? Can any glaze be more beautiful than a natural lichen layer? Testing over a few hard winters will confirm the body strength of the pot.

Containers should be in harmony with the bonsai tree. I like to match aspects of the pot such as glaze, clay body color, or oxided areas with the bonsai. I may be trying to match the bark, a bud, the leaf or flower color, spring or autumn hues, or winter twig or bud tones. This is a matter of personal taste, but ideally, the container should blend with the bonsai tree. Natural features such as clay texture, changes in glaze depth, imperfections in glaze or body surface, and color or tone variations may enhance the container. On the other hand, the pot should not dominate the bonsai; if carefully selected, it will augment the final image. If you make your own pots,

2–3 ● A divided pot with a pooled glaze to represent water.

2–4 ● The semi-vitrified (slightly porous) ceramic body provides a home for lichen, nature's own glaze.

matching clay, glazes, and pot shapes to specific bonsai produces countless hours of fun. I particularly like to match the shape of the bottom glaze edge line where it meets the oxided body to the underbranch lines of the tree.

You'll need to be very careful about selecting a pot with sufficient soil volume. A degree of compensation is possible with soil composition, and you may be able to find a shadier part of your garden or to stand the pot in shallow water and a gravel basin. However, I have found that under my once-a-day watering regime (adopted mainly due to work constraints), all trees will stop growing due to heat stress during hot summer days if the soil volume is inadequate. This is particularly true of beech, *Chamaecyparis pisifera* 'Boulevard', hawthorn, larch, and linden

(lime); it is also true of alder, azalea, apple, crab apple, *Cryptomeria,* European hornbeam, swamp cypress, willow, wisteria, and *Zelkova*. In severe cases this heat stress can progress to signs of leaf wilt. Even mild leaf drying is irreversible for linden (lime), wisteria, and *Zelkova*. They sulk for the rest of that season and, in the worst case, lose lower or shaded branchlets or branches. During the winter, larger soil volumes have the added benefit of cushioning the temperature fluctuations; the downside is that it takes longer for the soil to dry out. Using the soil mixes and winter protection I've recommended in this book, you should be able to avoid any of these problems.

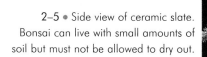

2–5 ● Side view of ceramic slate. Bonsai can live with small amounts of soil but must not be allowed to dry out.

2–6 ● Hand-textured ceramic slate with built-up edges to assist in providing a greater soil volume.

2–7 ● A concrete hand-textured finish improves the surface appearance.

2–8 ● The primitive style gives a natural look to this group and assists in retaining adequate soil moisture.

2–9 ● A close-up of the trunk.

2–10 ● The underlying handmade texture and the rich, multiple-oxide layers produce a lovely natural surface.

2–11 ● An example of a hand-cast drum-style pot.

An example of insufficient soil volume is the hawthorn pot **(2–12)** shown here. The bonsai dried out far too quickly each day; the leaf color would change from a rich dark green to almost yellow by the middle of the summer. By padding out the same mold, I was able to make a slightly larger pot **(2–13)**, increasing the soil volume by 50 percent while raising the pot height by only 20 percent and its depth (front to back) by 15 percent. To disguise any increase in pot height, I stopped the new glaze line higher up the pot wall. This left a deeper and shapelier oxide band to give the illusion of a shallower pot. The new top lip was also slightly deeper to keep it in proportion with the new pot size.

2–12 • The previous pot was not quite deep enough on hot days.

2–14 • Fiberglass and concrete pot by the author.

2–13 • The latest pot is designed for a larger soil volume.

or growing boxes to promote strong growth and vigor. As a tree matures and you refine its shape, the required volume of the soil reduces somewhat. You're looking for a balance between health and excessive growth or leaf size; if in doubt, err on the side of the larger pot. You can adjust the growth in part by soil formulation and by watering and feeding regimes. You should try not to buy a lovely container when you do not have a suitable bonsai tree to go in it. But for me, some things are too beautiful to resist. Well, it's my birthday soon and, after all, I can always just admire the pot. It also creates a great new challenge, to create a tree to suit that pot.

I've included some examples of superb pots by United Kingdom artists:

This tree was repotted at the correct time with the usual aftercare. It is now far happier and healthier. However, the pot is so shallow that missing one day's watering during the summer would be fatal.

Other bonsai species such as pine and juniper are tolerant of smaller soil masses; hence, the choice of pot size for these species is far less restricted. I've included an example of a small Scotch pine soil mass (2–14). Because the pot is coated with a fiberglass resin, it is totally nonporous. However, it does have a drainage hole that is 1¼ inch (3 cm) in diameter. The tree has grown in this pot in fairly full sunshine for five years. The smaller soil volume has a valuable role in controlling needle length. If the soil were to remain too wet during the summer months, long, new needles would form; this would create a very poor bonsai image, out of proportion to its overall size.

In general terms, the required container size changes with the age and maturity of your bonsai tree. Young, developing trees need larger, deeper containers

2–15 • Handmade ceramic pot by Dan Barton.

2–16 • Handmade ceramic pot by Dan Barton.

2-17 • Handmade ceramic pot by Bryan Albright.

2-18 • Handmade ceramic pot by Dan Barton.

2-19 • Hand-cast ceramic pot by the author.

2-20 • Handmade ceramic pot by the author.

2-21• Handmade ceramic pot by Gordon Duffett.

SOILS

The health of a bonsai is largely determined by the health of its roots, in particular, by the growing root tips that take up water and minerals for the plant's growth and survival. Air between soil particles is essential to provide the oxygen to promote root tip growth. Without oxygen, the roots will be forced to grow from the collar region of the trunk, just below the soil surface or not at all. Hence, soil must always be well aerated. Roots cannot split the oxygen from the water in the soil; they rely totally on an inter-granular air supply.

With a few notable exceptions (alder, swamp cypress, and willow), root tips will also die if they are waterlogged for a long period of time. They will suffer from a lack of oxygen and from a buildup of carbon dioxide. To compound the problem, new root tips in waterlogged soil are less able to withstand freezing than roots in well-drained soil. Roots in well-drained soil develop a brown protective coating after shedding excess water at the onset of freezing conditions; waterlogged roots cannot prepare for being frozen and, depending on the hardiness of the species, they will suffer (see section on Winter Protection later in this chapter).

If all this sounds worrying and awfully complex, just remember to include a minimum of 25 percent potting grit by volume in your soil mix. I use 3 to 4 mm grit. This improves aeration and avoids the risk of waterlogging. In addition, check that you have one or more working drainage holes in your container.

Grit itself does not retain any water; it is simply tiny, jagged pieces of stone. I have tried many substitute aggregates. However, I feel that the coolness of grit, combined with its aerating properties and the fact that it doesn't retain water in winter, makes it unbeatable. A side benefit of grit is that it discourages vine weevil from laying their eggs on my bonsai soil. Unfortunately, I have no corroborating evidence to back up my feelings in this regard.

Despite all the literature, I confess that only once in thirty years (as an experiment) have I sieved my bonsai soil. Instead of sieving, I rely on the addition of potting grit to provide the required aeration and drainage. I vary the proportion of grit to compost depending on issues such as pot size and depth, tree vigor and health, whether heavy root pruning has just been performed, how much control I want over leaf and new-shoot size, tree species, whether newly removed from a growing bed, and the stage of maturity of the bonsai.

In practice, I have only two mixes ready at any time, a basic mix and an ericaceous mix. All variations from that I blend as I pot. (See Appendix 2.)

When large pots are involved, using grit may make the bonsai too heavy. In such cases, I have successfully used 4 to 5 mm Perlag or volcanic pumice.

Clay minerals act as a reservoir for nutrients and provide a buffer for irregular feeding. Loam is mostly clay and sand plus some decayed vegetation. Peat contains few clay minerals; hence, nutrients leach very quickly from it. This is true of most organic materials, such as manure, bark, or fiber.

Mycorrhiza (the symbiotic relationship between the white or creamy strands and coatings of powdery fungus and the roots) is useful for the health of the tree. It prevents harmful pathogens from killing the roots and extends the root surface, significantly increasing moisture and nutrient uptake and, as a result, growth. Mycorrhiza is particularly helpful in soil that is deficient in phosphate. Once introduced into the soil (for example, by using rotted pine needles), this fungus stays with your bonsai. Mycorrhiza remains during repotting, as long as you don't remove the complete soil mass and do not use a soil sterilizer or fungicide. I encourage mycorrhiza in all my bonsai, but I have found it particularly beneficial for fattening up pine, spruce, and larch as well as some other coniferous species and beech. Most trees can live without mycorrhiza, but all trees will tolerate or benefit from it. It is proven to increase pine root branching and the life of pine rootlets.

I favor loam-based compost rather than a pure peat or pure clay based compost because loam seems to dry out less and reabsorb moisture better. This suits my once-a-day watering regime well. Unfortunately, this type of compost tends to be finer and less granular than in times past, but the grit compensates for this.

When I visit bonsai clubs, I hear many negative comments and concerns about soils. In recent years, experimenting with soils has become very popular. Many members have switched to imported granular clay soils. Unfortunately, after about three years these may lose their granular nature and become fine and compacted, leaving bonsai with little air between soil grains. When this happens, the bonsai lose vigor, creating a condition often referred to as the "death mix." As long as trees in this type of clay soil are repotted regularly (every two to three years), the granular structure will remain intact. Agents for coarsening clay-based soils such as potting grit or chopped sphagnum moss will help greatly. I am sure that with such additions, you can use these highly feed-retentive clay soils very successfully.

Experimentation is essential if you want to make progress. Perform trials on a handful of trees, but do not make wholesale soil changes that risk damaging your entire collection. I fell victim to this wholesale soil change approach when I substituted a highly water-absorbent granular product for my usual potting grit. Because 40 percent of my compost volume was now absorbent granules, the soil was too dry in summer and waterlogged in winter. Had I added only 10 percent absorbent granule and 30 percent grit, the result would have been fine.

If you do not know the acid or alkaline preference of a tree, a pH of 6.5 is a good starting point. Trees are generally fairly tolerant within one pH point of their desired range. However, trees on the extreme ends of the acid or alkaline range need special consideration. A few trees such as beech, holly, and yew have an incredibly high tolerance band (4 pH to 8 pH). Trees at the alkaline-loving end of the spectrum usually have a pH close enough to neutral to survive in neutral soil; on the other hand, the acid lovers such as azalea, arbutus, camellia, rhododendron, and spruce require further discussion.

The preferred general ranges for these acid lovers are	
azalea	4.5 to 6.0 pH
arbutus	4.0 to 6.0 pH
camellia	4.5 to 5.5 pH
Scotch broom	5.0 to 6.0 pH
ficus (fig)	5.0 to 6.0 pH
gardenia	5.0 to 6.0 pH
Laurus nobilis (bay tree)	5.0 to 6.0 pH
magnolia	5.0 to 6.0 pH
spruce	4.0 to 5.0 pH
rhododendron	4.5 to 6.0 pH

Acid lovers will quickly develop yellow leaves and eventually die if the soil is not acid enough or if the tree is constantly watered with hard (limey) water. Check the acidity of the soil and adjust it by adding peat, chopped sphagnum moss (3.5 to 5.0 pH), or sulphate of ammonia or Flowers of Sulphur to increase the acidity. Using ground limestone dissolved in water will eventually increase alkalinity. Burnt lime is much quicker acting, but it needs more careful handling. Allow a month or more for the adjustment to occur, then retest and continue adjusting if necessary.

REPOTTING

One of the most vexing questions involves the frequency of repotting. I want to start by citing two extreme, real-life examples to help explain my answer.

The first example is a tree I now own. Originally, it belonged to a dear lady whom I first met in April 1993. She had bought a 2-year-old 'Shimpaku' juniper bonsai in 1970. It was in a pot measuring 4¾ inches (12 cm) by 3 inches (7.5 cm) by 1¾ inches (4.5 cm) high. When I saw it in 1993, the pot was an oval approximately 12 inches (30 cm) by 8 inches (20 cm) by 2¼ inches (5.5 cm) high.

During this 23-year period, my friend repotted the tree just twice: once into an intermediate-size pot and then into its current oval pot. I was doing a bonsai demonstration at Birmingham Botanical Gardens in 1993 when she approached me. She was clutching a photograph and asked me what to do with her pride and joy. I suggested she bring it along to the Ambion Bonsai Club in Nuneaton, Leicestershire, where I was due to give a talk. She dutifully turned up at the club with the tree and her daughter. The tree was well fed, healthy, but in need of a complete makeover, which I happily performed as shown. I was so taken with the tree, I drew a possible after design, as shown on page 149. I also took several hardwood heel cuttings, which rooted.

Four years later (November 1997) my phone rang; it was my friend, now aged 85. Arthritis had rendered her unable to look after her tree any longer, so after a very embarrassing negotiation, I agreed to buy the tree for a fair price. It was a treasured Christmas present funded by my wife.

The fascinating thing about this story is that in 1997 the tree was back to almost the exact shape it was in when I first saw it in 1993. Until my friend explained her routine, I could not believe how healthy and vigorous it was and how much it had grown. This routine consisted of dunking the pot in a large bowl of water for two hours every day and dunking it in liquid feed, Chempak No. 4, for two hours every week. This is a high-potash liquid summer feed with a 15:15:30 N:P:K formulation.

This juniper had only had two repottings in 23 years. As you can see from the photographs, the root ball was very tightly gathered and was being forced higher and higher out of the pot, making it almost impossible to water it without dunking.

I was very worried about this special tree. My

2–22 ● The root ball shows a severe case of root-bound bonsai.

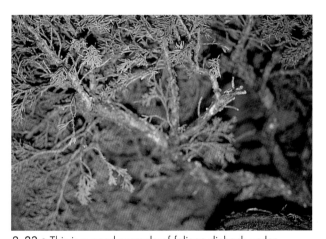

2–23 ● This is a good example of foliage dieback under branches.

2–24 • Notice the lack of root tips after removing the root-bound roots. This is a dangerous situation created by infrequent repotting.

2–25 • I trained, fed, and repotted this tree normally for 28 years.

once-a-day hose-watering regime would not keep this tree alive, even in November. I double watered (watered once, waited several minutes, and watered again) every day until February or March of 1998. Then, I was able to repot it into a larger pot. The tight state of the root ball made repotting dangerous because teasing the knotted roots out without breaking them was extremely difficult. The photographs indicate the size of the problem. My chief concern was in retaining sufficient viable root and root tips to ensure a successful transplant that would be able to support all that foliage. You can see that being so pot bound had resulted in the loss of some of the shadier underbranches.

The tree did survive. You can find the case history in Chapter 10, but the tree needed a good twelve months to settle in the new pot before I attempted a restyle. I promised my friend that if I wrote a book on bonsai I would include her prized tree in it. I would have liked more time to produce the final image, but I hope she likes the route her tree is taking.

Before drawing any conclusion, I'd like to share a second example. In November of 1970, I planted several seeds of *Cotoneaster horizontalis*. One germinated in April of 1971 (the larger tree); the other one germinated in March of 1972. The larger tree was trained normally **(2–25)**. I decided to experiment with the second tree by placing it in a tapered round pot and never repotting it **(2–26** to **2–28)**. It is pictured in its 27th year without a repot, a sickly specimen with an enormous root ball reaching far

2–26 • I trained and fed but not did not repot this tree for 28 years.

2–27 • A close-up of the swollen root ball of a plant that I trained and fed but did not repot for 28 years.

2–28 ● A comparison of the two trees.

Now that we've looked at these extreme examples, let's look at the key aspects of my normal repotting regime.

Typically, I repot my trees every three years. However, younger bonsai, small to medium bonsai in small pots, and vigorous growing species may need to be repotted annually. I leave older trees and those in larger pots alone for four or even five years.

I tend to leave pines five or more years between repots if they are in a medium to large pot. They seem to prefer this. Soil acidity tends to increase over time. Some trees, including wisteria and hawthorn, flower better if root bound, but this has to be carefully balanced against the risk of drought.

You learn from the previous season whether a tree is getting pot-bound by the ease with which it absorbs water and the pace of its new shoot and leaf growth. Slow growth, poor water penetration, and surface mounding of the soil **(2–29)** are sure signs you should repot next spring. Any delay in repotting vigorous species such as 'Jacqueline Hillier' elm, larch, and willow may cause loss of foliage areas next year. You should double water this year for the rest of the summer.

out of its pot. In contrast, its colleague is a healthy and vigorous specimen that spent several years of its early life in a large grow box. Both trees receive the same feeding regime; however, I sometimes double water the root-bound one.

2–29 ● Soil mounding is a warning sign that the roots are root bound and that repotting is overdue.

To summarize, here are the lessons from these two extreme examples of pot-bound trees:

❖ A tree can survive for many years without repotting, providing you give it extra watering, even if you only follow the normal feeding regime.

❖ The resulting tree will be very sickly and will exhibit much less growth and weak foliage, possibly showing several dead areas.

❖ With very individual watering and feeding regimes (involving increased feeding frequency and dunking rather than overhead watering), you can produce rampant growth and excellent health, even if the tree is heavily root bound.

❖ Repotting of such trees is highly risky with an increased chance of transplant shock and failure due to the tangled mass of long roots.

❖ Overfeeding negates the design process and causes excess growth.

No more than 25 percent of the soil is removed from evergreen varieties and rarely more than 50 percent for deciduous trees. However, you'll need to remove all the soil for deciduous trees at certain times, for example, when you are removing them from a growing bed, in cases of soil infestation, or when you are redesigning the root spread. Only the white or cream growing root tips absorb water and nutrients; other roots merely act as water conduits. It is important to remove a proportion of the old root to make way for fresh compost and the maximum number of new fibrous roots.

Before repotting, examine the general health of your tree. If it is sickly, examine the soil for waterlogging or infestation. If it is waterlogged, remove a fairly high volume (40 or 50 percent) of the soil, replacing it with better draining soil. Try to retain as much healthy root as possible. If the soil is infested you have a choice. You can remove all of the soil (only if deciduous), or you can dunk the tree in a bowl of appropriate insecticide for half an hour, fully submerging the soil and lower trunk. You can treat large infestations such as vine weevil or root aphid with chemicals (see the section on Pests and Diseases in this chapter), or you can remove as many of the insects as possible before replacing the soil with new soil appropriately pretreated with insecticide. A newly developed soil drench insecticide called PBI Provado Vine Weevil Killer will relieve these problems. Diluted and watered on the soil in the spring, it will provide several months' protection for bonsai roots by killing the deadly weevil grubs and root aphids.

When a tree is weak but not root bound, not suffering from soil infestation, and not suffering from any other soil deficiency, the safe strategy may be not to repot but to attempt to revive the tree by encouraging new root growth using bottom heat (see the section on Tree Reviving in this chapter).

Always repot in the spring unless there is a pressing need later in the growing season. If that is the case, you can repot in late autumn (early October in cool climates). I do not repot at any other times of the year, despite the possibilities of success if treated well.

I have seen instances of trees repotted in the height of summer for a sales event. They have struggled on, only to falter late the following spring, leaving their new owner to wonder what went wrong. It is often not until late spring, after the initial sap flow, that deciduous tree leaves flag due to some serious incident over the winter period (waterlogging plus a freeze and thaw) or during the previous growing season (drought for one day). The resulting dieback or death seems a very hard puzzle to unravel because of the delayed reaction.

The repotting time must be carefully tuned into the growth cycle of the bonsai. Repot in the spring just as the new buds of the bonsai are starting to swell. You need to act quickly before leaf burst. Evergreens are a little more tolerant than deciduous trees; junipers and pines are fairly accommodating, given the right aftercare. Larch is particularly intolerant of late repotting and must be repotted before bud burst (before you see green leaves beginning to emerge, while the swollen bud is still an unbroken sphere).

Other trees that require extra care when repotting include arbutus, birch, ilex, *Juniperus communis*, 'Nyssa', and 'Stewartia'. Remove less of the soil (20 to 25 percent maximum under normal circumstances) and less of the root for these trees. Give extra aftercare, including adding Superthrive (see later in this section), misting, protection, and shade. Secure the tree firmly in the pot.

If autumn repotting is necessary, repot deciduous plants immediately after the leaves fall; evergreens should be repotted at the same time of year. Some warm days will normally occur before the full onset of winter, allowing new root tips to establish themselves and to commence growth.

First, cover the drainage holes with plastic mesh. Then, sprinkle a thin layer, about ⅛ inch (3 mm), of potting grit in the base of your pots. For very deep pots, you can use more grit or pad the grit with lumps of broken up polystyrene foam or polystyrene worms to avoid excess soil mass. This reduces overall bonsai weight and soil waterlogging but can be a nuisance when roots tangle and weave into and through the foam. Place a layer of the soil mix in the pot, then add the tree. Fill in with more soil, shaking the pot to settle the soil. Prod the soil lightly with a stick to fill any cavities. Place a handful of pure grit under any heavily pruned and sealed root cuts that are over ⅜ inch (1 cm) in diameter to avoid root rot.

Firmly wire the tree into the pot. I like to loop a very thin wire through two drainage holes and tie the two vertical end pieces together over a padded branch fork or similar spot. This can be repeated two or three times. The key is to grip the wire with a pair of pliers and twist each vertical wire a half turn, creating a kink and increasing the tension in the wire. Repeat any number of times until all the guy wires are tense. Using string is not very successful because it doesn't maintain the tension. I often use electrician's plastic wire sheathing threaded over the wire or foam padding to avoid cutting into the trunk or branches with these wires. Sometimes, you can secure the tree lower down at its base, depending on its shape.

Always add Superthrive or a similar vitamin and hormone transplanting formula to your first watering of a newly repotted tree. On March 5, 1981, I received 165 bare-rooted larch seedlings from a mail-order nursery. They had been seriously delayed in the mail and were very dry and sickly on arrival. I planted them all and tied them in pots. I arbitrarily divided them into two equal groups. The soil was identical in both halves. I had spread and trimmed the roots of all the trees, and I had top trimmed the branches the same way. All the trees were watered thoroughly, then sprayed twice daily and protected from rain and excess cold. One week later, when the trees needed more watering, I watered half with a Superthrive solution (100 drops/gallon). I watered the remainder with normal water. Ten days later, I watered the first half with a solution of Superthrive (10 drops/gallon) again.

After two months, the two groups had equally high death rates. However, after three months, the trees that I had used the Superthrive on had twice the growth as the other group. After five months, I had lost 56 percent of the trees treated with Superthrive compared to 66 percent of the other group. After one year, the final death toll was 56 percent vs. 69 percent. Combined with the staggering difference in vigor, this convinced me once and for all of the reviving power of Superthrive. As a result, I always add Superthrive (10 to 50 drops per gallon) to the water for the first watering of newly repotted trees of all species. The exact dosage is not critical as long as it is within the range of 10 to 50 drops. These solutions are a bit pricey, but they are well worth the money.

Protect repotted trees from wind and severe cold. For at least four weeks, keep them in the shade. Try to retain good light levels but avoid direct sun. I move almost all my repotted bonsai under shade netting in my unheated hoop tunnel (a bent pipe with a plastic covering). I do this whether or not they are winter hardy on benches (see the section on Winter Protection later in this chapter). Cold greenhouses and hoop tunnels are warmer than benches (although freezing temperatures can occur) and, because there is no wind, they are ideal places for most newly repotted trees. However, I find scalelike junipers and hardy pines prefer a slightly cooler and airier situation, such as a sheltered garden area free from severe cold or drying winds.

Avoiding chilling winds combined with frozen soil is important for all repotted bonsai. All branches as well as leaves and needles transpire in winter and can be damaged if the soil is frozen for long periods between January and May. In particular, pine and cedar bonsai will show signs of needle-browning through the winter and early spring months. This is due to the cumulative desiccation damage, which is quite normal to some degree.

The problem is worse after you repot because the roots are not functioning normally. You must avoid severe needle desiccation by protecting your trees from wind and excess cold. I prefer to wait to repot pines until some of the buds are almost ⅜ inch (1 cm) long to get them further through the cold season. This reduces the potential desiccation time so that as daytime temperatures increase, root activity can begin again. You must not allow your old pine and cedar needles to become completely desiccated before the new spring growth forms.

The health of the old needles is what carries these trees safely through to the new season. Cedar buds should be well swollen and elongated but not yet burst when repotted. Unlike pines, they should be cosseted all winter in a cold greenhouse or hoop tunnel. Cedars react very badly to cold winter temperatures and can shed all their needles overnight during a very cold spell unless they are protected. Such needle loss may trigger the death of a tree. Cedars can also lose needles because of excess root removal during repotting. If a cedar tree looks weakened, it should be treated according to the suggestions in the Tree Reviving section of this chapter (see also the Overwintering section for more detail by species).

Do not feed repotted trees for at least six weeks. You should wait even longer to feed weak trees.

WATERING

Theoretically, bonsai trees should only receive sufficient water to retain the compact growth of new shoots and leaves and to keep the tree healthy. There should be no excess water. Most bonsai deaths and diseases are caused or triggered by drought. Hence,

2–30 • A maple glade at Weston-birt Arboretum, in Tetbury, United Kingdom.

watering your trees to a theoretically correct level means you must walk a tightrope between bonsai life and death unless you are at your trees' disposal every hour of the day. This is a frightening and unnecessary prospect. In essence, watering (like feeding) is a balance between too little and too much.

For most of the thirty years I've worked with bonsai, my watering time has been limited because of my long working hours. Consequently, I have always watered my bonsai just once per day with a fine spray nozzle on the end of a hose, preferably in the early morning rather than late at night. This gives the trees more of a water reserve to last through the hot days. If the forecast is for hot weather, I double water thirsty trees; that is, I water them and then, several minutes later, I water them again. This significantly increases the amount of water held in the soil.

One of the first problems such a daily regime raises is the question of whether to water a tree that is half dry. Even the best weather forecasters are frequently wrong. In late spring and summer, you only need one really hot day or a very windy day to dry out bonsai that are thirsty drinkers if they started the day with only half their total possible water reserve.

For this reason, in late spring and in summer, if there is any doubt, I saturate bonsai soil each morning. In early spring and autumn, I am more circumspect because the maximum daytime temperatures will be much lower and unexpected drought less likely. In winter, trees open to the cold and rain rarely need watering in Britain, but extra vigilance is needed to check trees regularly. A tree suffering from drought in winter dies just as surely as it does in summer.

The difficulty comes in controlling needle or new shoot length. Pines are perhaps the most affected. New needles will grow too long if the tree is over-watered. My approach here is not to worry about this in the developmental years when long needles aid growth and long shoots can be shortened or removed. Pay special attention to trees approaching their final-image stage when refinement of needle and shoot length becomes critical to the design. Segregate these trees and concentrate on more carefully controlling the soil volume, soil mix, watering, and feeding for this group.

Extra vigilance is needed in winter for trees sheltered from rainfall. It is easy to forget a tree pushed to the back, not noticing its soil has dried out. This happens even more quickly if winter storage temperatures are higher inside a hoop tunnel or cold greenhouse than the outside temperature.

The soil mixes I use allow me to get away with a once daily, generous, watering regime during the late spring and summer months. I can do this because I use fast-draining, water-retentive composts. Always water until you see the water draining freely from the drain holes in the base of the container. A few suggestions for compost mixes are listed in Appendix 2.

To avoid the risk of scorching the leaves, don't water in strong sunlight. I generally prefer to water the soil rather than the leaves. However, now and then, I water the leaves and the soil from above. Watering only the soil avoids any risk of mildew on susceptible species such as rowan, hawthorn, oak, apple, crab apples, and damson/plum. These suffer more when kept in shady, windless garden areas.

During my early years as a bonsai grower, mature trees shaded our garden. Mildew was endemic among my bonsai of the above species. I habitually watered all my trees from above with a hose, saturating the leaves and soil of all trees every day or so. Mildew appeared in areas on just the top surface of the leaves where the water had been lying. I cured the mildew problem forever by watering only the soil and by paying greater attention to the watering needs of each bonsai, targeting only trees that needed watering. I continued to use a hose, but I switched to one with a fine nozzle, watering one tree at a time.

In warm, airy, and fairly sunny gardens, mildew is unlikely. Thus, you can water the leaves and the soil from overhead. If your conditions are particularly cool or shady, you need to modify your regime to watering the soil only. Whether you use a fine nozzle on a hose or a watering can is an individual preference (and may depend on the quality of your local water supply). I recommend looking at each tree daily to tune into its requirements. If you still have a plant that develops mildew, begin applying a fungicidal spray treatment just as the buds are opening to arrest the problem as quickly as possible (see the Pests and Diseases section later in this chapter).

In a sunny garden during the summer months, I have successfully used an overhead watering system with an automatic timer to water my bonsai in the early hours of the morning. At this time of day, the risk of sun scorch is minimal. Using static spray heads on the end of a standard hose covers a fairly small bench area well. Larger areas require a standard pipe feed line and a much smaller set of feeds to individual spray heads to divide the main pressure and to increase the area being sprayed. Using multiple water computers timed to come on at differing times allows you to cover larger areas if one system is inadequate.

Automatic sprinkling is very wasteful on water since it must run for long periods to reduce the risk of wind depriving some trees of water. It also waters all areas surrounding your bonsai. It is better to program two separate spray times to effectively double the water and to allow for some changes in wind direction. Sprinklers may be a good solution when you're away on vacation, but get someone to check your trees daily. Water supply failures, battery failures, broken pipes, wind changes, and the like are all possible hazards. In addition, someone should check to be sure that the spray has not missed any bonsai.

I am not a fan of automatic sprinkling. It results in excessive shoot and leaf growth. In addition, liverwort and moss abounds in excessively wet soils. Having said that, I used it for three or four summers when time was very pressing. Nowadays, I only hand-water using a fine spray nozzle on my hose. I find I can control shoot length and diameter and leaf/needle size far better. This is essential in the later stages of completing your bonsai design when mistakes cannot so readily be pruned away. A very important additional benefit is that you get to look at each tree every day to check that all is well. I have not tried alternatives such as drip irrigation or gravel plus waterbeds.

In the final analysis, watering is an acquired skill, based on experience, observation, and vigilance. With experience, you will become sensitive to the needs of each tree. Those that are weak or newly transplanted must not become waterlogged; those whose new growth is potentially too coarse and vigorous need special control of their water supply.

FEEDING

The key to successful feeding of bonsai is finding the balance between too little and too much. This is a great deal simpler in practice than the following might suggest, but I believe we need to understand the basics first; I've included a simple methodology. Correctly fed bonsai rarely fall prey to serious diseases. They also have increased insect resistance.

Allowing soils to dry out seriously lowers a plant's insect and disease resistance; it also reduces nutrient uptake. High acidity or alkalinity locks nutrient minerals in the clay. As a general rule, you should aim for a pH of 6.0 to 7.0. The leaves contain most of a plant's minerals, except magnesium, which is stored in the trunk. Therefore, leaves are excellent indicators of nutrient deficiency and of health. Examine the color, shape, and size of the leaves. Look for necrotic areas or other problems and refer to a reference book.

The Soil section of this chapter explains the importance of clay in the soil as a reservoir for nutrients. Roots easily absorb liquid feed and quickly leach it. On the other hand, solid feed moves through the clay mineral stores to the roots and is longer lasting. Liquid feed gives a more even soil distribution, but it is easier to overfeed with it than with solid feed. Having said that, I have experimentally hyper-dosed plants by using too much surface feed, specifically quick-release granules.

Overfeeding, using liquid or solid feed, has a catastrophic effect on plants, called plasmolysis, in which the water flows from the roots to the soil. This is the opposite of normal plant behavior, in which water travels from the soil to the plant by osmosis. Osmosis works when the root tips contain higher concentration of salts (minerals) than the surrounding soil. The water naturally migrates to the higher concentration. Excessive feeding can increase soil salt levels beyond that of the root tips, causing plasmolysis or loss of water from the plant. This in turn produces flaccid (limp) leaves and shoots, a dulling of the plant's color, collapse, and death. To prevent this problem, delay feeding newly repotted trees for six weeks. Feeding for weak trees should be limited until they regain vigor.

The Soil section in this chapter also contains an example of overfeeding of a 'Shimpaku' juniper, leading to excessive growth and the loss of bonsai design. Generally, deciduous trees require twice the quantity of feed (every 10 to 14 days vs. every 21 to 28 days) required by evergreens. Among the evergreens, I consider the non-needled juniper bonsai to need the most feed. Hence, this example of overfeeding a non-needled juniper is doubly interesting for me because it indicates the level at which overfeeding is harmful to shape but not to physiology. The feed requirements among trees can vary greatly, as can their preference for high- or low-nitrogen feeds. Oaks for example require little nitrogen; maples and beeches need medium levels of potash and lime.

In the middle of September of 1980, I conducted a large experiment using Sudbury liquid fertilizer, sold separately as 45 percent nitrogen, 45 percent phosphorus, and 45 percent potash (leaf and stem, root, and fruit and flower, respectively). I divided a large growing bed into two parts and made up two feeds, feeding half the bed with a 0:1:1 ratio and half with 3:2:2 for the remainder of September and every seven to ten days during the 1981 growing season. The outcome enabled me to compare the no-nitrogen type feed with a high nitrogen type. The bonsai common to both beds were Scotch, mugo, and Japanese black pines; *Acer palmatum, ginnala,* and *pseudoplatanus* 'Brilliantissimum'; *Malus cerasifera; Ulmus parvifolia* (Chinese elm); *Juniperus chinensis; Zelkova serrata,* and European hornbeam. I also had sycamore, small-leaved linden (lime), common hawthorn, Japanese red and white pine, European larch, and pyracantha in the high-nitrogen bed only. I had deodar cedar; *Juniperus × media* 'Plumosa Aurea', *Cryptomeria japonica* (Japanese cedar) and Kurume azalea in the no-nitrogen bed.

In summary, the no-nitrogen regime helped the Scotch and Japanese black pines grow better. It reduced the severity of woolly aphis attack and reduced winter needle discoloration between January and the end of May compared to pines in the high-nitrogen group. The deciduous trees all grew better on higher nitrogen, especially linden (lime), although the leaves were not as dark as in the no-nitrogen deciduous group.

What surprised me most was that, despite the above differences, all trees, whether evergreen or deciduous, seemed happy with both feeds. Although significant differences can be teased out by careful experimentation, using normal-strength liquid feed every seven to ten days seems to work well for all trees. This is true whether the feed contains high nitrogen or no nitrogen. The garden bed remains healthy and all plants grow and prosper.

During the growing season, I feed my mature potted bonsai collection using liquid feeds only. I use full strength during the growing season except for the first feed, which is half strength. I feed them at approximately ten to fourteen day intervals. I always make sure the soil is wet before applying a liquid fertilizer. In the spring, I individually feed trees with a watering can to avoid waterlogging weak or newly repotted trees. In the summer months, I sometimes use a watering can to target different feeds to different trees, but I often use a hose applicator that mixes water with a reservoir of concentrated liquid fertilizer (mine is 25 times concentration). Because I always drench foliage (not flowers) and soil with hose applicators, I feed early in the morning to prevent the strong sunlight from scorching the leaves. I try to fertilize when I expect a spell of warm weather.

I vary between a liquid feed of 10:10:27 and either an extract with seaweed and sequestered iron (0.72:2:3), Miracle-Gro (15:30:15), a (12.5:25:35), or a liquid fish emulsion (5:2:2). None of these feeds is very high in nitrogen; nevertheless, I taper off nitrogen feeds by the end of August and use exclusively 0:10:10 liquid feed during September to harden off shoots so they are ready for the winter cold. Evergreens and flowering deciduous bonsai get a further feed in October.

Winter hardiness in trees is a balance between the hormones that promote their growth and the hormones that inhibit their growth. Nitrogen feed in late season is particularly bad for evergreens because it affects inhibitor levels, reducing winter hardiness. Many commercial feeds contain an assortment of trace elements, but if in doubt, apply a trace element Frit in early spring.

My flowering and fruiting trees are targeted during the growing season with only low-nitrogen feeds to encourage flowering and fruit production. I also target pines and junipers with lower-nitrogen feeds. Flowering and fruiting trees and acid lovers also get one fine sprinkling of bonemeal on the surface of the soil in November or December each year and a trace element Frit in January or February.

Acid-loving species such as azalea, rhododendron, camellia, spruce, and some other conifers benefit from use of a no-lime release fertilizer to avoid disturbing the acidity of the soil. Now and again, I use liquid feed (30:10:10) for such trees and occasionally across my entire collection, but it is a very high-nitrogen formulation, which I would not use after the middle of the summer.

Large fruit-bearing trees such as apple, crab apple, and mulberry must not be fed during fruit set until the fruits are about half size to avoid fruit drop. After this period, trees drink a great deal, and watering and feeding should not be ignored.

Signs of overfeeding are a crystalline layer on the surface of the soil, or if mossed, a green or black surface slime.

I have had very good results with thickening young trees in growing boxes containing well-rotted pine needles combined with Osmocote six- to nine month slow-release granules (18:11:10). Sprinkle a little on the soil surface, especially around the edges of the pot, but do not crush the granules because this hyperdoses the roots. I used a teaspoon in a 5-inch (12.5 cm) pot and six teaspoons in a 22-inch (55 cm) wide growing pot. Do not use any other feed in combination with these granules.

In 1977, a friend gave me the idea of combining Osmocote with rotted pine needles in deep growing boxes. Apart from its slow release characteristics, one of the secrets of the success of Osmocote is its ability to increase nutrient release in both hot and wet soils, providing nutrition at the optimum time. The latest generation of granules are even smarter (PBI Time Release—twelve-month formula). They have a polymer coating and only respond to heat. These granules do not respond to the waterlogging that can occur during rainy periods and in winter. They should also be less prone to nutrient excess or breakage of the granule. It is worth experimenting with these new granules. Try adding them to bonsai compost for trees in training or in growing-bed soils at repotting time. Fork them under the surface of the soil four to six weeks after repotting in the case of more delicate bonsai or if you have removed much of the old soil.

SUN AND SHADE

Without sunlight, trees in nature do not grow. With too much sun, all the water evaporates, and everything turns to desert. This section is another of those balances between too much and too little.

Some trees in nature such as birch, cedar, *Cryptomeria,* eucalyptus, juniper, larch, oak, and pine thrive in sunlight. Their leaves or needles are well adapted to reducing transpiration loss. Others such as beech, fir, hornbeam, sycamore, yew, and some hollies thrive in heavy shade and can grow quite well under gloomy forest canopies. Amazingly, some species such as yew and juniper are adapted to both extremes.

In the British Isles, 1989 was a hot summer, causing a drought and a ban on watering. This was followed by another hot summer in 1990 with temperatures of 95° to 105°F (35° to 40°C) recorded in July and August. Late in the summer of 1990, even some very mature deciduous trees died. Hornbeam and beech were most affected, but larch, birch, laburnum, and hawthorn were also badly affected.

When you grow a tree as a bonsai in a relatively small container, the soil temperature and moisture levels fluctuate to a much greater degree than a tree planted in the ground. This affects winter hardiness and summer heat stress. The tolerance range of both is markedly reduced from that of a tree in the open ground. The section on care, cultivation, and winter protection in Appendix 1 details the requirements for individual bonsai species. Remember that hot sun or winter cold can kill young seedlings in one day, even though as a mature bonsai specimen, they may well survive these same conditions.

Perhaps summers in cool climates have been warmer recently and the ozone layer thinner. Trees most affected by this heat are hornbeam and beech, then larch, laburnum, and hawthorn, then swamp cypress, willow, wisteria, linden (lime), *Zelkova*, and finally maple. Obviously, small or shallow-potted bonsai and those grown on rocks or in a weak condition are all susceptible, too. Even growing beds can suffer in very hot weather with the loss of small base buds or shoots of trees; in particular, I find that the lowest pine shoots and buds are lost in such conditions. To avoid this, significantly reduce the top foliage masses of growing bed subjects in hot summers.

In particular, Japanese, European and hybrid larches that normally would survive unharmed on sunny benches all day (albeit only just), have significantly suffered leaf scorch in recent years, especially on exceptionally hot late spring or summer days when the temperature is 86°F (30°C) or more. This scorch can be very serious and can be followed by leaves shriveling in some branch areas, leading to a selective leaf loss. Next year's buds in these leafless areas attempt to grow toward the end of this season to compensate, leaving the tree still producing new, weaker shoots in September when it should be going into hibernation. Branch areas may be noticeably weaker the following spring, as illustrated (April 1998). Even worse, some branch areas or shady underbranch areas fail to grow and must be removed, crippling the tree shape. Mild bouts such as the one illustrated are curable with vigilant double watering and perhaps some local foliar-feed spraying the following season. This tree was much improved the following May, but it required a further year to recover fully.

I am trying to underline how important some shade is to many bonsai species. In particular, deciduous ones are vulnerable, unless you are prepared and able to rush out and water bonsai several times each day. Larches are common victims of heat stress. I have one twin-trunked, hybrid larch that has been almost dormant for many years despite feeding and daily watering. It is in a very shallow oval pot, and during even moderately warm summer days, the soil dries quickly. In hindsight, I see that heat stress stopped the normal shoot extension for so many years that I began to think it was a runt. I moved it into a cool, semi-shaded spot where it now thrives **(2–31)**. I have a second, shallow-planted, Japanese larch raft-style group. The friend who sold it to me warned me that it kept dying back. It is

2–31 ● After placing this tree in a cool, semi-shaded position, it has returned to a normal growth pattern after years of dormancy caused by heat stress.

wonderful to see the lush, vigorous, new growth on these two problem trees due to being placed in their cool and semi-shaded microclimates.

Even though there may be no outward signs of heat stress, such as leaf scorch or wilting, there may be no growth; this is another symptom of heat stress. Lower and underbranch dieback are also symptoms of heat stress from the previous year.

I want to add a word of caution to redress the balance. In my very shady garden, my bonsai survived for many years but never grew due to a lack of sun. They were sickly looking, leggy, and prone to mildew and branch dieback. In such shady conditions, it is impossible to successfully thicken bonsai even in growing beds. All trees in growing beds and deep boxes should be exposed to full sun each day.

2–34 • The reduction in vigor of the lowest branch is due to heat stress.

When I moved to a much sunnier garden, the benefits were improved growth, trunk thickening, leaf/needle color, more compact new growth, and improved prospects for such sun lovers as pine and *Cryptomeria*. However, in May of my second sunnier growing season, I noticed a severe lack of bud growth at the rear of some of my trees, especially damson, European larch, and willow. The big change in growth had evidently occurred mostly on the sunny side, leaving the weaker rear side to die in the face of greater competition than previously experienced.

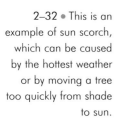

2–32 • This is an example of sun scorch, which can be caused by the hottest weather or by moving a tree too quickly from shade to sun.

2–33 • The underbranch spring dieback was created the previous year by heat stress from too much sun or from being root bound.

2–35 • Careful extra watering and moving the tree to a semi-shady location have helped this tree recover the vigor in its lower branches.

Initially, I saw this as a signal to turn my trees regularly, but the situation eventually stabilized. This highlighted the need to wean weak trees from shade to sun, and to turn them regularly for a season after a significant increase in sun exposure. I do not routinely turn my bonsai trees nowadays, providing they are in the open in a sunny position and not close to a wall.

I had a similar experience one year when I moved a Japanese yew, which I had owned for many years, from a deep shade area where it had stayed for many weeks to a full sun situation. It was a blazing hot first day, and the yew leaves literally scorched and bleached. The tree died a few weeks later. I grow many yews, often in full sun all summer, but I will never make that mistake again. Yews need weaning from prolonged deep shade to full sun. To a lesser extent other tree types such as *Cotoneaster horizontalis*, Hinoki cypress, Chinese elm, *Acer palmatum*, wisteria, and *Zelkova* are prone to leaf scorch if moved from shadier winter protection straight into full sun. Wean them into full sun over several weeks.

The section at the end of this chapter details the ideal location for many of the popular bonsai species I have grown. I have come to the conclusion that unless you are lucky enough to have a partially shady garden, you need to consider building artificial shade using shade netting or similar ideas to protect some of your bonsai from the sun.

PESTS AND DISEASES

Bonsai that are well cared for are mainly disease free; insects are more of a nuisance, but they prefer weak trees.

If you follow the care and cultivation methods in this book, your bonsai will hopefully "live long and prosper." In the Prevention section of this chapter, you'll find advice on what actions to take to minimize the risk of attack by pests or diseases, reducing the need for chemicals or other solutions. You'll also find a table of suggested treatments for each pest and disease.

To avoid burning the leaves, do not spray chemicals in bright sunshine. When treating existing infestation or disease, spraying once will probably not cure the problem. You'll need to adopt a program of respraying as per instructions.

Identification of pests and diseases is beyond the scope of this book. If you contact suppliers, local agricultural schools, gardens centers, or associations, they will often supply very comprehensive information booklets. In Appendix 1, I have tried to identify the most common pests and diseases faced by each species and to recommend appropriate actions in this section.

If, like me, you do not practice preventive spraying, then when problems do occur, you must act quickly to identify the type of problem and use the correct solution. Chemical solutions should normally be applied at the recommended strength; however, weak trees, delicate new foliage (larch and maple, for example), or aggressive chemicals may occasionally justify a slightly greater dilution.

Continual changes in the availability of chemicals due to bans, new discoveries, and the like make any specific recommendations difficult. I have tried to concentrate on sprays and treatments harmless to garden-friendly larger insects such as bees and ladybugs and, where possible, modern and/or safer chemicals not so likely to be banned. Older stalwarts such as lime sulphur, malathion, and permethrin are banned or will eventually be unavailable in Britain and in many other areas of the world.

Fortunately, the amount of chemicals required in bonsai care is very small, reducing the risk to oneself and to the environment. However, you should seek organic solutions where effective. In fact, the application of some preventive insecticide sprays can increase the risk of insect attack by upsetting the natural predator balance. Where possible, I have recommended sprays or treatments such as pirimicarb that are harmless to garden-friendly larger insects, including bees and ladybugs. Sprays harmful to these garden-friendly insects should only be applied in the early morning or the late evening during flowering periods, when bees and other insects are less active.

Disease

Diseases play a vital role in the ecosystem of our ancient forests by decomposing and recycling weak, dying, and dead trees, providing light and nourishment to the survivors. Although man assists by thinning and pruning, the trees have now built a remarkably good defense mechanism against such pathogens, providing they are healthy.

One of the main keys to avoiding disease in bonsai is to avoid drought. You also need to ensure that your bonsai are free from leaf litter or other debris and that all unhealthy shoots are promptly removed, sealed, and burned. Additionally, all surrounding flora and areas should be free from diseased material. One of the most common sources of infection is old tree stumps or wood left in the ground. When you find a fairy ring in a lawn, the center of it will probably be a dead cherry tree, a buried stump, or a tent peg. If a tree dies in a bonsai group, remove it, including the roots, to minimize the risk of infection.

You can treat bonsai with very effective multipurpose fungicides. You can also use them prophylactically, spraying them routinely to protect trees from attack. Long-lasting, multipurpose, nonsystemic treatments such as copper fungicide and bordeaux mixture are still useful as preventative treatments. However, they both use a great deal of copper, causing their own low-level soil contamination. Copper-based fungicide can occasionally adversely affect certain species, such as *Malus*. A multipurpose fungicide is generally the most effective preventative measure.

Clearing up fungal or bacterial infection after the onset of a disease is far more difficult than preventing one; in some cases, it is impossible. I have been able to keep my trees healthy enough to avoid virtually all such infections, but this may not be possible in some parts of the world where climate and other factors increase disease virulence. A good prophylactic fungicide is mancozeb, which will prevent disease. However, it will not cure it once established. Once infection takes a hold, I prefer a systemic fungicide myclobutanil. It will be more effective when sprayed at bud burst and repeated as required. The latter is both a preventive and curative treatment.

Peach leaf curl is an example of a fungus that can be minimized or averted by protecting trees under plastic or glass to avoid the cold and wet spring environments in which peach leaf curl thrives. Attacks of peach leaf curl should be treated at bud burst, then every fourteen days with mancozeb, and again when the leaves fall.

Bacterial attacks are far less prevalent than fungal ones. However, because bacteria are much smaller than fungi, they can only enter through wounds or crevices. Fireblight is the most serious bacteria. It attacks the *Rosacea* family (apples, crab apple, cotoneaster, cherry, hawthorn, *Prunus,* quince, *Sorbus acuparia,* and pyracantha). You must cut all the affected shoots or trunks back to healthy wood seal the wound. Burn all affected material. This is especially important if you live in an area in which commercial plants or fruit are being grown.

Coral spot, common on maples and beech, used to be confined to dead shoots, but nowadays, it is spreading to healthy tissue. You'll need to cut well back into healthy wood, seal the wound, and burn all the affected material.

Algae buildup on branches (more common in the countryside where city pollution fails to suppress it) is best removed by gentle brushing with a diluted soap solution.

Soil Problems and Treatments

Insect infestation such as root aphis or vine weevil, and fungal attacks such as jelly molds normally require saturation of the soil, using a watering can. Better still, immerse the tree in the appropriate insecticide, fungicide, or sterilizing solution. Some diseases such as verticillium can survive in soil for over ten years, but sterilizing the soil destroys them.

Jeyes Fluid is a gentle soil sterilizer I have used successfully on some species. I use one teaspoonful per gallon to discourage root aphids, worms, and wood lice from soil. It kills moss. You can also use it as a winter branch wash, as a soil drench against black spot, and as a sterilizing agent for the soil.

Armillatox is a very powerful cresylic acid soil sterilizer. It kills green plants if applied to leaves or green shoots or if too strong a dose reaches the growing root tips. I have successfully used it to clear some bonsai problems (for example, black spot, jelly or other soil molds, and soil infestations such as ants). By careful experimentation, however, I have found that Armillatox applied at the appropriate dilution is very effective. I generally start at 100:1, but I have reduced this to 50:1 and even 25:1 in some cases. Apply it on the soil only, avoiding the foliage, trunk, and green shoots. You may prefer to submerge the pot in a large container of the dilute solution. Armillatox has also been advertised as a treatment for honey fungus, phytophthora, club root, white rot, and vine weevil. I have not tested its effectiveness in such circumstances. It will, of course, kill surface mosses and mycelium.

Used with caution at 50:1, I have successfully sprayed some deciduous branches with Armillatox before bud break (on *Acer palmatum*, Chinese elm, Guelder rose, hawthorn, larch, wisteria, and even the bark only of pine and juniper, but not tender variants) in February to remove moss and algae. You'll need to experiment carefully. A substantial brushing with a dilute soap solution (such as heavily diluted liquid soap) is still required after two weeks to remove the dead white debris. In fact, my larches have been successfully sprayed at 25:1.

Honey fungus is usually fatal, but a healthy tree can fight the soil-borne pathogens for many years, especially with the help of a strong sterilizer such as Armillatox.

When watered onto soil, a new systemic insecticide called PBI Provado Vine Weevil Killer relieves this weevil problem. Vine weevil grubs are a serious and hidden threat to bonsai and to other plants in small containers. The larvae live in the soil and are capable of quickly killing a tree by eating all its soft new roots.

Diluted and watered on the soil, PBI Provado can now provide six months' protection for bonsai roots by killing the emerging weevil grubs. Its systemic action also has a marvelous side effect of killing sap-sucking insects such as green and black aphids, whitefly, and sciarid fly for a period of one month or more after application. Although not advertised as such, it also discourages leaf hopper, woolly aphis, adelgids, mealybug, leaf miners, thrips, spruce aphid, capsid bugs, and scale insects. Provado is also b.i.f. (beneficial insect friendly) and does not harm bees, ladybugs, etc. (Please read the Pests section below for more information on vine weevil prevention.)

Pests

Although most insect attacks are a nuisance and may weaken a plant, they are not normally fatal in themselves unless the infestation is intense (for example, in hot weather) or unless treatment is delayed. Deciduous trees have a better chance of survival when their leaves are attacked than conifers, and they normally recover more quickly. Insect attacks increase the chance of viral, fungal, and bacterial infections carried from plant to plant by these creatures, which can enter the plant through damaged tissue.

Vine weevil is a far more serious pest during the summer months. Its eggs are capable of lying dormant for up to four years before the larvae emerge. These can kill a bonsai very quickly as they eat through the young roots. The first sign of trouble is likely to be foliage wilting due to a loss of roots. However, by this time, the condition is life threatening. Mature vine weevil beetles, easily seen at night by flashlight, only eat leaves and are not nearly as harmful to bonsai as the grubs. They lay eggs in the soil that will emerge as deadly root-eating grubs.

Prevention is the best policy for vine weevil grubs. Two possible strategies exist. The first is to use a soil additive that contains chlorpyrifos in slow-release, dark green granules. If evenly distributed throughout the soil, they will give two or more years' protection against hatching vine-weevil larvae. The additive has no systemic properties and does not fight sap-sucking insects. Take care when handling this granule and treated soils.

The second approach is a water-drenching treatment with PBI Provado Vine Weevil Killer. This provides six months' protection against vine weevil and one month's protection against sap-sucking insects (see more details above). In cooler climates, March would be a good time to apply PBI Provado because vine weevil larvae should be controlled during their active growing period, and sapsuckers need to be controlled for a month or so.

An alternative beneficial insect-friendly treatment for non-sapsucking aphids and mites not killed by Provado is Bio Naturen, an organic leaf spray formulation based on rapeseed oil. This has the added bonus of turning the leaf surfaces shiny. The summary of chemical treatments, which appears later in this chapter, suggests possible treatments for specific problems and a suggested priority sequence of chemicals, preferably starting with beneficial, insect-friendly options.

Animals

Rabbits are a real threat to bonsai, and they are not very fussy. They will chew off the leaves and young shoots of most species. Single podiums must be at least 1½ feet (0.5 m) high; benches must be about 3 feet (1 m) high. Squirrels favor larger trees, particularly sycamore and red maple, stripping off large areas of bark from high branches. They are less inclined to attack bonsai on benches near ground level, but you should keep an eye on them.

Of course, you'll keep domesticated grazing animals behind a fence and away from your bonsai. However, wild animals such as deer can visit at night and devastate your plants. The level of danger these animals represents varies by location. However, raising the height of your benches can help if animals are a potential hazard.

Prevention of Pests and Diseases

Avoiding extremes is the key to pest and disease resistance. The following actions will greatly reduce the risk of attack:

❖ Above all, provide a regular water supply. Severe drought and pot-bound roots weaken a tree's resistance, leaving it open to pests and disease. Loam-based composts are good for moisture retention, and grit helps to keep the soil cooler.

❖ When mixing composts, use good, sterile soil mixes such as those recommended in this book.

❖ Avoid waterlogged and compacted soil, especially in winter. Beware of adding too many water-retaining aggregates or granules; I use potting grit mainly, and I use a maximum of 10 percent water-retaining additives. Fine soils such as clay or loam without grit or similar aeration will become too compact (see Soils in this chapter).

❖ Correct any soil deficiencies and soil pH imbalances, ensuring that the water you use is not too acidic or alkaline. Ideally, it should be soft and free of impurities.

❖ Avoid wide temperature variations, which produce cold damage or heat stress (see Winter Protection in this chapter and in Appendix 1).

❖ Avoid still, damp air and excessive shade. Equally important, avoid excessive wind exposure.

❖ Feed trees with a low-nitrogen feed to avoid soft growth. Organic feeds are claimed to increase resistance compared to artificial feeds, but I have used predominantly artificial liquid feeds without problems.

❖ Some organic matter (humus) in the soil is vital for insect and disease resistance.

❖ Do not water the leaves of species that are prone to mildew.

❖ Add mycorrhiza to conifer (including larches) and beech bonsai soils.

❖ Remove all decayed leaf litter, branches, and debris, especially over winter because this matter can create a good breeding ground for fungal infection.

❖ Provide good soil drainage and surface soil hygiene, especially with species prone to fungal infections.

Often, fungal and viral infection start in wounds that are not cleanly trimmed or sealed. These infections can be passed on when a diseased bonsai has contact with another bonsai. Opinion is divided over the need to seal wounds. Some contemporary studies indicate that the natural healing mechanisms of a tree are superior to sealants. This may be true for healthy trees in healthy surroundings or where the cost and difficulty of such sealing is significant. However, in orchards or gardens with nearby diseased trees or material, sealing has a very important role. I strongly recommend you seal all bonsai trunk, branch, and root-pruning scars to ensure that all crevices and wounds are filled. This creates a barrier for the many waiting enemies.

❖ Choose varieties that will thrive in your area. Be aware of a tree's sensitivity to pollution, infestation, disease, wind resistance, etc.

CHEMICAL TREATMENT SUMMARY
(B.I.F. = Beneficial Insect-Friendly)

Choice rating and examples are based on a priority of b.i.f. first, followed by other effective, but less insect-friendly options. There are many chemical options; this is not a definitive list, just my suggestions:

Pest or Disease	Prevention or Cure (P/C)	1st, 2nd, or 3rd Choice	Treatment	Comments	B.I.F. (Y/N)
Pests					
Adelgids	P&C	1	Imidacloprid	Soil drench	Y
	C	2	Bifenthrin	Spray	N
Ants	P&C	1	Cryselic acid with care and experimentation		N
Aphids (including Spruce, green and black)	P&C	1	Imidacloprid	Soil drench	Y
	C	2	Rapeseed oil	Spray	Y
	C	3	Pirimicarb	Spray	Y
	C	4	Bifenthrin	Spray	N
Root aphid	P&C	1	Imidacloprid	Soil drench	Y
	P&C	1	Cryselic acid with care and experimentation		N
Borers			Clear out, prune off, and burn all affected material		
Capsid bugs	P&C	1	Imidacloprid	Soil drench	Y
	C	2	Bifenthrin Less effective than the systemic action of no.1	Spray	N
Lacebug	P&C	1	Imidacloprid	Soil drench	Y
	C	2	Bifenthrin Less effective than the systemic action of no.1	Spray	N
Leaf hopper	P&C	1	Imidacloprid	Soil drench	Y
	C	2	Bifenthrin Less effective than the systemic action of no.1 Use water jet on cuckoo-spit as soon as it appears	Spray	N Y
Leaf miner	P&C	1	Imidacloprid (Emphasize prevention; cure is difficult)	Soil drench	Y
	C	2	Malathion	Spray	N
Mites (including blister mite)	C	1	Rapeseed oil	Spray early	
	C	2	Bifenthrin	Spray early	
	C	3	Permethrin	Spray early	Y

CHEMICAL TREATMENT SUMMARY (*Continued*)

Pest or Disease	Prevention or Cure (P/C)	1st, 2nd, or 3rd Choice	Treatment	Comments	B.I.F. (Y/N)
Mealy bug	P&C	1	Imidacloprid	Spray early	Y
	C	2	Bifenthrin	Spray early	N
	C	3	Permethrin	Spray early	N
Red spider mite	C	1	Rapeseed oil	Spray early	Y
	P&C	2	Imidacloprid	Soil drench	Y
	C	3	Bifenthrin	Spray early	N
Sciarid fly	P&C	1	Imidacloprid	Soil drench	Y
Scale insects	P&C	1	Imidacloprid	Soil drench	Y
	C	2	Rapeseed oil	Spray	Y
Thrips	P&C	1	Imidacloprid	Soil drench	Y
	C	2	Rapeseed oil	Spray	Y
	C	3	Bifenthrin	Spray	N
Vine weevil grubs	P&C	1	Imidacloprid	Soil drench	Y
	P&C	2	2 chlorpyrifos	Soil additive	Y
Whitefly	P&C	1	Imidacloprid	Soil drench	Y
	C	2	Rapeseed oil	Spray	Y
	C	3	Bifenthrin	Spray	N
Woolly aphid	P&C	1	Imidacloprid	Soil drench	Y
	C	2	Malathion	Jet spray early	N

Diseases

Pest or Disease	Prevention or Cure (P/C)	1st, 2nd, or 3rd Choice	Treatment	Comments	B.I.F. (Y/N)
Anthracnose		1	Clear out, prune off, and burn all affected material		
Black spot	P&C	1	Myclobutanil		
	P	2	Mancozeb		
	P&C	3	Cryselic acid with care and experimentation		
Canker		1	Check for woolly aphid first and treat as above		
		2	If possible, cut out or off, and burn affected areas		
		3	Otherwise keep		

CHEMICAL TREATMENT SUMMARY (*Continued*)

Pest or Disease	Prevention or Cure (P/C)	1st, 2nd, or 3rd Choice	Treatment
Coral spot			Clear out, prune off, and burn all affected material
Fire blight			Clear out, prune off, and burn all affected material
Gray mold (Botrytis)	P	1 2	Improve air circulation Mancozeb
Honey fungus	P&C	1	Cryselic acid with care and experimentation
Mildew	P&C P	1 2	Myclobutanil Mancozeb
Needle cast		1 2	Keep tree healthy Use foliar feed to sustain needle vigor if necessary
	P&C	3	Benlate and copper fungicide sprays alternately
Peach leaf curl	P	1	Mancozeb
Rust	P&C P	1 2	Myclobutanil Mancozeb
Silverleaf (true—dark-stained inner wood)		1	Clear out, prune well into healthy wood, then burn all affected material back to healthy wood
Silverleaf (false—no dark-stained inner wood)			No action required
Scab	P&C P	1 2 3	Avoid still air and dead leaves Myclobutanil Mancozeb
Verticillium wilt		1	Clear out, prune off, and burn all affected material
	P&C	2	Try sterilizing soil with cryselic acid

IDEAL STARTER SPECIES

A newcomer to bonsai needs a bonsai tree that can stand up to a little inexperience in the areas of watering, feeding, and winter care, as well as one that will respond to shaping when wired or pruned.

Junipers are an outstanding genus for this, especially species such as:

> *Juniperus sargentii* (Sargent's juniper)—if you can find this uncommon species
>
> *Juniperus chinensis* (Chinese juniper)
>
> *Juniperus* × *media*—in particular the cultivars 'Shimpaku', 'Blaauw', and 'Plumosa'
>
> *Juniperus virginiana*—in particular the cultivar 'Burkii' (Virginia juniper).

Pines are another excellent genus, especially the following species:

> *Pinus sylvestris* (Scotch pine)
>
> *Pinus thunbergii* (Japanese black pine)—requires some winter protection.

Among deciduous trees, I would recommend the following for their vigor and toughness:

> *Acer ginnala* (Amur maple)
>
> *Carpinus betulus* (European hornbeam)
>
> *Larix eurolepis* (hybrid larch)
>
> *Larix decidua* (European larch)
>
> *Malus cerasifera* (Nagasaki crab)
>
> *Viburnum opulus* (Guelder rose).

You can leave all of these trees outdoors all year round with the exception of the Japanese black pine, which needs a cold greenhouse or some protection from the worst winter cold.

GROWING FROM SEED

This approach allows you to control the growth and shape of your bonsai from the beginning. It is a very rewarding and inexpensive way to grow species, some of which may be hard or even impossible to obtain as mature bonsai specimens. Unlike cuttings (discussed next), plants grown from seed have unique features; they are not clones of the parent plant.

Tropical and subtropical seeds are very easy to germinate. Temperate region trees are not so easy. They require a high level of moisture to germinate. Some need a period of winter cold. Ninety percent of northern trees need a low-temperature treatment of 34 to 39°F (1 to 4°C). This low-temperature treatment increases jacket porosity and increases the supply of oxygen to the embryo, assisting germination. Some seeds require one or two winters of freeze and thaw to germinate. *Acer griseum* typically requires two winters, unless you carefully remove the shell and the fawn or brown diaphanous inhibitor membrane from the seed, in which case it might germinate in ten days.

A wealth of specialized information exists on the subject of optimum cropping and early germination using acids, boiling, scarring, artificial freezing methods, etc. On the other hand, you can get acceptable results by letting natural bacteria, the elements, and time do their work. However, notching hard seeds on the edge may speed up the process (for example, of ginkgo, *Rosaceae*, and legumes).

If you are storing seeds, you should partially dry them. If they are too dry, the embryo dies; if they are too wet, fungus develops. The shelf life varies, depending on species. A few seed types cannot be dried below the moisture level at which fungus thrives (25 percent) for fear of killing the embryo seed. For example, *Acer saccharinum* (sugar maple) seed embryo dies if the moisture level drops below 36 percent. Such seeds should be sown shortly after you collect them.

Some seeds rarely contain an embryo. *Acer griseum* (paperbark maple) is such an example. Only certain of these trees are fertile; some others are but only very rarely.

For the above reasons, I prefer to sow seeds as soon as they are picked, if possible. However, I soak them in water for 48 hours first. Seeds are best sown in moist, but not soaking-wet sphagnum peat. This peat is more acidic than most peat types. The resulting germination rates are generally far better than sand, which compacts too much. Apply a fungicide soil drench initially, such as Chestnut Compound.

I usually place these seed trays in the open air on benches to receive all the elements. Placing a thin plastic covering above them is helpful, but do not place it directly on the soil. A transparent plant cover is ideal to keep the water out but let in the air. If you are using a cover, shade the seeds to avoid condensation and do not let the soil dry out. If temperate tree seeds do not germinate that year, leave them exposed to the winter elements to benefit from the freeze/thaw.

The winter care of germinated seedlings requires far more thought in the first two or three years of a plant's life than later years. Treat all temperate seedlings as needing a minimum of cold greenhouse protection for the first three years (more for certain species) and use smallish pots to avoid waterlogging. After three years, you can default to the recommended long-term care in the Overwintering section of this chapter and in Appendix 1.

TAKING CUTTINGS

Cuttings provide an opportunity to create new plants from those that you feel are particularly suited to bonsai without losing any of the characteristics (such as color, size, bark, bud, shoots, etc.) exhibited by the parent.

A wealth of information on timing and methods for taking cuttings exists. I find that March to May is a good time, although whenever I find myself pruning interesting shoots off bonsai, I feel it is worth taking cuttings. Early season cuttings have more time for root establishment before winter and require the same winter care as seedlings for the first three years.

Select firm, healthy shoots from vigorous 1- to 5-year-old areas. I prefer to take heel cuttings where a shoot is torn from its joint with the branch or trunk giving a heel. This may need a little trimming to remove frayed edges. However, good results are also obtainable by cutting off the tip growth. It is helpful if this has a ⅜-inch (1 cm) hardwood basal section. You may also cut sections through long shoots, cutting at an angle just under and into a bud node; leave at least one other dormant bud above that.

For deciduous cuttings, strip off the big leaves from the cutting but leave one or two smaller ones. Remove all the leaves below the ground. For evergreen cuttings, strip off only those leaves that would end up below soil level. The length of the cutting is not too important, but I typically use 2¼ to 4¾ inches (6 cm to 12 cm). Without delay, soak the

cutting in a liquid fungicide. Shake off the excess moisture, then put it into hormone rooting powder. I use a strong hormone rooting powder on hardwood heel cuttings, but I use a less strong form in April and May for soft shoot cuttings. Use a dibble to make a hole in the compost to set the cutting at an angle. Firm the soil lightly around the cutting. Hormone rooting powder, like all other chemicals, must be handled according to the manufacturer's directions.

Plant the cutting in a mixture of 50 percent peat and 50 percent grit or perlite and water well. Water with a fungicide such as Cheshunt Compound initially to avoid damping-off. Cuttings live temporarily on their carbohydrate store, so early production of roots is important. To help this process, cover the cuttings with a thin plastic layer and mist the cuttings regularly. Bottom heat is really beneficial in encouraging early rooting. Shade the cuttings initially, then gradually move them toward the light. Take care to avoid excess condensation, which can encourage fungal growth such as damping-off.

Popular species from which cuttings are easily taken include:

Junipers such as:

Juniperus chinensis (Chinese juniper)

Juniperus communis (common juniper)

Juniperus × media and in particular the cultivars 'Blaauw', 'Plumosa,' and 'Shimpaku'

Juniperus sargentii (Sargent's juniper) and in particular the cultivar 'Burkii' (Virginia juniper).

Maples such as:

Acer buergerianum (trident maple)

Acer davidii and its faster-growing, larger-leafed clone 'George Forrest' (snakebark maples)

Acer ginnala (Amur maple)

Acer palmatum (mountain maple) and several of its non-dissected, non-variegated cultivars.

Other easily started species include:

Carpinus betulus (European hornbeam)

Escallonia

Jasminum nudiflorum (winter jasmine)

Salix babylonica (weeping willow)

Ulmus parvifolia (Chinese elm)

Viburnum opulus (Guelder rose)

Wisteria (try *Wisteria floribunda* 'Macrobotrys')

Zelkova serrata (gray bark elm).

WIRING

For me, wiring is a means to an end rather than an art form in itself. My objective in wiring is to change the shape of the trunk, branches, and new shoots into an aesthetically pleasing form as quickly as possible and with a minimum of damage to the bonsai. Although it may be overstated, I am comfortable with my reputation as the world's worst wirer. My trees are not exhibited while under heavy wiring, but I wire for the tree, not the viewer. My technique aims to minimize wire marks and unnatural bonsai.

My reputation probably derives from my very loose wiring and from my use of far heavier wire than most would choose for a specific task. By wiring heavy and loose, I feel I can achieve a much better shape because the wire will not move, and the extra gap allows the wire to remain until the branch angle is well set. In addition, the extra wire diameter doesn't cut into the bark as much. I anchor the wire well and keep the first turn from trunk to branch looser than the rest because the most susceptible part of the branch is its fork with the trunk. Rapid growth can strangle a branch easily at this junction.

My preferred time for heavy wiring is April or May. At this time of year, the sap flow is good, although it may continue through until the end of July or early August (see Appendix 1 for details by species). After this time, deciduous trees and, to a lesser extent, evergreens become less flexible because the sap flow slows. Branch brittleness continues from September through February or March in the British Isles and in cooler climates. Typically, wiring is not used during this period. Certain conifers such as larch, non-needled juniper, and vigorous pine species will tolerate winter branch wiring on warm days.

Once the heavily wired branch is set, I always crop off the wire in single turns to avoid any damage to the tree. This is a more expensive approach, but aluminum and copper wire are easily recycled.

I confess to having made some heavy wire marks despite this loose wiring technique due to negligence or lack of vigilance. Time is a great healer, particularly on some pines, but thin-barked evergreens and all deciduous trees take many years, if ever, to heal. Some people say pine bark can be made more interesting after wire marking, but this is a risky strategy. I prefer natural bark platelets to any artificial scarring, although in time, the two converge.

Another area of particular importance for me is fine wiring new shoots early in the season as they grow from ¾ to 1¾ inch (2 or 3 cm) onward. For new-shoot wiring, I use thin section wire and great care; new shoots of some species are very brittle at the base, particularly yew, trident maple, wisteria, and pine candles. Clearly, if you are reducing the length of the shoots (by cutting or pinching them), this shoot wiring technique is not as appropriate, although I still often use it on the pruned new shoot. In combination with shoot reduction, using fine wiring in the early growth season is a good means of steering new grow, new branches, and new trunks. It ensures that the new shape is changed into an interesting and appropriate form early in its life.

As you will see in the chapter on bonsai design, a great deal of my growing involves adding on rather than reducing. Occasionally, I have restyling bouts of wholesale thinning by pruning and wiring. Such a policy allows trees to consolidate and gain vigor between restyling bouts. New-shoot wiring can look unsightly, but I think it is essential. The resulting branch detail, with its twists and turns, plus the correct angle setting of twigs is, thus, ensured early on. Hence, fewer design compromises are necessary. You gain extra inches out of some otherwise straight new shoots by bending them and forming attractive shapes. This is particularly valuable during the first growth surge of the season, which is longer than the second. (Note that some bonsai, such as beech and Japanese white pine, have only one growth per season.)

Some trees dislike fine-twig wiring to remain over the winter. More tender types need to be completely unwired during the winter. While wired, fine-twigged and thin-barked trees need protection from strong sun to avoid fine-twig damage (see Appendix 1 for details by species).

PRESEASON SHOOT-TIP TRIMMING

Most fine-twigged and vigorous-growing deciduous bonsai benefit from a trim just prior to bud burst. You selectively prune back the branch tips to just above a bud. This encourages budding and twig ramification and stops the foliage mass from growing too large in comparison to the trunk size. Typical bonsai that benefit include *Acer buergerianum, Acer palmatum, Acer campestre*, birch, beech, cotoneaster, elder, elm, hornbeam, liquidambar, Stewartia, willow, and *Zelkova*.

PRESEASON BUD REMOVAL

In recent years, I have had a great deal of success using this technique in reducing the size of large-leaved common horse chestnut and sycamore (*Acer pseudoplatanus*) bonsai and in promoting rampant budding. This procedure requires complete tip bud removal just as it swells **(2–36)** but before it bursts. Detailed photographs of the technique, its outcome, and reservations are documented in the case studies of these two species. You should only use this technique on vigorous trees during their development, and you should not repeat it for three or four years. No total leaf removal is performed in the same year as bud removal.

2–36 ● This is a preseason bud removal technique.

EARLY SEASON NEW-SHOOT PRUNING

The earlier the new shoot or candle is pruned, the more compact the new growth will be. This produces a smaller shoot diameter, a shorter shoot (between nodes), and smaller leaves or needles. Do not remove all the new growth, just half or two-thirds of it. Be aware that a few species such as beech, Japanese white pine, and San Jose junipers do not respond well to 100 percent new shoot removal.

Most new shoots should be pruned when they are ⅜ or ¾ inch (1 cm or 2 cm) long. This is typically done in May in cooler climates. Plucking with your fingertips is the preferred method. You can twist and pull pine candles when they are small by gently holding the base of the candle in one hand (between two fingers) and removing half to two-thirds with two fingers of your other hand. If you use pruning scissors, you can more accurately determine where the cut will be, but the result tends to be more unsightly if some needles or leaves are cut through and die back. If you are exhibiting a tree, particularly a conifer, try to finger-prune only. If you use scissors, take great care not to cut through stray leaves or needles or to leave odd shoot stubs sticking out.

Why is early new-shoot pruning so beneficial? It catches the new shoot at a shorter length and smaller diameter, which means that it has less vegetative mass. This reduces the amount of resource that the remaining shortened shoot has to produce to make additional new leaves and shoots. The result is that the new shoot is smaller in diameter with shorter internode lengths and smaller leaves.

A good example is what happens when you leave a new shoot or candle on a vigorous pine to grow unchecked. It can become a 2¼ to 4¾ inches (6 cm to 12 cm) long, which will have a shoot diameter larger than the shoot it is projecting from (inverse taper) and excessively long new needles. By the end of the season, it is a total liability on your bonsai; it is out of scale and will need removing unless you are looking for vigor, not shape. A good example of a deciduous tree is common beech, which has just one big growth push per year. It develops a long silky, snakelike shoot, up to 2¼ to 3½ inches (6 cm or 9 cm) long, which appears over a few days, just like magic. You need to be vigilant in order to catch these new shoots early and to reduce them to two or three leaves. At this point, they are in miniature, and the resulting shoot and leaf compactness is very rewarding. Follow the early shoot-pruning approach on all parts of the bonsai as required.

Most deciduous trees are apical (top) dominant; so are many evergreens, including *Abies, Cryptomeria japonica, Chamaecyparis pisfera* 'Boulevard', and most pines. However, a few bonsai subjects such as azalea and Kyohime maple can be basal dominant. In weak or underdeveloped areas of the tree, new shoots may be left longer or left unpruned. On the other hand, dominant areas must have the new shoots pruned more heavily, thus retaining overall balance in tree vigor and avoiding local branch dieback in weaker areas.

Theories on timing abound. One example of such a theory is starting from the top or bottom of the tree and/or delaying one or two weeks between pruning weak and strong areas. My approach is based on examining trees several times a week in the early growing season, and basing early shoot pruning on each new shoot's size (its stage of development), the vigor in that area of the tree, and the overall design plan.

You'll want to make decisions on whether or not to prune on a shoot-by-shoot basis as soon as the shoot reaches the target size.

For each species of flowering bonsai, you can find many special pruning regimes. My best advice is to explore these in detail to maximize the care of your own specimens. A good general rule is to prune back new shoots to two or three leaves shortly after flowering. A few (such as pyracantha, willow, and tamarisk) benefit from very early spring pruning of old wood because it encourages compact new growth in the coming season. Do not use this early old-wood pruning for most of the early flowering trees (for example, crab apple, hawthorn, winter jasmine, forsythia, apricots, and cherries) or you will remove the flower buds formed on the previous season's wood. You can sparingly prune the new shoots of vigorous flowering trees such as pyracantha, cotoneaster, and Nagasaki crab before flowering if the tree is a little untidy and you wish to neaten it up to exhibit it. However, do not remove too many flower buds.

Some flowering trees are encouraged to grow long sacrificial branches through the summer. This takes the majority of the tree's vegetative growth and encourages other, shorter shoots to be even more compact. It is only from the compact shoots that next year's flowers will grow (for example, apple, crab apple, hawthorn, pear, pyracantha, and wisteria). The best times to remove these large sacrificial branches is after leaf fall or, better still, in February of the following year, leaving all the short shoots alone to bear flowers.

I do not routinely prune the new shoots of young trees in growing boxes or beds. I do, however, perform structural pruning regularly to balance strength and shape and to reduce excess growth mass in hot periods. This helps to avoid the dieback of lower, weaker areas. Incidentally, pruning techniques do not reduce the size of the flowers or the fruit.

MID-SEASON PRUNING

Keep an eye on emerging new shoots throughout the main growing season. For nonflowering trees, prune new shoots following the instructions in the Early Season New-Shoot Pruning section above. Some bonsai continue to produce shoots throughout the season (for example, Hinoki cypress, *Cryptomeria*, and junipers) and need continuous monitoring.

Some deciduous trees, such as trident and Amur maples, and to a lesser extent *Acer palmatum*, love to send vigorous new shoots from the base of a branch. These look a lot like suckers. If these shoots are not removed, the whole branch with all its detailed branchlets may die. Similar vigorous shoots can emerge from trunks and branch tips and should also be removed quickly if they are not required to balance vigor throughout the tree.

Some bonsai trees produce many suckers from the trunk base. For vigorous trees prone to suckers, such as *Acer ginnala*, cotoneaster, apple, crab apple, elder, Guelder rose, and yew, these suckers do not threaten the future of the bonsai too much. One or two can grow as sacrificial branches for a few seasons in order to fatten the trunk base. Do not leave too many suckers on at one time because this does not work effectively. It simply diverts energy from the main bonsai trunk and branches.

Heavy fruit or cone-laden branches can be severely weakened or killed unless you remove some of the fruit. This is a common problem with crab apple and larch. To be safe, remove 50 percent of the fruit or cones from heavily laden branches. You should do this early, during their formation.

LATE-SEASON SHOOT PRUNING

Late-season pruning of the current season's growth shortens or eliminates each of that year's remaining growth shoots, which were pruned earlier in the year. In general, this late pruning stimulates more prolific spring budding the following season, promoting more buds, sometimes called cluster budding. The resulting new-shoot growth is smaller the following season.

Some growers leave the current year's shoots unpruned throughout the season, removing them all late in the season. This exaggerates the reaction discussed above and promotes a greater number of spring buds the next season. You should use this technique carefully and only on very vigorous trees. The technique weakens some trees. Use it only on selected species and then only every second or third year. Use it less frequently, if at all, on older trees. Fruiting and flowering trees are sometimes pruned late in the season to promote fruit or flower (see Appendix 1).

Late-season pruning is a useful technique for some pine species (see Scotch and Japanese black pine case studies), but it must be done with care and knowledge of the species. If in doubt, experiment on small areas first. I have found it very useful for Scotch, Japanese black, shore (*Pinus contorta* var. *contorta*), and mugo pines, which are vigorous growers. I would not use it on Japanese white or red pines.

Late-season pruning is a popular technique for larches, but I do not recommend it because it produces prematurely old and arthritic-looking knuckles on these wonderful trees. In addition, it prematurely thickens, weakens, and kills the branches. True, you get a denser tree in the short run, full of needlelike foliage, but this peaks and becomes ugly and disproportionate within a very few years. Larch trees can be made into beautiful bonsai in five to ten years without this technique. You will only be able to keep an acceptable image for a further fifty years with a combination of early and mid-season pruning and by avoiding large-scale late-shoot pruning. Dormant buds are the lifeline for future larch branches and branchlet replacement. Please leave them on your inner branches as a future insurance policy. I have had one of my larches almost ruined by thoughtlessly removing dormant buds. You do not see many examples of larch in bonsai literature; I hope that this will change (see Larch Case Studies for more information).

While I tidy up odd shoots at the end of season, I do not routinely prune late-season shoots on any of my bonsai species other than the above three vigorous pines, *Acer buergerianum* (to avoid winter twig dieback), and some fruiting or flowering species as indicated in Appendix 1.

HEAVY PRUNING

Normally, I use heavy pruning to redesign a tree radically, usually one under development. I prefer to use heavy pruning while repotting in the spring although you cannot be quite as radical with evergreens as with deciduous bonsai. After repotting, one or two years must elapse for the tree to regain vigor before I do any further heavy pruning. I prefer to perform heavy pruning and the restyling of trees that I haven't repotted in April or May when the sap flow is good and the wounds start to heal quickly during the growing season. These wounds then tend to continue to finish healing better over the coming years.

Some trees, such as maple, birch, mulberry, and pine, bleed more than others. To be safe, do your heavy pruning in January or early February to limit the amount of bleeding. However, all the trees discussed as case studies have been heavily pruned in the early growing season just before bud burst. Normally, this heavy pruning is combined with repotting and root pruning with no ill effect (including *Acer palmatum*, *Acer buergerianum*, and various pine species). Trees must be vigorous, and large wounds must be initially sealed, preferably with a sealant that retains a fluid, lubricating quality. According to one school of thought, you should prune maples heavily in June so that the wound healing (and bleeding) is slightly less vigorous and the final callus is more refined with fewer bulges. I do not practice this, but it seems a good idea for vigorous maples.

Ideally, you should do your heavy pruning at repotting time, especially the first potting from a growing on bed into a large pot or box. This would typically be February or early March, extending no further than early April in Britain and cool climates. It would correspond to early bud swelling time (see Repotting section). The combination of heavy root removal and heavy branch removal works well if you seal all the wounds above and below ground and if you place pure gravel under heavy root cuts to avoid root rot.

Heavy pruning using a saw usually leaves a very flat wound which, if not dressed, produces an unsightly scar after healing, as shown in **9–22** and **9–26**. Always try to gouge out and undercut the edge area of large wounds with a power tool or a small hand cutter, as illustrated in **16–14**, before sealing. This will produce a smooth final contour once the wound has healed.

When a leader with a small diameter is grown and thickened (for example, to extend a pruned trunk), the new leader angle should be established early. Either make it a radical angle or, in the majority of cases, angle it to continue in the same direction as the pruned trunk. If you use this technique, your eye will not be drawn to this union in the future. You can then start any change of direction or curve slightly higher than the union.

Case History

Trident Maple on a Rock

This *Acer buergerianum* (trident maple) example clearly illustrates how effective radical pruning can be.

2–37 ● I pruned off all this trident maple's branches because they were all pointing upward (May 1989).

2–38 ● After I pruned off all the branches, it was time for a fresh start (1989).

2–39 ● After six weeks, the new shoots were well established.

2–40 ● After fifteen weeks, the tree was almost back to where it started.

2–41 ● Only two or three branches survived this pruning. The wiring of the lower left branch was the critical factor (April 1990).

2–42 ● Notice the new growth developing five weeks later. Fine wire loosely applied to new shoots helps to direct the new shoots.

2–43 ● This was the situation a few months later (September 1990).

2–44 ● Pads and the pad height were forming as branchlets grew. Notice that the vertical growth tendency is present again (June 1991).

2–45 ● Here's the tree after I scissor-pruned the new growth and wired the new shoots (June 1991).

2–46 ● After repeated prunings and after wiring the new shoots, this is the tree's appearance only four years and four months after the initial image (September 1993).

LEAF REMOVAL

In the early years of bonsai growth and development, this technique is not useful because it can reduce tree vigor. Leaf removal is ideal as a tree is developing toward its final shape. At that time, it will reduce leaf size over a two- or three-year period.

This technique is only used on deciduous bonsai. It involves the wholesale removal of new leaves, retaining the leaf stalk and the bud in the axil of the stalk. Typically this is performed in May or early June once the first leaves have developed. It must never be practiced on evergreens or weak deciduous bonsai. Even healthy deciduous trees should only have their leaves totally pruned every other year or so, depending on the health of the tree. After a few weeks, the new shoots from the dormant buds will grow, producing smaller shoots and leaves and better autumn color. Do not do a total leaf prune in July or later because the resulting new shoots need time to harden before winter. In fact, they may not emerge at all that year.

Never perform total leaf removal in the same year as the early bud removal technique described in an earlier section of this chapter, or the tree may be badly weakened. You will find that after the leaf size has been reduced for two or three years, less, if any, total leaf removal will be required to maintain the leaf size.

USING GROWING BEDS OR CONTAINERS

I cannot tell you how many times I have suggested that the proud owner of a spindly seedling or young bonsai should grow it in a deep container or growing bed for five or ten years. Initially, this suggestion is met with horror or disappointment because it effectively dispatches the owner's highly valued tree to the sidelines for five or ten years. I understand the reaction, but from bitter experience I know there is often no alternative but to begin developing a decent trunk and core branch system sooner rather than later.

In choosing a growing bed, pick an open, sunny area, preferably one that faces south and is sheltered from the cold north and easterly winds. The bed can be ordinary garden soil if you have good soil that is rich loam. Raised growing beds, above ground level, are a blessing when you need to weed or prune.

If deep containers are easier for you than growing beds, I prefer to make or acquire wooden rectangular boxes rather than use the many pots and containers that are available. Angling the sides slightly inward toward the base is a nice touch, but it is not essential. Feet on the box are useful to reduce insect colonization and to stop the box from rotting at the base.

Select a section of pressure-treated wood ⅝ to ¾ inch (1.5 to 2 cm) thick. You want it to last for five to ten years. Use thick timber for the baseboard and make plenty of drain holes. The box should be 6 to 8 inches (15 to 20 cm) deep and at least 12 inches (30 cm) long and wide. The typical grow boxes I have used are 6 inches (15 cm) deep, 20 inches (50 cm) long, and 14 inches (35 cm) wide. It helps to incorporate carrying handles because these boxes are heavy.

If the box is deeper than 6 inches (15 cm), increase the grit by one or two parts to avoid waterlogging. Extra deep containers that are over 8 to 10 inches (20 to 25 cm) are risky at this stage. Waterlogging is a distinct possibility with a root volume that is small compared to the pot.

Plant the seedling at the correct spring repotting time. Take extra care to spread out the roots in a good radial form. Prune any tap root or overly dominant side root to encourage branching of the roots near the trunk and a good basal taper. Angle the trunk if you wish. Always spread the roots not only outward but sloping slightly downward from the trunk base to create an interesting root surface shape and to encourage formation of trunk basal taper. Remember the future scale of the tree and avoid having a tree whose roots spread only a little then dive vertically into the soil like claws or knuckles. If you are planning to grow a root over a rock, bury the rock along with the tree roots in the wooden box or in the ground design (see Case History —Trident Maple on a Rock earlier in this chapter).

Water the trees well, initially with a Superthrive solution (10 to 50 drops per gallon). Protect boxed trees from shade and wind for four weeks. Six weeks after planting, sprinkle Osmocote slow-release granules onto the surface of the soil in the bed or box. Do not break the granules (see Feeding section of this chapter). You should not apply any other feed when using Osmocote. Apply fresh Osmocote every April or May once you see that the tree is growing again.

For deciduous trees, this occurs shortly after leaf burst. If you prefer to use some other solid or liquid feeds, that is fine; I simply suggest Osmocote based on my own good results.

Water as required, but remember that even the garden growing bed will benefit from occasional watering to maintain healthy surface roots during hot, dry spells.

Sun is another important factor in thickening trunks. Keep the trees exposed to full sun during the summer. Frequent turning should not be necessary for grow boxes, providing all sides of the tree see good levels of light. In the case of the growing bed, planting trees a good distance apart, say 2 feet (60 cm), is helpful to avoid shading lower branches and adjacent trees.

Mindful of the eventual tree shape, you will need to shorten or remove branches and remove dense top growth to retain the vigorous lower buds and branches. The secret to developing a good trunk taper and major branch shaping is to grow, cut back, and grow again in cycles.

Heavy trunk and branch pruning is best done in April or May, using smaller diameter side shoots to replace larger diameter trunks or branches. The replacement branch must then be allowed to grow long and thicken for one or more years until the diameter of its base is less than its host branch. However, it should not be so small that it looks like a big step down in diameter. At that point, you prune it back, perhaps to within an inch (2.5 cm) or so of its host, depending on your projections for its future shape. By repeating this prune-and-grow process a few times, you can develop a shapely, interesting trunk or branch with a good taper on a small scale. All you need is patience and an eye to the future, earmarking future replacement shoots and maybe wiring them in advance into a good angle.

Retaining long sacrificial branches near the wounds and bases of thickening trunks and branches accelerates the healing and thickening processes. Pruning certain growing shoots back to a dormant bud is also very useful for encouraging well-placed future replacement shoots.

I recommend winter protection for boxed plants, as detailed later in this chapter and in Appendix 1. Trees have a little more tolerance in these deep pots than normal, shallow bonsai containers.

I have not repotted or removed trees for root pruning during this growing period whether for five, ten, or fifteen years. Usually, the greatest growth occurs a year or two after the tree gets a good hold of the soil or a good root formation. During the following few years, the growth is prolific, and you need to prune back any excessively thick branches, trunk, or visible surface roots. You may need to do some broad skeletal wiring. If you are aiming for a fine and very well rami-fied surface root formation, then removing the tree in the spring every two or three years for root pruning is a good idea. Replant the tree and treat it the same way you did for the initial planting. Use the aftercare procedure discussed above.

It is possible to wait too long before removing these trees. Without careful monitoring, you can suddenly find that surface roots, trunk, or branches have thickened to a point where they are ugly, and you have lost the tree shape you wanted. Once the trunk and major branch shape is good and the bigger wounds have made some progress toward healing, the tree is ready for removal. You can then develop slower growing finer branching, and any remaining wounds can heal once you've removed the tree.

When removing trees from a growing bed, you can prune the roots and branches as described above, as though you were going to plant the tree in a growing box. Instead, you return it to the growing bed. Shade the tree for a few weeks and ensure that the soil is sufficiently watered. This reduces the trans-plant shock. The following year, you can move the tree to a container with less shock.

FROM GROWING BED OR BOX TO FINISHED IMAGE

In early spring (see the Repotting section in this chapter for the exact timing), you can repot those plants that are ready for the next stage. Plants grown in growing boxes move into shallower bonsai pots. These may be intermediate, deep pots before you move them later into the shallower final-image containers. If you judge that the volume of the roots you have removed will not shock the tree too much, you may repot it directly into the final-image container.

Plants grown in growing beds usually require some major root removal so that they will eventually fit in an acceptably shallow container. It may be better to stage the heavy root removal over two repots if the loss of fibrous root at this stage looks too great. You need to prune back the top growth on deciduous trees to a shape from which finer, ramified branching can grow, pruning back to well-placed dormant buds.

I avoid too much heavy cutting back of top growth on evergreens, preferring to remove a maximum of one-half the foliage (usually only one-third) at this time. I also try to avoid the loss of too much soil from around the root. This first transplant from the growing bed is the riskiest time for pines and cedars (*Cedrus*) because the foliage may weaken and drop. By using a larger pot, you'll pretty well ensure your success, even following heavy root removal. Of course, you must retain plenty of volume of fibrous root, and you must firmly wire the tree into the box to avoid root damage. For evergreens, you

may need to move much of the growing-bed soil with the tree during this first move in order to reduce shock. Deciduous trees will withstand total soil removal if that is necessary to reorganize the roots. Some of the case studies indicate the typical root volumes that were successfully removed. For species susceptible to root rot, you'll need to remove any garden-bed soil over the next few repots to ensure proper drainage (see Appendix 1).

I treat pines as a special case with regard to reducing foliage because their first transfer from a bed to a box is critical. After the first move, subsequent repotting of pines should be routine. I prefer to repot even my largest pines after candles have started to emerge from the bud. The candles may be up to ⅜ inch (1 cm) long.

I apply Superthrive to all transplanted trees and care for them as discussed in the Repotting section.

Case History

Scotch Pine, Slanting Style

I have always wanted to produce a Scottish highland pine image, and this is the closest I have come. Grown from seed thirty years ago, this tree was used as a styling demonstration at the April 1999 exhibition, Joy of Bonsai 1999.

You have to watch to see if snow is forecast with this gravity-defying style. A moderate snowfall is enough to send the tree and pot toppling. A strategically placed broom under the crown does the trick, but it does spoil the image somewhat!

2–47 ● I removed the tree from the growing bed after 9½ years of thickening. The lower trunk taper was good, and its apical dominance was now threatening the vigor of the lower branches (April 1990).

2–48 ● The tree after I removed 25 percent of its foliage.

2–49 • Notice the potential daughter trunk. It needs encouraging.

The larger volume of foliage seems to help buffer the transition. Incidentally, I never remove old needles from my growing-bed pines; they help thicken the plant and reduce shock during the transition to a container (see Pine Case Studies for more detail).

The high level of grit in this soil mix is based on the depth of the pot used. Notice how the future daughter tree has already been identified. By looking ahead to the future design, you can prune carefully, retaining this shoot and giving it a little more light to develop.

Always use Superthrive on transplanted trees and anchor them firmly in pots. Give aftercare according to the instructions in the Using Growing Beds or Containers section of this chapter.

2–50 • Here, I've wired and lifted the daughter trunk, removing unwanted branches and foliage that were shading out the daughter.

2–51 • I was so pleased with its progress after a year that I reduced the foliage by 50 percent and repotted it in an intermediate pot. Typically, I would wait two years before attempting this (May 1991).

I prefer to remove no more than one-third of the top pine foliage (even if I have removed up to 50 percent of the heavy root), relying on good shading and wind protection to protect the pine from dehydration. A hoop tunnel (a bent pipe covered with plastic) may help for a short spell, but it is not vital and was not used in this example.

Little or no wiring or detailed training is necessary at this stage. You can wire in April two or three years later, once the pine is vigorous again. Notice how securely the tree is tied into the plastic pot.

By providing shading and misting daily for four to six weeks, the pine's roots re-establish themselves.

2–52 • The pine is shown after I restyled it, nine years after I removed it from the growing bed and 29 years after the seed germinated (July 1999).

GARDEN-CENTER STOCK

Garden centers are an excellent place to find suitable material for developing into bonsai; normally, their trees are modestly priced and grown in a container. You can enjoy hours of fun examining the beds. Try to find specimens that have a good trunk base and shape, even if the trunk needs shortening. Look for neat, compact foliage, and, if it is a flowering tree or shrub, wait to view flower size, shape, and color to avoid disappointment. If you are selecting young stock, look for good basal trunk taper.

The choice of suitable species found at garden centers is endless. You'll find maple, cedar, cotoneaster, *Cryptomeria*, fir, juniper, pine, pyracantha, quince, spruce, wisteria, yew, and countless others.

Specialist bonsai nurseries today often have dedicated growing beds for the more popular and specialized bonsai species. This is another very cost-effective option, although you may need to time your visit for spring or autumn because some of the trees will not be root wrapped.

COLLECTING FROM THE WILD

This common hawthorn (*Crataegus monogyna*) was rescued from the wild just before an area of rock was to be quarried (see Hawthorn Case History in Chapter 12).

Some of the finest bonsai are collected from nature following years of restricted growth and sculpturing by nature's hand. Perhaps their roots have been restricted by rocky or boggy terrain, or they've been exposed to salty winds. They may have been "trimmed" for decades by grazing animals. The hostile conditions found at high altitude, such as drought, snow, and gales, produce many masterpieces. One or more of these circumstances and, of course, time can produce wonderful specimens. Some of the best examples of such collected wildlings in the British Isles are common juniper, English yew, hawthorn, larch, Scotch pine, and sloe (*Prunus spinosa*). However, the list is endless.

I do not like removing such natural wonders from their habitat unless some catastrophic event, such as a road being built, land being cleared, etc., is threatening their existence. In any case, you should obtain written permission before removing such a tree. Often, landowners are glad to help. Many times these trees are located in areas where their absence wouldn't be noticed. It might even be beneficial.

What upsets me is when such a tree is removed at the wrong time of year or not enough thought is given to its care. I also hate to see such a tree radically redesigned or sold as a potential bonsai the same year it was dug up without allowing the roots to settle down for at least two years to ensure its future. You should only collect such trees with permission, and you should plan carefully how you can transport your specimen. If the operation is successful, the tree should live far longer in its new container than in the wild, and it is sure to have many admirers.

The best time to dig up a wildling is in early spring, just prior to bud burst. It is also possible just after the leaves fall, but I would then use bottom heat to encourage new fibrous root formation and to discourage winter waterlogging. Older pines seem to benefit from being dug up after the buds have started swelling and have extended up to ⅜ inch (1 cm) or even a little more. In Britain, this typically occurs at the end March to the middle of April.

Case History 1 in Chapter 13 documents the successful collection of a Scotch pine wildling, removed in the middle of June. Note how the tree growth has been held back by transplant shock, despite extensive aftercare. Late removal is not recommended.

Dig a deep trench all around the tree and then undercut the root ball. Collect the maximum amount of fibrous root and keep the root ball intact by wrapping it in burlap or plastic and tying it together. Such a root ball may be very heavy, and you may need a friend to help load it into your vehicle. Prune back the top selectively, removing up to a third of the foliage mass. Ensure that the soil has some moisture, spraying the tree regularly to reduce transpiration loss.

Pot the tree as soon as possible in a large grow box or container (see the Repotting and Growing Bed sections). Treat it like a developing bonsai just removed from the growing bed. However, be sure to anchor the tree, mist it several times daily for two months, and protect it from any wind. Do not feed it for at least eight weeks. If you are doubtful about its survival, plunge the tree, including the container, into a soil-warming box specially made for reviving trees (see the Tree Reviving section at the end of this chapter).

Such trees normally settle into containers very well after a couple of years if they are handled correctly. However, a few remain delicate for many years until they develop a good root structure again. The most notable delicate example in the British Isles is the common juniper (*Juniperus communis*). A needle juniper form can still be temperamental after five or more years in a container.

Once established in its natural habitat, common juniper is so robust, even in the hottest situation with the poorest and driest soil, that it appears baffling that this tree has such problems in re-establishing its equilibrium in a shallow pot. However, very deep roots support the drought resistance in its natural habitat, and morning mists compensate for the heat. Just because a tree adapts over time to such hostile conditions is no indicator of its instant adaptability to a shallow container set out in the blazing sun.

To transplant this species successfully from the wild, I consider bottom heat essential for at least the first three months. In addition, you need to create a plastic windbreak surrounding the tree to establish a stable root system with a minimum of transpiration loss. Shade the tree and mist it twice daily for eight weeks. Using a hoop tunnel for protection might help. You'll have to compensate for the drier hoop tunnel environment by misting more frequently in order to avoid foliage dieback. A cool, shady corner of a garden is an ideal spot, perhaps under trees. The bottom heat will protect the roots from cold and frost. A loosely fitting plastic sheet over the soil surface on wet days will stop soil waterlogging. A deep pot is essential to avoid massive soil moisture variations and to maintain good drainage. Be sure that the surface roots don't dry out or become overheated.

In years to come, you can slowly reduce the pot depth. However, if you envision a shallow pot, you'll need a much higher loam content to maintain the soil moisture. For extra insurance, try to keep your future pot design ideas on the deep side. An alternative successful collection of a common juniper is described in Case History 1 in Chapter 10.

TRUNKS

Often the sole purpose of a growing bed is to develop a thick trunk. Of course, you know that you'll rebuild a new branch structure after transplanting the tree to a container. This potting is essential in some fine-branching designs because the growth energy of the tree must be slowed down enough so that it produces much smaller diameter shoots. You can strip the branches of deciduous trees overnight at the appropriate time of year, as shown in this Chinese elm example. On the other hand, evergreens must always retain foliage. Hence, such an operation can only be done in stages of branch replacing and branch shortening (see the Scotch Pine Case Studies).

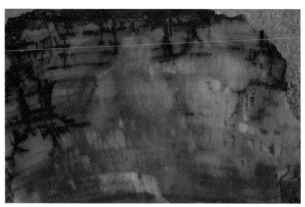

2–53 • A petrified tree slice from Arizona displayed at the Flourissant Fossil Park.

2–54 • A Moreton Bay fig at the Royal Botanic Gardens, Sydney, Australia.

Overview—Chinese Elm

Ulmus parvifolia is a very attractive tree from China, Korea, and Japan. It is rarely planted as a specimen tree. Compared to most of the elm family, it is a small tree.

This tree makes an excellent bonsai subject because of its small leaves, fine twigs, deeply fissured bark (on Japanese strains), and ready trunk basal flare. Although deciduous in cooler climates, its leaves linger at the end of the growing season, revealing its evergreen tendencies in warmer climes.

As a bonsai, it is normally very healthy, but it occasionally suffers from mite damage, which results in galls. These should be removed and burned in June. The trees can be susceptible to root rot if the soil drainage is poor or if the garden soil remains after several repots. I use well-draining soil for medium or deep pots.

Prune heavily at repotting time in the middle of February or early March. The tree will produce buds from old wood. Prune and thin out the new shoot length to a point where the shoot will divide. This increases ramification. Budding is prolific along new shoots.

Keep spring light levels high to avoid leggy (etiolated) shoots. Remove any such shoots to encourage shorter, compact shoots to sprout.

After you've pruned, wire new shoots as needed. Remove any unwanted heavy sucker-type branches that emerge from the trunk or from a branch base. The latter are worse because they will eventually kill the branch if you don't remove them.

Although Chinese elms are very accommodating trees, they must not be exposed to winter cold on benches; they require cold greenhouse or hoop tunnel protection to avoid serious damage or death.

Leaf scorch can occur after repotting unless you are careful to wean the bonsai slowly from shade to sun over a period of four or five weeks. The tree will recover from such damage, but it looks unsightly. This species likes sun exposure except on the hottest days, but the trees benefit from a deeper than normal pot to avoid drought.

Case History 1

Chinese Elm from Cutting

2–55 • This is a 10-year-old tree from a cutting. It was dug up from a friend's growing bed (1992).

2–56 • I acquired this beautiful potential bonsai tree and removed all the branches (May 1992).

2–57 • Five weeks later, I had many new shoots to choose from. I wired and cut a select few and removed the rest.

2–58 • I pruned off the heavy roots and wired the new ones in place where possible (February 1993).

2–59 • I had too many branches to choose from. Notice the disturbing upward trend of the branches (February 1993).

2–60 • A close-up of the branches (February 1993).

2–61 • Time to thin out and wire before new shoots emerge. This method maximizes the new season's growth where it is required in just about a dozen branches.

2–62 • This is a sketch of my proposed design.

2–63 • The growth was substantial (October 1993).

2–64 • The tree gets an additional pruning (December 1993).

2–65 • The tree in 1997.

2–66 • This winter image identifies refinement work still to be done (November 1998).

2–67 • The continuation of the usual pruning and wiring work.

2–68 • It is becoming a charming bonsai only seven years and seven months after I gave it a total branch strip to bare trunk (July 1999).

FOLIAGE MASSES

At Reddich Bonsai Club, a young man named James, new to bonsai, stopped me in the middle of a club talk. He asked me, in the self-assured and direct manner that only youngsters seem to possess, "Why do you keep talking about foliage pads? Do all trees have them?" His question was brilliant. I paused to think, and at last I recalled my "waterside larch" as I was probing my gray cells for a sensible answer. This larch was trained in a weeping habit with no obvious pads. The young lad was right. I knew by his question that he didn't think all trees had pads!

It is easy to get into a rut, to oversimplify when explaining bonsai development. The term "foliage pad" now conjures up images of lollipops or blobs of foliage such as the stylized and pompon bonsai referred to in Chapter 1 and oversimplifies the natural tree image I am trying to create and recommend.

Hence, I prefer to use the term "foliage masses." However in this book, I do occasionally still refer to pads to help identify the basic building block that you develop on each branch in most designs. These need to interrelate and balance with all the other pads in the design. The following sketches of a Scotch pine (in the U.K. referred to as Scots pine) show a simplified pad arrangement that developed into a foliage mass arrangement (**2–69** and **2–70**). This shore pine (**2–71**) is projected with a foliage-mass based design (**2–72**). The trick is either to merge several pads into foliage masses or to avoid pads and to develop foliage masses from the beginning.

2–69 ● A sketch of a Scotch pine based on use of foliage pads.

2–70 ● A sketch of the same tree using foliage masses.

2–71 ● A sketch of a shore pine tree before designing.

2–72 ● The proposed design of the shore pine based on the use of foliage pads.

Case History

European Larch, Weeping Style

This waterside larch is an example of foliage masses as opposed to pads. At one stage, when I could not analyze what was wrong with this larch design, I broke the foliage masses down into three smaller shapes. This mechanism suggested a five-area solution to me (see the Bonsai Design section in Chapter 3).

2–73 ● You can make out three arches: one to the left, a higher one to the right, and the top one covering the crown.

2–74 ● I modified this tree to a five-arch design over the next four years.

WINTER PROTECTION

This subject is dear to my heart. My initial approach to bonsai growing was that if trees could not survive all year on benches, then the hobby was too complicated for me. All my trees were exposed to the worst elements for many years, and the learning experience was great, as was the eventual death toll.

2–75 ● Bonsai overwintering on benches in my garden (Christmas 1990).

Over the years, I have very successfully modified my winter protection strategy into two broad groups:
❖ species that stay outside on benches all year.
❖ species that need an unheated cold greenhouse (or unheated well-lit garage or hoop tunnel).

For simplicity, I shall refer to these as on benches or in a cold greenhouse.

The winter survival of your bonsai depends on knowing the tree type and the correct environment for that species. When winters are really cold, I may move one or two benched trees into cold greenhouse storage.

Be sure to take the adverse conditions in your locale into account. For example, be aware of frost pockets in low ground or rapid reheating in spots that face south or east where the morning sun can rapidly thaw and damage tender plants and flowers. For this reason, locate your cold greenhouse or hoop tunnel in a shady place not warmed by the sun in early winter or in spring. Failing that, you should provide overhead shade netting.

The best hardiness teacher is experience. However, I see the value of hardiness zone numbering, initiated by the United States Department of Agriculture

(USDA) in the 1930s. It has since been adopted and adapted in Europe, Australia, and other areas.

In the zoning system, trees are given a hardiness number from 1 to 11 (arctic to tropics) indicating the average annual minimum temperature that a tree type will survive in the wild. Corresponding world zone maps define these areas.

Most books and references, including this book, use the following USDA zone classification and average minimum temperatures:

Zone 1	below -50°F	below -45.6°C
Zone 2	-50 to -40°F	-42.8 to -40°C
2a	-50 to -45°F	-45.5 to -42.8°C
2b	-45 to -40°F	-42.7 to -40°C
Zone 3	-40 to -30°F	-40 to -34°C
3a	-40 to -35°F	-39.9 to -37.3°C
3b	-35 to -30°F	-37.2 to -34.5°C
Zone 4	-30 to -20°F	-34 to -29°C
4a	-30 to -25°F	-34.4 to -31.7°C
4b	-25 to -20°F	-31.6 to -28.9°C
Zone 5	-20 to -10°F	-29 to -23°C
5a	-20 to -15°F	-28.8 to -26.2°C
5b	-15 to -10°F	-26.1 to -23.4°C
Zone 6	-10 to 0°F	-23 to -17°C
6a	-10 to -5°F	-23.3 to -20.6°C
6b	-5 to 0°F	-20.5 to -17.8°C
Zone 7	0 to 10°F	-17 to -12°C
7a	0 to 5°F	-17.7 to -15°C
7b	5 to 10°F	-14.9 to -12.3°C
Zone 8	10 to 20°F	-12 to -7°C
8a	10 to 15°F	-12.2 to -9.5°C
8b	15 to 20°F	-9.4 to -6.7°C
Zone 9	20 to 30°F	-7 to -1°C
9a	20 to 25°F	-6.6 to -3.9°C
9b	25 to 30°F	-3.8 to -1.2°C
Zone 10	30 to 40°F	-1 to 4°C
10a	30 to 35°F	-1 to 1.6°C
10b	35 to 40°F	1.7 to 4.4°C
Zone 11	above 40°F	above 4.5°C

The extra divisions in the zone (the *a*'s and *b*'s) and Zone 11 were recently introduced.

You can find a world of information on hardiness on the Internet (try searching "hardiness zone").

Zone numbers apply to trees growing in the wild; in the British Isles or in similar climates, any tree in Zone 8 or lower will normally survive our winters. For bonsai trees in pots in cool climates, any tree in Zone 4 or lower will, in theory, survive on open benches. For climates above Zone 4, use a cold greenhouse or the equivalent. Zone 8 and above are warm temperate or subtropical. Plants will usually need some winter heat to avoid subzero temperatures. The zone number has to be reduced drastically to work for bonsai because the small containers result in rapid temperature and moisture fluctuations, greatly reducing the tree's hardiness.

I need to add a word of caution at this stage. Some big climatic differences mean that we cannot just take the zone numbers at face value. While these zone numbers are a useful guide, they are based on minimum average winter temperature. However, these are not the only variables that affect vegetation. Local climate characteristics, such as the average summer temperature (much lower in cool climates), moisture, wind, soil, late frost, and pollution, have a marked influence.

If you are using hardiness numbers for trees or shrubs planted in the open in cool climates, you need to subtract one from the plant zone number. A tree designated as Zone 8 should, in theory, survive in most cool climates. In fact, it needs to be a Zone 7 category plant to survive comfortably, chiefly due to colder summers in these climates.

The genetic composition of the plant and the climatic profile of its country of origin are other variables. For example, a birch from Siberia will not behave like its European equivalent. The plant experiences only winter or summer in Siberia and has a short growing season. That area has no equivalent to our spring. Hence, once warm spring weather occurs, the plant begins to grow, only to be damaged or killed by a spring frost. The European equivalent is better able to withstand the drastic temperature fluctuations characteristic of temperate zone springs.

We can use the genus Larix (larch) as an example of how to use hardiness zone numbers. People often presume that they are hardy on benches, but to be sure, you must examine each species:

Larix decidua (European larch) is Zone 2 or -50 to -40°F (-46 to -40°C)

Larix eurolepis (hybrid larch) is Zone 5 or -20 to -10°F (-29 to -23°C)

Larix kaempferi (Japanese larch) is Zone 7 or 0 to 10°F (-18 to -12°C)

The hybrid (*L. eurolepis*) has an intermediate hardiness between its European and Japanese parents.

Using Zone 4 or less as a definition of hardy, we see that only European larch is actually hardy on benches. This zoning is slightly different from my experience; I have found the hybrid to be fully hardy on benches. The Japanese larch, as suggested by the zone number, needs cold greenhouse protection in cool climates. However, these are among the last trees I bring in, probably after snow or maybe at 23°F (-5°C), typically at the end of November or early December (**2–76**). In very cold winters, Japanese larch trees are on the edge of survival if left on benches. You'll see symptoms of this as red margins on the emerging spring leaves.

2–76 ●
Japanese larch is not fully winter hardy on benches in my area, but it benefits from a chill before moving to shelter.

Larch (and any temperate zone tree) can die from extremes of overprotection. I kept my first larch and spruce seedlings indoors for their first winter. By February, they were sprouting new shoots and looking great; by March, they were dead because they never had winter rest and hardening.

Taking one more example, maples are often assumed to be hardy as bonsai on benches in the British Isles. Bitter experience has taught me that few are.

Acer buergerianum (trident maple) is Zone 6 or -10 to 0°F (-23 to -18°C)

Acer ginnala (amur maple) is Zone 2 or -50 to -40°F (-46 to -40°C) to Zone 4 or -30 to -20°F (-34 to -29°C)

Acer griseum (paperbark maple) is Zone 5 or -20 to -10°F (-29 to -23°C)

Acer japonicum (full moon maple) is Zone 5 or -20 to -10°F (-29 to -23°C)

Acer pseudoplatanus (sycamore) is Zone 4 or

-30 to -20°F (-34 to -29°C)

Acer palmatum (mountain maple) is Zone 5 or -20 to -10°F (-29 to -23°C)

In practice, only *A. ginnala* and *A. pseudoplatanus* are hardy on benches, and this agrees with the zone numbering.

The hardiness zone numbers are only a guide to tree hardiness. They are not a substitute for practical experience when growing bonsai. Appendix 1 lists typical bonsai hardiness zone numbers and, more important, is a practical guide to bonsai hardiness. Based on my experience, you can categorize bonsai:

❖ hardy on benches
❖ hardy on benches, but protect when really cold
❖ hardy in cold greenhouse or hoop tunnel

Placing a tree, including the pot, into sheltered ground and submerging the pot totally helps greatly. Typically, it will improve hardiness by two zone numbers, making Zone 6 or less trees hardy as bonsai if placed in sheltered garden soil. The control of watering, insect infestation, etc., makes this method unsuitable on a large scale.

Roots are one of the main keys to winter survival. Waterlogging is bad for bonsai. During winter, the root tips of most species will die if they are waterlogged over a long period. The problem is a lack of oxygen and a buildup of carbon dioxide. To compound the situation, new root tips overwintered in waterlogged soil are less able to withstand freezing than are roots in well-drained soil. In well-drained soil, roots develop a brown protective coating after shedding excess water at the onset of freezing conditions. Waterlogged roots cannot prepare for being frozen. Consequently, they suffer more damage. For bonsai species categorized as bench hardy and open to winter rain and snow, soil drainage is the key to survival because you have no way to control watering during the winter months (see the Soils section in this chapter).

Later in the growing season, using a feeding regime with low or no nitrogen assists in tree hardiness (see the Fertilizing section in this chapter). Nitrogen feeds late in the season interfere with growth inhibitor levels. Thus, they reduce winter hardiness, particularly for evergreens.

Light is also a factor in the winter hardiness of bonsai. Usually, we say that deciduous trees are hardy without light, although I have seen less twig dieback in good light for susceptible species. On the other hand, evergreens (broad-leaved and coniferous) need at least low light levels during the winter to retain maximum hardiness. Storing evergreens greatly reduces their hardiness.

Above all, winter hardiness is a balance between the hormones that promote growth and those that inhibit growth. Warm spring days, especially long spells, are harmful to bonsai. A few warm days will lull the tree out of its hardiness. If this weather is followed by freezing cold and winds, the tree has insufficient time to regain full hardiness; thus, root damage results. Full hardiness may take several days to return after warm weather.

Fluctuating winter temperatures are also more damaging than consistently low ones. Roots typically stop growing below 36°F (2°C) and only restart once this temperature is exceeded. If the temperature drop is small, for example, from 36°F (2°C) to 30°F (-1°C), growth restarts in a few days. If the temperature drops more severely, such as from 36°F (2°C) to 20°F (-7°C), this delays the start of root growth for several weeks. If warm weather returns, it is more harmful to the foliage.

Desiccation of evergreen foliage (especially *Cedrus* and pine) is a significant factor. Cedars react very badly to cold winter temperatures and can shed all their needles overnight during a very cold spell if they are not protected in a cold greenhouse. Unless repotted, Scotch pines are perfectly hardy on benches, although many other pine species are not. All branches, leaves, and needles transpire in the winter, and they can be damaged if the soil freezes for long periods. From January to May, pines and cedars will show signs of needle browning due to cumulative desiccation damage. This damage is quite normal to some degree. The problem is made worse if insufficient foliage is left on the tree or if, following a repot, the roots are not functioning normally.

Observe all bonsai emerging from winter. Buds that are slow to swell or are reddened rather than the usual green are danger signs. Emerging leaf margins that are red are another indication of cold or frost damage caused by a lack of protection.

For all the above reasons and from experience, I never transfer trees from cold greenhouse or hoop tunnel to open benches until the first of May (in England). Many growers are tempted into transfer-ring earlier, but I believe it is best to avoid late frost and cold damage.

Keeping light levels high during the winter avoids elongation of new shoots, particularly of deciduous trees. These weak, pale, etiolated shoots look like watercress and are particularly evident on Chinese elm, trident maple, and *Zelkova*. If your storage light levels are insufficient to avoid etiolation, just prune off these shoots as you transfer the trees to open benches. To avoid leaf scorch, keep the trees in shade for two or three weeks if the storage light levels were low (see also the sections on Sun and Shade in this chapter).

The transfer from a cold greenhouse to benches may require temperature acclimatization unless you are able to introduce colder air into your cold greenhouse or similar storage area. I now use a cross between a hoop tunnel and an air house. It has a netting skirt that comes to just below bench height. Normally an air house is used for summer strawberry growing or the like. Purchasing an air house and substantially lowering the horizontal rails provides winter warmth and summer cool. The plastic cover was long enough to extend down one side to form a roll-up blind to regulate the draft. During the winter, this blind is partially or completely shut. In the spring, it helps to acclimatize bonsai, depending on temperature. This and the high light levels allow me to transfer bonsai straight from my air house to benches, providing no bright sunshine is forecast for a few days. A final benefit of the air house variant of a hoop tunnel is that it becomes possible to over-winter bonsai that would be prone to mildew attack in an unventilated hoop tunnel.

2–77 • Casting hoop tunnel uprights into submerged concrete blocks or, in this case, to an extension of wall footings, adds security against damage for sites exposed to high winds.

2–78 ● It's helpful to erect the benches first to avoid ripping the cover with the long wooden rails.

2–79 ● I laid an entrance path on flooring sand complete with underground services (electricity and water).

2–80 ● To increase the security of the tunnel against high winds, cast eyebolts in concrete and use them to anchor tensioners with the help of many strands of wire looped around to form a rope.

2–81 ● Locate the tensioner in a hole drilled on the top side of the angled strengthening tubes.

2–82 ● An old pull-down projector screen makes a useful photo backdrop.

2–83 • Olly owl the Ollytunnel mascot.

I grow a wide variety of temperate trees as bonsai. I've summarized my winter hardiness experiences by species in Appendix 1. As a general rule, variants and cultivars (often developed for finer leaf shape or color) tend to be less hardy than the commoner species or genus itself. Typical examples are *Fagus sylvatica purpurea*, which is far less hardy than *Fagus sylvatica* (common beech) and *Acer palmatum* 'Butterfly' (Zone 6) when compared to *Acer palmatum* (Zone 5).

AUTUMN COLOR

Here are some ways to improve the autumn color of deciduous bonsai:

❖ Expose to full sun in late summer and autumn to maximize the sugars in the leaves

❖ Expose leaves to cold air and frost to trap sugars in the leaves

❖ Remove leaves early in the season to prompt a smaller set of new leaves (deciduous trees only)

❖ Keep the soil drier late in the summer (a risky strategy).

TREE REVIVING

Lack of root function due to root tip damage can occur when trees are underprotected, and a lovely, warm spring week is followed by a sudden subzero spell. Trees newly collected from the wild or repotted trees are also susceptible, especially if too much root is removed or temperatures plummet. Waterlogged soils,

root rot, soil infestation, overfeeding, and severe drought are among the many other causes. All of these can produce symptoms such as lack of leafing, collapse of existing leaves, or desiccation of needles. Milder cases can be caused by heat stress, indicated by a lack of new-shoot growth and by foliage damage from the leaf tip backward. If the existing leaves remain healthy-looking, the heat stressed bonsai will normally recover, providing it is positioned in a shadier spot (see the Branch Weakness section of this chapter).

In severe cases, I recommend a bottom heating system to stimulate root growth and revival. If the soil is infested or diseased or if the roots are rotting, you'll need to correct these conditions first. Dunk the complete root ball of infested or diseased trees in a large bowl of appropriate insecticide or fungicide for an hour or more. Prune off all the rotted roots back to healthy live root; seal the cuts and replace the disturbed soil with faster draining, high grit content soil (see the Pests and Diseases section of this chapter).

A typical bottom heat box is a large custom-made wooden box having the usual drainage holes and, preferably, handles. It is located in a shady, sheltered spot outdoors. Fill it with one-third potting grit (3 to 4 mm) with a thin compost layer above. Place the 15-watt soil warming cable in a snaking pattern on the compost. Bury it with more soil, until the box is about ⅔ full. Then, pass the thermostat through a hole in the box and align it with the soil surface ¾ inch (2 cm) above the cable. Wire the thermostat, following all safety guidelines carefully. I made a hinged all-weather box over the thermostat to keep out the damp. The box is now ready and on standby for any emergency. To revive a tree, remove it from its container or keep it in the container and place it in the box on the grit. Add more grit to fill the box.

2–84 • This is an undersoil heated box used for reviving trees.

Case History

Atlas Cedar—Needle Drop

2–85 ● I removed too many roots from this atlas cedar when I repotted it. The result was almost total old-needle drop (April 1990).

2–86 ● Three weeks later, you can see new shoots emerging.

2–87 ● After an additional four weeks, the fresh, new foliage is well established, but there is evidence of some dead branches, too.

The cedar illustrated had been mistreated twice. The first time, I removed too much root in the spring of 1990 as I sawed through the root ball in the most cavalier way. This is not recommended because you may end up with a tree with no connected roots. I should have reduced the size of root ball more over the years. The tree recovered without the use of bottom heat, but as you see from the photographs, it lost some useful branches.

I stored my cedar on garden benches over the winter. The tree had fully recovered its strength when the next problem occurred. Unfortunately, spring 1992 was a defining year for cedars in the British Isles. In a normal year, new blue cedar needles appear in April or May, but a warm spell followed by cold and very strong cold winds in late spring desiccated the old needles and, on the trees affected the most, even the 1-year-old needles were lost. Many collectors lost cedar bonsai that year. Fortunately, some trees recovered naturally. My cedar remained dormant until the middle of July when I decided to utilize a heat box.

As you can imagine, I now protect them in a cold greenhouse. If a combination of one spring night of cold temperature, prolonged frozen soil, and cold, desiccating winds can prompt almost total old needle drop, it is time to modify my winter protection.

By the twelfth of July, that year's buds were still dormant, although they were very slightly swollen. Something was needed to save this evergreen tree, which cannot survive for long with no new foliage at all.

I placed the tree in the box and topped it off with grit. I added a plastic soil cover that was loose enough to let in air. It stopped rain from waterlogging the already wet soil. I set the thermostat at 75°F (23°C). In cold weather, it may take a few days to reach this temperature.

Two weeks after placing the tree in the box, the buds were very swollen; two weeks later, new needles appeared. After four more weeks (the middle of September), I started to dial down the thermostat; this process took two weeks. In November, I placed the tree in winter protection. Although the tree was weakened, I had saved it. Within two years, it was fully vigorous again.

2–88 • To avoid waterlogging the soil, use a plastic soil covering if you keep the tree outdoors.

2–89 • Last year's needles were dormant or dying, and this year's buds were still dormant in July due to a warm spring spell followed by sudden subzero temperatures and dessicating winds.

2–90 • After four weeks, the tree is recovering, but it is still slow to drink, as evidenced by excessive liverwort present on the soil surface.

2–91 • Two years later, the tree is fully recovered.

I had a similar experience with the hawthorn case studied in Chapter 12. On April 22, 1979, slightly green buds were visible, but they were not opening. It was as if they were in a suspended state. This was due to a combination of excessive root removal at repotting time (because the tree was root bound) and a warm spell, which was followed by a very cold spell.

I followed the same procedure as above, except that I set the thermostat for a soil temperature of 70°F (21°C), and I erected a plastic windbreak around the box.

For the next two days, the buds continued to shrink slightly, then they stabilized. Four weeks later, the tree leafed and was saved. Its brother (collected in the same place and at the same time two and a half years previously) had been in the same condition, but untreated, it remained dormant for a total of fifteen months. When it did leaf, 90 percent of its branches were dead, proof of the power of bottom heat.

Branch Weakness

Branch weakness rather than root weakness can have a number of causes. Among these are having too much vigorous foliage in dominant areas, leaving trees in too much shade, exposing them to too much sun, drought or overwatering, insect damage (above and below the soil), wiring that is too tight (branches on fast-growing trees such as pines can strangle), overladen fruit or cones (especially crab apples and larches), underfeeding (junipers are particularly prone to this), overfeeding (all the foliage and young shoots normally collapse), too little winter light (for example, *Acer burguerianum*), or by having too little space between branches.

Uneven foliage vigor is common for plants such as azaleas, *Chamaecyparis pisifera* 'Boulevard', *Cryptomeria*, and Kyohime maples. They need to have well-balanced foliage strength to avoid excessive dieback in their weaker parts. This requires selective pruning of new shoots during the growing season (and occasionally more radical spring structure pruning) to even out the vigor in all parts of the tree.

Excessively heavy foliage areas can also cause lower branch dieback in very hot spells. This can result from leaving all of this season's growth on trees. The branches can also be shaded out if you don't give them sufficient room for air and light. Larches are susceptible to this low branch dieback in hot spells (see Chapter 11). Avoid such problems by providing partial shade in summer, by pruning excessively long new growth, or by correcting an inadequate water supply for the soil. An example of lower branch dieback on larches is illustrated in Case History 3 in Chapter 14.

Lack of sunshine will cause some sun-loving bonsai such as birch, *Cryptomeria*, and pine to experience dieback, especially on the lower and under-branches. Others will grow weaker and will have longer new growth.

If the lower branches on a cascade-style bonsai are weak, angle the pot with wedges to raise the affected branches. Spray weakened foliage areas with a liquid feed that is suitable for foliage, but use it in a slightly weaker solution. I use Phostrogen. Apply it once every two or three days, spraying only the weakened areas; repeat this process throughout the growing season.

Heat stress from too much sun is a common problem. I have one hybrid twin larch (Case History 3, Chapter 11) that has been almost dormant for many years despite feeding and daily watering. It is in a very shallow oval pot. During even moderately warm summer days, the soil dries quickly. In hindsight, I realize that heat stress stopped the normal shoot extension for so many years that I began to think it was a runt. When we moved to another house, our new garden was not all open to full sun; it has a cool, semi-shaded valley in which the tree soon resumed normal growth.

Correct obvious problems. For instance, move trees out of extreme shade or full sun, remove tight wire and some fruits or new cones, correct foliage mass imbalance, improve light to shaded-out branches, correct soil problems, etc. If the tree was overfed, keep applying water to leach the feed out of the soil and shade the tree; if the tree was underfed, improve the feeding regime.

Drought will quickly weaken a tree, leaving it open to foliage and branch dieback and to insect and disease attack. In particular, avoid drought for maple, *Arbutus,* azalea, birch, *Chamaecyparis pisifera* 'Boulevard', hawthorn, common juniper, larch, linden (lime), magnolia, *Nyssa,* poplar, *Taxodium,* and willow.

Waterlogging will weaken a tree, especially during cold winters. This can create the ideal conditions for fungal attack, especially on types such as beech, birch, crab apple, gingko, holly, *Lonicera,* mulberry, and oak that are prone to this type of attack.

In all such cases, ensure that the soil is only sufficiently moist (check Appendix 1 for guidelines by species), not waterlogged. The foliage should be misted in hot weather, and the tree should be protected in a well-lit, cold-greenhouse type environment during the winter months. Repeat remedial treatments until the tree's vigor returns. This may take several seasons.

Insect infestation is covered earlier in this chapter under the section on Pests and Diseases.

Overladen fruits or flowers can affect many bonsai, including azalea and camellia flowers and apple, crab apple, Chinese quince (*Chaenomeles chinensis*), and larch fruits and cones. An example of a crab apple overladen with fruit is given in Case History 1 in Chapter 4.

Underfeeding can cause a loss of lower branch vigor as discussed under the Feeding section earlier in this chapter.

Overfeeding is unlikely to result in selective loss in branch vigor. However, extreme overfeeding can cause rapid dehydration, collapse, and death of a bonsai. Such a situation is rare, especially if you are using liquid feeds. I have only witnessed it due to an experimental overapplication of quick-release feed granules (see Feeding section earlier in this chapter).

3

Principles & Process of Bonsai Design

KEY DESIGN PRINCIPLES

Designing bonsai is essentially decision making, based on sound principles. Once your decisions are made, the process is usually easy, but please do not start unless you have a clear plan.

To create your very own bonsai from start to finish, try reading the aims and goals discussed in Chapter 1 and the key design principles listed below. While I am not conscious of them every minute, they are the basis of all my decisions when I am creating or maintaining bonsai. They are the key that unlocked my hands and released a skill that eluded me for the first ten or more years of bonsai growing.

When reading these principles, imagine that you have a partly developed tree in front of you and that you have decisions to make. This may be the first design phase, or you may be stuck on what to do next with an established bonsai. By the end of today, you hope to have planned, pruned, wired, and shaped it to create the first design steps toward a future masterpiece. Better still, bring in a tree right now and try applying the following principles to it.

1. Aim for a Natural Bonsai

The goal is to present a natural bonsai. Remember the definition presented earlier:

> A natural bonsai is one that has no obvious man-made elements to jar the design, such as an ugly, chopped trunk, branches, or stumps. It has no wire marks or sudden big changes in taper, texture, or refinement. The trunk and major branches in particular will have a pleasing taper and shape. It does not have a long straight, uninteresting trunk or branches; rather it has interesting curves or directional changes. It does not possess unconvincing areas of dead wood or overlarge leaves or flowers. It is three dimensional, containing many areas of interest and viewing angles. It also has a pleasing, treelike shape, evoking images of trees in nature, allowing you to cross that tree/bonsai line in some way.

3–1 • Douglas fir and foxgloves at Pico Arieiro, 5,900 feet (1800 m) above sea level, Madeira.

The early stages of a beautiful tree.

Avoid any evidence of the hand of man or woman in the final image even though the development process will require much handiwork.

2. Look for Outstanding Natural Features

Every potential bonsai is unique. It is up to our imagination to select some bend, twist, or angle that makes the tree in front of us different and to build on that difference. Our job is to avoid a "formula tree." As you examine a feature, imagine how you might echo it and/or reverse it (possibly on a smaller scale). You might want to emphasize it or complement it within the design.

Case History

European Larch—A Rule Breaker

The European larch illustrated here had one outstanding feature: a long, sweeping branch off an inner trunk curve. This is a definite rule breaker in most bonsai books. As it turns out, this feature has been the making of the tree. Over the first fifteen years, I felt it necessary to double the trunk height to 22 inches (55 cm), wiring a small branch shoot upward to make the new trunk. The extra height was required to make the longish needles on the tree look more in scale. This was a long but rewarding action completed by 1988.

The tree then developed branch masses. Very heavy wire was used loosely on the top trunk for the next few years to force it to lean further to the left. The long, downward-sweeping branch was also loosely heavy-wired to get the right curve; it had tended to droop too much under the weight of the foliage. Today, the wire has been removed without any scarring, the trunk taper is smooth, the bark is maturing, and the image is far more natural.

3–2 • The trunk height has doubled in the past fifteen years. Now it is time to analyze the foliage arrangement to improve the presentation (1988).

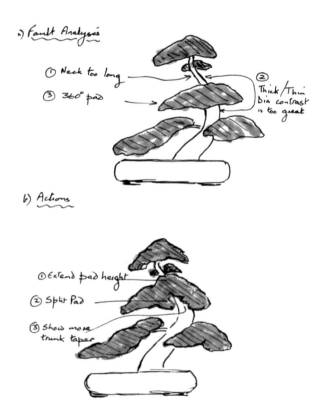

3–3 • Sketches showing the design weaknesses at present and the proposed corrective measures.

3–4 • I heavy-wired the trunk top to lower the top left branch (1990).

3–5 • I enlarged the rear pad below the crown to the left to fill the gap (1991).

3–6 • This is the winter image (1992).

3–7 • Nine years after I sketched the proposed design, the image is much improved (1997).

3. Find the Front

Examine the trunk, root, and major branches. Angle the tree in all directions and settle on a front. Mark this by placing a wire or stick in the soil vertical to the new design angle. The decision process should also take into account many of the other factors listed below. Do not necessarily follow the typical advice that the "crown must come forward." This is a device that adds the illusion of depth to the tree. It is very well illustrated, in extreme form, by the side and front views of this attractive white pine (**3–8** to **3–9**). Selecting a front based simply on a forward-pointing crown severely restricts your design options. If a design looks good, you can easily create perspective by placing some branches forward and some toward the rear.

If there are two possible fronts, mark them both and develop the future design around both possibilities, keeping one as the main front.

3–9 ● This is a front view of the imported white pine.

4. Examine Growth Energy

Most trees are apically dominant, growing stronger at the top than the bottom. A word of caution though; others, such as Kyohime maples and azaleas, can be basally dominant. Study your subject tree and analyze whether it has a natural growth imbalance. This affects your final design, as you may need to radically thin down and shorten strong areas in order to rejuvenate weaker ones. If possible, discard very weak branches from your future design to avoid disappointment if they fail to respond to training.

5. Create All-Round, Three-Dimensional Images

Think ahead to the time when the tree is nearer completion. Imagine how well your proposed design will look from other viewing angles. Had you planned to remove branches that instead can be moved to improve the all-round look without spoiling the primary (front) viewing angle? At least leave them there for now and review them as you are shaping the tree. Please do not arbitrarily remove chunks of foliage and branches just to "see the wood for the trees." You are sure to lose a vital branch.

Do not design a two-dimensional tree that

3–8 ● Here's a side view of an imported white pine showing an amazing trunk angle that greatly improved the perspective when viewed from the front. (Bonsai courtesy of Malcolm and Kath Hughes.)

3–10 ● This close-up shows the three-dimensional aspects of the bonsai design.

disappears when you turn it sideways. Build in lots of front-to-back movement and depth as shown here.

6. Maximize Eye Movements

Look for a strong line, but don't ignore other areas of interest. Don't oversimplify the design. The success of a bonsai design lies in the mental reaction of the viewer; this is a function of eye movements and the resulting brain stimulation. You want to stimulate the eye to make as many movements as possible. The key factors are:

❖ Initial Point of Focus—The tree should have an initial point of focus. Normally, that would be an interesting trunk or trunk basal flare, preferably near the center of the object.

❖ One Strong Line—The eye should be strongly led along one line, for example, a long branch, a tall trunk, or a long cascading trunk. The eyes will follow lines first, although they will join points to make a line. I've included a charming cascade hawthorn to illustrate the importance of a strong, artistic line.

3–11 ● A lovely example of a cascade hawthorn bonsai. (Photo and bonsai courtesy of Dan Barton.)

❖ Several Smaller Lines or Shapes—Other lines, such as branches, should then draw interest. These lines should invite the eye to study interesting detail, such as shapely foliage pads, sharp or shapely bends in branches, interruptions in trunk line using small foliage pads, or attractive negative areas.

The thumbnail schematic in my notebook charts the expected eye movements for the proposed design.

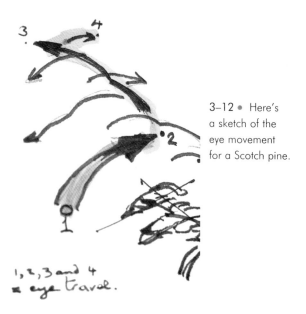

3–12 ● Here's a sketch of the eye movement for a Scotch pine.

❖ Extra Detail or Texture—Interesting shapes or colors of small leaves or needles add extra interest for the eye. Strong sunlight contrasting with the background, for example, yellow on black, green on maroon, or blue on brown also adds extra interest. The finer the detail, the larger the tree image appears.

❖ Diagonal Lines—Try to angle your trunk and branches to add interest. Horizontal and vertical lines are less stimulating, although they are more restful to the eye. Horizontal lines such as the soil and the container create stability low in the image. In general, diagonal lines are more stimulating.

See how much more interesting the front of this pine is compared to the back. The difference is due to a strong dynamic line (echoed by an interesting pot line).

❖ Curved Lines—These are attractive to the eye and evoke feelings of speed.

❖ Line Ratios—To obtain a good asymmetric balance, split a line using a 2:3 or 3:5 ratio rather than

3–13 ● The front view of this very small and difficult tree shows how it was improved by emphasizing the diagonal branch line, echoing the line of the pot.

3–14 ● The back view of this tree shows how boring it is without some interesting feature.

3–15 ● The side view shows the tree has good foliage depth from front to back.

❖ Symmetrical Tension—This tension stops the flow of eye movements, creating a kind of road-block, causing the eyes to oscillate between the two equal stimuli, but not allowing them to move on. An example would be branches or a fork in the trunk that are opposite each other (bar branches) and that create two equal lengths and foliage masses. You need to remove or disguise one side or the other to create asymmetry. In the case of a catapult-shaped trunk, rotate it until it looks like a single trunk and an asymmetric branch. This symmetrical tension occurs also with the 1:1 line ratios discussed earlier.

❖ Perspective—If you imagine looking at a tree through a fish-eye lens, the perspective is exagger-

3–16 ● This tree in training has a jarring bend in the middle of the trunk.

a 1:1 ratio. In this developing European larch, the trunk shape changes half way up. This creates an uncomfortable feeling for the viewer (3–16). When the ratio changed, the image improved.

❖ Repetition of Shape—The eye will search for repeating shapes (such as foliage pads or strong angular branches or bends) around the bonsai. The image is most effective if these repetitions are a good distance apart, forcing the eye to examine the detail between each repetition.

ated. All the branches would radiate upward at the top of the tree, horizontally in the middle, and downward toward the bottom. Angling lower branches down more than higher branches and having a nicely tapered trunk add to this illusion.

As demonstrated perfectly by the dahlia flower, **(3–17)** exaggerated perspective applied to foliage clouds within the foliage pad produce large clouds at the bottom front, becoming slightly smaller as you go

3–17 ● The dahlia flower shows how effective an exaggerated perspective can be.

higher and nearer the top center of the pad. Detailed branch wiring gives branches and pads an exaggerated perspective, aiding in the illusion of a large tree. This also adds dynamic line.

❖ Internal Frame—A frame focuses interest inside it. Forest groups can benefit from a well-profiled canopy top, combined with the underside of the container to frame the subject. Pay particular attention to the bottom canopy line when styling a forest group. Great patience is required to align and prune shoot tips to form a smooth outline (with a few natural irregularities) around the whole tree, but this sharpens the image

3–18 ● This beautiful tree shows excellent twig profiling, creating a beautiful outline tree frame. (Bonsai courtesy of Ian Stewartson.)

spectacularly. Just picture a solitary English oak or elm in winter and recall the fine tracery and the imaginary line around the edge of the crown. This technique of combining precision with variety is illustrated in this winter image of a unique trident maple raft.

❖ Symmetry—A formal upright tree with a symmetrical design will only work if it is precise in its symmetry. The trunk must be perfectly upright, and the branch structure must be precisely arranged.

7. Draw the Current Shape (the "Before" Image)

Start with a light drawing of the current shape of the tree, using the proposed front and planting angle.

8. Draw Your Proposed Image (the "After" Image)

Superimpose a realistic final image over a copy of the current image based around the core parts of the tree that will remain. As you have already seen, some of my designs have involved total branch removal. For the purposes of understanding these design principles, let us assume we have a more compliant imaginary tree in front of us with many small branches waiting to be bent into shape. It is not important whether you can or cannot draw; do the best you can. If the drawing turns out really well, sign it! You may need several attempts to get a satisfying image, but you should always be honest regarding the core (immovable) trunk and branch positions. If you really struggle with drawing, you can follow my directions for the projection method in the Setting Your Own Goals and Agenda section of Chapter 1. If you cannot find a good image, leave the tree for another day.

9. List the Negatives (Faults)

Some people prefer to accentuate the positive. I believe passionately in concentrating on removing the negatives. I encourage people to say to me, "That branch must go," or "Nice tree, pity about the pot." Be open to all ideas, but be your own person, too. Only adopt an idea if you are convinced it is a good one.

Identifying negatives allows you to move from a current poor design position to a proposed better position. Such a leap also means you already understand what is right in a design (the positives), and it forces you to find the path to move toward this in your design. This means you must make decisions.

Case History

European Larch—Mother and Daughter

3–19 ● This tree needs a design review (1990).

Several years before I took this photograph of a European larch, I had a great idea. I wanted to shorten the trunk. The idea was to produce a strange, new, curved flying top trunk that is typical of larch. Unfortunately, the whole design was not working. I listed the following faults in my notebook:

❖   Trunk ugly at the top; neck too long; bend is crude.

❖   Lower trunk too straight and long.

❖   Scar on lower right-hand side of trunk distracts the eye.

❖   Lower mother branches too heavy and uninteresting.

❖   Linear or triangular branch pads conflict with curved trunk, especially the apex.

❖   Daughter tree or branch has no movement, no dynamic direction.

❖   Daughter neither in front nor behind mother, appears flat.

❖   Some bar branches (opposite); one bad one on left of and just below sharp trunk bend.

❖   Pad top profiles should be curved, not sloping lines, to match curves in trunk.

❖   Insufficient horizontal layers or lines in pads and insufficient detail within the pads.

Wow! Where's the trash can?

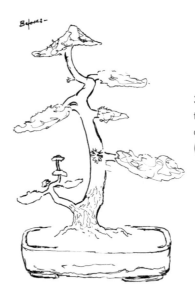
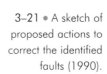

3–20 ● A sketch of the tree showing several design weaknesses (1990).

3–21 ● A sketch of proposed actions to correct the identified faults (1990).

10. List the Proposed Actions

It is hard not to be depressed by a list such as the one described on the previous page. You'll need to address each negative and consider how to resolve it. I came up with the following action list and proposed design, which turned out to be very close to the eventual tree shape. This included many new branches that did not exist at that time, but they were easy to develop from existing pads. Imagine my joy when a picture of this tree won the first *Bonsai Magazine* photo competition only two years and four months after its redesign.

3–22 ● This is a close-up of the lower right side of the trunk where I removed a major branch.

❖ Round periphery of crown should match gentle trunk curves; remove the arrow head.

❖ Extend the left-hand side of the crown downward to form a suspended pad to hide long neck and reduce distance between top pad and next pad below. Enlarge the rear branch behind the long neck to fill in the gap between crown and lower branches. Extend top right-hand branch pad to the left to cover some of the ugly top trunk bend.

❖ Split top left branch at neck base into two pads to add interest, mask parallel branch lying under it, and create a sheltering feel over the daughter. (It's always good to link mother and daughter trees with a subtle feeling of parental protection.)

❖ Enlarge the center shoot into a pad to cover and visually split the long, straight trunk.

❖ Make two pads from the lowest right-hand branch.

❖ Reduce height of daughter and emphasize diagonal trunk movement to counter the general trunk direction of daughter and echo the angular movement in mother's neck.

❖ Widen the lowest daughter pads and extend right-hand pad in front of mother trunk to give a more three-dimensional look. Leave the option to extend further and cover scar, although the scar should disappear with time. (As this picture six years later shows, time did heal the scar.)

❖ Try to form a series of horizontal areas at differing heights, all pads to be domed on top, and create several multiple pad clusters that are also broadly domed as a group.

3–23 ● The pads have improved, and the image has developed markedly (1994).

Although I think the proposed design was originally overstylized, it provided a route map, a goal. Over time, I merged the pads a little to produce a more natural look without losing the underlying rhythms.

3–24 ● The pads are less defined and are becoming foliage areas rather than pads (1999).

3–25 ● European larch trees usually turn straw yellow, but this year this one turned golden tones more typical of Japanese larch.

DESIGN PROCESS

Armed with the above principles, it's hands-on time. Place the tree on a turntable at a comfortable height. Use a plain background and place your drawing in view. Rather than wire the whole tree, wire just the trunk and core branches as required. Look at the whole tree and home in on the most interesting part, where you can develop a theme. This may be an attractive branch angle or a pad shape. Prune and wire this local area as needed. Then, keep working on its design, varying the angles, pad shade, underbranch line, etc. until you are pleased with this area.

Turn the tree around and look at it from the rear. Make any changes that feel right. Turn the tree sideways and repeat this process from both sides. Look at the front view again. Make any adjustments to return this frontal view to a pleasing design. You will have a lovely three-dimensional area that looks good from all sides.

You are still following the drawing, but you should feel free to find inspiration as you are designing. The drawing is a good map but it is only a tool. Sometimes, extra ideas occur to you while you're working on the tree. Sometimes, a radical idea comes accompanied by an overwhelming conviction. Check it carefully, but I find such overwhelming ideas are usually sound and just require the boldness to act.

3–26 ● *Picea 'Nidiformis' on a homemade rock.*

Some stylists make the mistake of removing too many inner branch shoots and buds. The result is an "arm-waving" bonsai with bare branches and bunches of foliage only at the tips. This is particularly common with subjects such as *Chamaecyparis pisifera* 'Boulevard', spruce, and some junipers that often have their most vigorous foliage at the branch tips. Not only does this detract from the final image, it leaves no future options to replace, shorten, or ramify branches.

Continue wiring, applying this method in other areas. Start at points where a repeat design beckons, perhaps a smaller or mirror image. Ensure that no two pads are on the same horizontal line and that the most prominent pads are in good diagonal opposition and in overall balance.

Continue turning the tree frequently, pruning and wiring until the design is complete.

If this is an interim design, be content that you have positioned the major branches and allowed for new growth outward and upward as the pads grow and develop. The three views of this Scotch pine show the importance of continuous turning. The side view illustrates the ease with which you can spot a misplaced branch and correct the problem, using this repeat turning technique.

Tall, Slanting, Mother and Daughter Literati Bonsai

3–27 ● Front view

3–28 ● Back view

3–29 ● Side view

INSPIRATION

3–31 • The amazing trunks of the palm lily from Mexico found in Santa Barbara, California.

3–30 • This is Inspiration Point in Bryce Canyon National Park, Utah. The naturally eroded limestone is 8,200 feet (2,500 m) above sea level.

Earth is crammed with heaven and every common bush on fire with God.
But only he who sees takes off his shoes, the rest sit and pluck blackberries.

—Elizabeth Barrett Browning

3–32 • These are lichen-overed maple trunks in the shade of other Westonbirt Arboretum giants.

These fantastic limestone pinnacles were photographed from Inspiration Point, 8,200 feet (2,500 m) above sea level at Bryce Canyon National Park, Utah. I overheard one sightseer say to her friend, "Oh, no, not more rocks!" Well, that's a vivid illustration that we each see beauty and find inspiration in different things. I wanted to include this small section of images in the hope that you will find some inspiration here.

The stimulation obtainable from scenes in nature is infinite. Often we try to translate the thoughts provoked on such occasions into our bonsai designs. I have tried for years to create a stately lone Caledonian Scotch pine image and a young coppice of dancing, flowing, constantly changing larches with their bizarre pointed trunk tips and outrageously long branches flying in all directions. It matters not that I have not succeeded; I have had hours of pleasure trying.

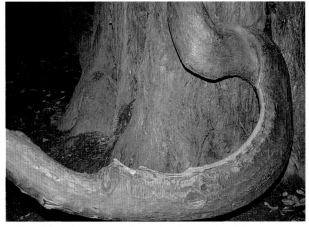

3–33 • I found this bizarre branch at Westonbirt Arboretum, Tetbury, United Kingdom.

3–34 • The fascinating trunk and lower branches are from a western red cedar I photographed at Westonbirt Arboretum, Tetbury, United Kingdom.

3–35 • I found these two magnificent trees at a crossroad on Levada walk.

3–36 • I took this at the National Bonsai Exhibition at Cliffe Castle, Keighley, Yorkshire (July 1994). (Right-hand bonsai courtesy of Colin Lewis.)

3–37 • This is an example of the waterside weeping style.

4

Crab Apple—from Seed to Flowering Tree

4–1 ● Here's a good shot of a Nagasaki crab apple.

OVERVIEW

Crab apples are wonderful deciduous bonsai subjects, offering a profusion of spring flowers and autumn fruits. You may choose from many varieties, but base your selection on the size of the flowers and fruits and on the color. Some crab apples are fully hardy, some need winter protection, but all benefit from a degree of cold, 45°F (7°C) or less, to encourage flowering. Crab apples are easy to grow, but their roots will rot in wet soils, and they dislike limey soils. They thrive in deep pots with well-drained loam-based compost.

Most crab apples are very healthy, although some varieties are prone to mildew or apple scab in still air. Place them in a sunny, airy position. Partial shade is beneficial on the hottest days in mid- to late summer to avoid leaf burn.

Water the soil, not the leaves or flowers, to minimize the risk of mildew and to improve pollination. Pollination is also improved by avoiding damaging heavy rain, air frosts, and insect sprays during flowering. You should also ensure good sun exposure and an outdoor placement. Watering the soil well during flowering encourages pollination, too. Watering is even more important as the fruit grows.

If mildew or apple scab is present, spray every other week from bud burst to the end of the summer as discussed in the Pests and Diseases section in Chapter 2. Remove all dead leaves from the soil and burn them. Scale insect can be very debilitating. Remove it physically or paint it repeatedly with methylated spirits as per Chapter 2.

Trees requiring repotting should be transplanted in the spring, typically in February or March, just prior to bud burst. All heavy root pruning should be accomplished with clean cuts, leaving no ragged edges. If the branch is over ⅝ inch (1.5 cm), seal the cut and add some pure grit under the cut to discourage root rot and root gall. Root rot is normally fatal, and the *Malus* genus, which includes apple as well as crab apple is, in my experience, more prone than any other genus to root rot from large wounds. However, a year or so after the pruning, the high

A fruit-laden Nagasaki
crab apple after its wonderful
spring bloom.

risk has passed. Thereafter, routine fine-root pruning of *Malus* does not present a high risk of root rot if you use well-drained soil mixes. Root gall does not seem to harm crab apple, but unsightly lumps appear around root cuts at the soil level. Ideally, you should remove the affected root and burn it. Improved drainage discourages root gall bacteria.

Crab apples flower on old, short shoots. They benefit from early new-shoot pruning back to two or three leaves after flowering. Leave some long sacrificial shoots unpruned until you remove them the following February. This practice encourages some shoots to grow shorter. Heavy trunk or branch pruning is best done at repotting time in February or March, but you should retain all the short shoots to maximize flowering.

To encourage flowering, surface dress the soil with bonemeal each November or December and water in a trace element Frit in January or February. Then, apply a little low-nitrogen feed (in a low strength) often during the growing season. Liquid feed is beneficial during the growing season, excluding the flowering period, until the fruit is half size. This helps to avoid fruit drop. As an alternative, apply a quarter of a teaspoonful of rapeseed to each corner in March when the flower buds are just starting to swell. Then, wait until the fruit is half size and repeat the dose at three-week intervals until early September. Do not apply rapeseed when crab apples are in flower or for the first five weeks of fruit formation. Do not allow a heavy crop of apples to go full term. When in doubt, halve the number. Overladen fruit weakens trees and can kill them (see Case History 1).

You can harvest crab apples once they are ripe (in October or November). Crush them in order to remove the seeds. Immediately plant the seeds outdoors (see the Growing from Seed section in Chapter 2). Seedlings should appear the following spring. Because *Malus* freely hybridizes, interesting blends of leaf color, flower, and fruit will appear. Flowering may take up to twenty years for crab apple seedlings, although I have seen flowers appear in under ten years. Some seedlings will be prone to mildew or root gall. Obviously, you should discard these. Dip any seedlings planted in an area contaminated with root gall in copper fungicide before planting them and avoid any root pruning.

Perhaps the best species for bonsai is *Malus cerasifera* (Nagasaki crab), which is fully hardy on benches, providing it is in good health. There is an exciting choice of *Malus* varieties to experiment with. *Malus halliana* (Hall's crab) is popular for its vigor, interesting trunks, and small fruits, but the fruiting is sparse, and hand pollination is required to be certain of fruit. In addition, Hall's crab requires some winter protection.

Case History 1

Parent Nagasaki Crab Apple—Branch Dieback

I purchased this as a 30-year-old imported bonsai in 1978. After sowing seeds from this parent in 1978, I had a wonderful crop of seedlings in the spring of 1979. Twenty-five respectable potential bonsai trees grew; two of these are featured in Case Histories 2 and 3 that follow. The parent crab suffered a bad attack of scale insect, but this was followed by an extraordinarily rich crop of over one hundred apples in 1986. Sadly, at the time, I did not understand how this heavy crop would weaken the tree.

The effect is evident in this picture (**4–2**) from the spring of 1988, showing dead lower branches on both sides. The left-hand side of the tree became very weak, and I needed an action plan to save this tree.

It took three years to stabilize and a total of ten years to regain its full vigor. This involved the following steps:

❖ Provided winter protection in cold greenhouse for eight years.

❖ Removed all fruit in the middle of May for eight years.

❖ Fed to encourage vegetative growth and pruned off most growth from the strong side of tree in the middle of the summer for five years, leaving the weak side mostly unpruned.

❖ Treated any fungal or insect attack immediately, as above.

❖ Provided sun exposure, except on hottest days.

4–2 ● The branches are weak and suffering from dieback because I didn't thin out the excess fruit the previous year.

4–3 ● It took nine years of careful management for this tree to recover balance and vigor.

4–4 ● A fruit-laden tree following flowering.

After nine years, the tree is back to full vigor, as shown in these spring and autumn pictures. I need to remove all fruit now to rest the tree and to avoid repeating history. The lesson is that if you have a heavy crop, you must always remove half of your crab apples in May or June to avoid weakening or killing the tree. Then, once the best display is over, remove the remaining crab apples. Try planting their seeds, too.

Case History 2

Red-Leaf Crab Apple from Seed

4–5 ● Notice the lovely red leaves on this Nagasaki crab apple seedling, which has hybridized with a red-leaf *Malus*.

In fifteen years, I developed this tree into a bonsai from the parent discussed above. As you can see, it has a pink flower and an attractive red leaf as a result of a natural cross-pollination. Although early in the season only a few leaves may show red, by mid- and late summer, all the leaves are a distinct pink or red, as illustrated. All other crabs in this generation had green leaves. The growing sequence was as follows:

❖ Crab apples harvested in October and November of 1978; crushed and seeds removed.

❖ Seeds promptly set 2 to 2½ inches (5 or 6 cm) apart in seed trays as per Growing from Seed section in Chapter 2, then left outdoors in the open to undergo winter freezing and thawing cycle.

❖ Seeds germinated, spring of 1979.

❖ One-year-old seedlings root pruned (tap root removed) and transplanted into open, sunny, growing bed in spring 1980 as per Growing Beds section in Chapter 2.

❧ Trunk shortened after fourth year in growing bed; wound roughly ground into a shape that allowed good callusing; new leader encouraged to grow long and vigorously.

❧ After six years in growing bed (spring 1986), 7-year-old tree dug up; tree 6½ feet (2 m) tall. Branches and new trunk leader severely shortened to 20 inches (50 cm); diameter roots of 1¼ inches (3 cm) to 2½ inches (6 cm) sawed off to permit planting in shallow pot; all wounds were clean cut, then sealed.

❧ Trunk diameter similar to parent tree.

❧ To avoid root rot, handful of grit used under all major root wounds.

❧ First potting should have been done in March when buds were just starting to swell, but first potting was delayed until late April when crabs were already just leafing; far too late, but crabs are more able to stand late repotting than most deciduous trees.

❧ Due to late potting, existing leaves collapsed, looking very flaccid for several weeks despite shade and misting; required two months before second set of strong leaves formed. (Then I knew the tree would survive. I do not recommend repotting crabs after bud burst.)

❧ Three other crabs were treated identically, but once the top and roots were pruned and sealed, these were placed back into the garden bed without container, given water, and misted; remarkably, they showed no ill effects (no leaf droop) with minimal shading. (This is a useful technique for reducing transplant shock after severe pruning, but it should not be necessary if trees are removed prior to bud burst.)

The tree is pictured in the spring of 1988. Notice that the new trunk leader is far too small in diameter compared to the main trunk. An extra two years in the garden bed would have cured this far quicker than the time in a shallow container. I used knotting instead of proprietary wound sealant in those days, as witnessed by the paint runs. I now use Kyonal or Lac Balsam sealants.

By May 1, 1994, this 15-year-old tree was looking far better. From seed to flowering tree took ten years. As is true of all its offspring, it is fully hardy on benches, even in the severest of winters.

4–6 ● Notice that the new trunk leader is small in comparison to the main trunk (1988).

4–7 ● Here you can see where the knotting sealant has run (1988).

4–8 ● Two more years in the garden bed would have increased the diameter of the upper trunk (1988).

4–9 • A winter image (1998)

4–10 • The tree design is developing after three years.

4–11 • Six years after I removed it from the garden bed, this tree looks lovely in flower.

4–12 • These are the roots of a crab apple.

Case History 3

Crab Apple from Seed—Horizontal Style

Sadly, this tree has not yet reached a final image after twenty years, but I include it because of its potential within the next few years. I have always wanted a crab apple with a long, almost horizontal trunk and branching under which fruits dangle like Christmas tree decorations. This seedling showed exceptional trunk taper, vigor, and an unusual orange bark hue from an early age. Unfortunately, it has always had crown gall root damage, but this has not interfered with the tree's health or design. It is also prone to

4–13 • I developed a lovely taper on this garden-bed crab seedling by selectively pruning the trunk and the branches.

mildew, which must be caught early, as mentioned in the Overview section earlier (see also the Watering and the Pests and Diseases sections in Chapter 2). The main growing stages were:

❧ As in Case 2, Nagasaki crab apples were harvested October and November of 1978; apples crushed and seeds removed.

❧ Seeds promptly set 2 to 2½ inches (5 or 6 cm) apart in seed trays as per Growing from Seed section in Chapter 2, then left outdoors in the open to undergo winter freezing and thawing cycle.

❧ Seeds germinated in spring of 1979.

❧ One-year-old seedlings were root pruned, taproot was removed, and tree was transplanted into open, sunny, growing bed in spring of 1980 as per Growing Beds section in Chapter 2.

❧ Five years later, trunk was significantly shortened and heavy, low branch removed; large wounds were shaped and sealed with non-drying sealant to allow good callusing; new leader was encouraged to grow long and vigorously to help seal wounds.

After twelve years (March of 1992), I removed this 13-year-old tree from the growing bed. It was 6½ feet (2 m) tall. I washed off the root ball and reduced the length of the roots, which were up to 2½ inches (6 cm) in diameter, in order to permit the use of shallow containers in the future. I reduced the height of the trunk and pruned the tree down to the core trunk and the branch required to ensure all this season's growth would be directed toward new branch development. The wounds were not fully callused, but because the trunk proportions were right, it was the correct time to remove the tree from bed to container.

To avoid root rot, I used a handful of grit under all the major root wounds, and I sealed all the wounds.

The picture of the tree taken in April of 1998 shows the new branches in need of pruning. After twelve years, the tree has started flowering, but it has never been allowed to fruit.

This tree (as with the full progeny) is totally hardy on benches even in the severest of winters.

4–14 •
This is a seedling I dug from the garden bed (March 1992).

4–15 •
Here, it is pruned and ready for potting (March 1992).

4–16 • Six years later, it's time for more selective pruning (April).

4–17 • This is a shot of the tree after pruning. It is developing nicely now, but sadly no final image is available yet.

5

The Natural Beauty of Wisteria

5–1 ● A close-up of the tree in flower.

OVERVIEW

This deciduous climber, although not tall enough to be recognized as a tree, is occasionally grown as a tree with a little support. Often it is successfully grown as a solitary specimen, as witnessed by this old tree **(5–2)**.

The haunting fragrance and graceful trailing flower racemes make wisteria a delightful bonsai subject, especially in April, May, and June. This genus is fairly free of disease and pests. It quickly develops old gnarled trunks and branches, especially when initially grown unabated in sunny ground near a wall that protects it against cold north and east winds.

Wisteria bonsai need protection from winter cold to minimize branch dieback. You can use a cold greenhouse or hoop tunnel for this purpose. Wire the current year's shoots carefully because they are prone

5–2 ● This is a lovely wisteria grown as a solitary plant in a suburban garden, Birmingham, England.

Close-up of the first delightfully perfumed
Wisteria flowers from a garden-stock plant turned
into a naturally styled bonsai.

to snap or break off at the base. Wire a little loosely, using thick wire after flowering. Once the branch shape is set, remove the wire, preferably before the onset of winter to avoid chilling the branches. Wiring old wood is risky; wisteria become very brittle and are prone to cracking and splitting. Removing the wire before winter helps to avoid branch dieback, although cold greenhouse or hoop tunnel protection will allow you to leave the wire on first-year shoots.

Wisteria bonsai grow well in loam-based soil. However, you always need to retain some soil moisture. In order to flower, they need full sun and plenty of water in the growing season, especially to aid pollination during flowering. Above all, after flowering, they need a high-feed regime. Use deep pots and stand them in a shallow dish of water. However, this vine is prone to branch dieback.

The flowering improves when wisteria roots are pot bound, but this is not essential to the process. Sprinkling bonemeal on the soil surface in November or December is also helpful. After flowering, give wisteria a low-nitrogen feed. Use this after flowering and throughout the growing season, every seven to ten days, more frequently than you would for the average bonsai.

Growing long, sacrificial branches through the summer aids in the production of other, shorter shoots. Wisteria flower on old, short shoots. They benefit from pruning new shoots back to two or three leaves immediately after flowering in addition to retaining some long sacrificial shoots. These sacrificial shoots are shortened or removed the next February or March before flowering. Leaving tendrils as additional sacrificial branches is quite acceptable, and flowers will be encouraged to form at the branch base near the trunk. Some people prefer to prune back sacrificial branches by ⅓ late in the summer, leaving the remainder to be cut in February or March. This is not a practice I employ.

Common methods of reproducing are seed, shoot or root cuttings, and layering. Seeds take a long time to flower. The flower quality is variable and may be disappointing. Taking root cuttings at repotting time, typically February or March, is very successful. Woody cuttings can be taken at the same time, but you'll have better results with half-ripe shoots in August. Layering is best done in the middle of the summer and, like cuttings, guarantees the same flowering and other growth characteristics as the parent.

Wisteria sinensis (Chinese wisteria) is the most common species for bonsai. However, many other varieties exist, offering a range of flower color, including white, pink, blue, and mauve. I have successfully used *Wisteria floribunda* 'Macrobotrys' (lilac) and *Wisteria floribunda* 'Premature' (pink). *W. floribundas* are also known as Japanese wisteria.

Case History 1

Wisteria floribunda 'Macrobotrys' from Garden-Center Stock

'Macrobotrys' is a vigorous, fragrant wisteria cultivar, highly suitable for bonsai. This plant is approximately seven years old. It was purchased for its flower color, its curved trunk, and the swollen trunk base, which is a little ugly. Four years after its purchase, the plant developed sufficiently for it to be a first-prize winner in a *Bonsai Magazine* photographic competition.

5–3 ● This is how the plant looked when I purchased it from a garden center (early spring 1990).

5–4 • Once bare rooted, it is apparent that almost all the fibrous root is at the bottom of a long, thick taproot.

5–5 • I removed most of the taproot, leaving very little fibrous root. I treated the taproot wound with hormone rooting powder to encourage further rooting (early spring 1990).

5–6 • I planted the top and watered it with Superthrive (approximately 10 to 50 drops/gallon). I shaded and protected it from the cold for six weeks (spring 1990).

5–7 • The branch-tip cuttings removed from the repotted plant are worth taking.

5–8 • The tree shoots have grown significantly (early March 1992).

5–9 ● It's time to prune the branches (March 1992).

5–10 ● This was the plant's first flowering.

5–11 ● Four years after the initial styling, this picture won first prize in the UK *Bonsai Magazine* photographic competition.

Case History 2

Wisteria floribunda 'Macrobotrys' from Root Cutting

This 4-year-old root cutting taken from the plant in Case History 1 is beginning to develop. However, a period of fattening up in a garden bed prior to potting would have been beneficial. Because the parent plant had commenced its flowering cycle, the root cutting continues flowering; such is the case with all vegetative propagation techniques. This and the high success rate are the main attractions for taking wisteria root cuttings.

5–12 • Treat root cuttings the same as branch cuttings. Cut cleanly with a sharp knife, dip the cutting in water, and dress with Hormone Rooting Powder No. 3.

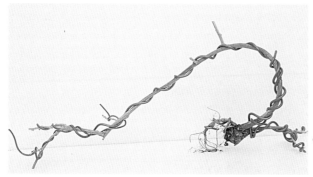

5–13 • You can wire the tree into a preliminary shape if required.

5–14 • Pot up.

5–15 • Eight years later, here's a display of the parent plant (center) and two root cuttings (May 2000).

6

Cedar—a Stunning Tree for All Seasons

6-1 ● Blue cedar in the garden, Herefordshire, England.

OVERVIEW

This is an architecturally stunning evergreen genus. The most striking of the four cedar species is cedar of Lebanon (*Cedrus libani*), second is the blue variety of the atlas cedar (*Cedrus atlantica glauca*). Both are hardier than the Cypriot cedar (*Cedrus brevifolia*) and the Deodar cedar (*Cedrus deodara*), although no cedar can be considered hardy as bonsai. *C. deodara* is the least suitable for bonsai because of its long needles. The other three species and their numerous varieties make wonderful bonsai subjects.

Trees from seed can take forty to fifty years to cone on their short shoots, but several forms are grafted and may bear fruit sooner. Cones are really of secondary interest to the wonderful foliage.

Cedars thrive in a sunny position during the growing season. The needles are adapted to low transpiration. They do not consume vast quantities of water, but they must have a sufficient amount. The soil mix should be well drained to avoid waterlogging, but at the same time, it needs to be fairly water retentive. Well-drained, loam-based composts suit cedars better than peat. Winter protection is crucial. In particular, avoid long bouts of frozen soil combined with cold, desiccating winds that dehydrate the tree, desiccate the foliage, and may encourage root rot. Exceptionally cold spring temperatures following a few warm days can be fatal for cedars growing in containers. They may temporarily lose some of the hardiness they've developed and experience total needle drop overnight early in the spring, many weeks before new buds burst. Such trauma can kill or, at a minimum, weaken cedars because they lose their source of energy (photo-synthesizing needles) and suspend bud growth for several weeks, even months. You can avoid this trauma by using a cold greenhouse for protection. The tree still experiences the subzero temperatures but without the desiccating winds. One respected bonsai grower places all of his cedars, complete with pot, into a sheltered outdoor garden, burying the containers completely. This successfully avoids needle drop and winter damage. The temperature fluctuations of the soil are far less severe under these conditions.

Another cause of cedar needle drop can be transplant (repotting) shock. This can occur when you remove too much root or when the weather following repotting is adverse and you don't provide sufficient protection from wind and cold. For this reason, transplant cedars later

Blue atlas cedar photographed seven years after being purchased as a garden-center tree.

rather than sooner, waiting until the buds begin to swell to minimize the time between transplanting and new buds shooting.

If your cedars do suffer needle drop, see the Tree Reviving section of Chapter 2 for a real-life example of how to overcome it.

Do not be put off by the above. It is easy to manage the overwintering of cedars to avoid needle drop. Simply follow the information given above and use a cold greenhouse or a hoop tunnel until at least the first of May in cool climates. These trees are then very easy to look after. They are not prone to disease or to damage from insects, and they take well to container life and to new-shoot pruning. In addition, they need little work on the foliage in order to look wonderful year after year. At times, they look almost plastic.

Reduce new shoots to one-third their length when they are ¾ or 1¼ inches (2 or 3 cm) long unless you are leaving the shoot unpruned for design purposes. Needles will turn brown if you cut through them, so take care to angle the scissors at the same angle as the needles. Point the scissor blade tips inward, toward the shoot base. I prefer to perform heavy branch or trunk pruning when I repot in April or May.

Wiring is best done early in the summer on new or 1-year-old shoots because these set easily. Older shoots are springy and need thick wire; they may take several years to set. Branches and trunk soon become very rigid, so select your plants carefully. Because new shoots are brittle at their base, you should anchor the wire to the trunk well away from the target branch and keep the wire a little looser at the branch base.

Inspirational examples abound in our stately homes. How wonderful it would be to see a cedar of Lebanon bonsai with all the character of those candelabralike, flat-topped parkland specimens.

Case History 1

Blue Atlas Cedar from Garden-Center Stock

When I purchased this 9-year-old typical garden ornamental, it was 8 feet (2.5 m) tall. I always chuckle when I recall getting the tree back to my car in the parking lot and not being able to fit it in the trunk. Eventually, I broke off the top 20 inches (.5 m) of the trunk and discarded it, much to the horror of some onlookers. Why should I worry? I still had enough for a bonsai and a substantial Christmas tree.

This case study highlights how not to treat cedars. It includes two examples of needle trauma. The first was caused by excessive root reduction and the second by winter cold. Despite these two traumas, this tree reached a good finished image seven years after I purchased it at the garden center. Needless to say, this tree now has winter protection every year following its near death experience. Please read this case history in conjunction with the Tree Reviving section in Chapter 2.

6–2 • I was attracted to this garden-center plant after noticing a fork low on the trunk where a side branch had grown almost vertically (September 1989).

6–3 • I also liked the folds of bark near the trunk base, reminiscent of the base of a mature monkey puzzle tree on which the sheer weight of vertical bark appears to collapse like a loose stocking folding around an ankle.

6–4 • The lower branches are wired roughly, and the root ball is reduced to half depth with a saw (knowing there are plenty of roots still attached to the trunk). This was a rather drastic root reduction for a cedar and not something I recommend (spring 1990).

6–5 • The trunk angle was fine and was too thick to change significantly without causing major damage.

6–6 • This is a close-up of needle trauma due to excessive root removal.

6–7 • After seven weeks, the tree is stable, but notice the dead branches. These were a direct result of the severe root pruning (June 1990).

6–8 • Six years after I purchased it, the tree is looking beautiful, despite its early problems.

6–9 • This is the image seven years after purchase.

7

Chamaecyparis

OVERVIEW

This small genus of American, Taiwanese, and Japanese false cypresses now includes variants and cultivars of every shape, size, and color, which are prized as garden ornamentals. Although the Lawson cypress (*Chamaecyparis lawsoniana*) is the most famous of this group, the two Japanese forms, Sawara cypress (*Chamaecyparis pisifera*) and Hinoki cypress (*Chamaecyparis obtusa*) are, in my view, more suitable species for bonsai despite their slow growth rates in containers. They are both readily obtainable as container-grown garden-center stock. However, because their growing requirements are different, I willl discuss them separately.

Hinokis (*Chamaecyparis obtusa*) are an easier and more vigorous species to grow than Sawaras. Hinokis demand a little less water and are more tolerant of drought, although it is not good policy to let them dry out. They require no winter protection because they are fully hardy on benches all year in the British Isles and cool climates unless the weather turns really cold. Like Sawaras, they may show a winter discoloration (reddening of foliage) **(7–1)**, especially if exposed to full sun in the growing season. They are relatively disease- and insect-free.

Do not remove more than 20 percent of the root at any one time and do not let the trees become too root bound. Drastic root reduction is risky to their health. Once repotted, secure the tree in the pot to avoid further root damage and shade the bonsai for several weeks. Hinokis, like yew, dislike sudden full-exposure sun after a period in deep shade. Therefore, you should gradually acclimate them to sun to avoid scorching the foliage and weakening the tree. They grow perfectly well in full sun, although the leaf color is darker and more attractive in partial shade.

You can pinch new growth between your fingers early in the growing season to form a ginkgo-shaped profile, which is the ideal. The top growth of Hinokis is very strong and must be trimmed to rebalance the tree's vigor.

Dense cultivars like *Chamaecyparis obtusa* 'Nana Gracilis' require very little new-growth pinching. They do, however, need to be thinned out

7–1 • 'Three trunked' showing reddening of leaves in winter.

Chamaecyparis pisifera 'Boulevard' styled after being in a
pot for 17 years. More work is required, but this is an
acceptable beginning.

by selectively removing some leaf fronds every two to three years on young vigorous plants. You can thin older specimens every four to five years. Use scissors to introduce daylight and to show off the lovely branching bark texture, which peels with age. I think of this as a haircut every few years. Although the tree can look a bit sparse immediately after the treatment, it soon grows again and looks far better for it. Do not tip prune with scissors as this creates an unsightly brown mark across the frond. Careful, selective removal of the inner foliage over the years reveals a wonderful branching detail reminiscent of a Lebanon cedar. The styling of Case History 2 on the next page was influenced by the Lebanon look.

Wire loosely early in the season at repotting time (February or March) until April. Wire marks are unsightly on this species, and they take quite a while to disappear. Thicker branches are slow to respond to wire bending and require thick wire and plenty of patience. You can avoid such problems wiring branches while they are still young. Do your heavy pruning at repotting time.

Sawara cypresses (*Chamaecyparis pisifera*) live in damp ground in nature. This is reflected in Sawara bonsai, which dislike drought. Some conifer leaves are well equipped to fight dehydration. However, Sawara bonsai, which continue to produce juvenile foliage throughout their lives, soon suffer leaf desiccation if the soil is allowed to dry out. This shriveling of the foliage is sudden and permanent, leading to a frustrating season or two, waiting for fresh soft growth to reemerge and for the bonsai form to be reestablished. Because Sawaras are apically dominant, the lower branches and the underbranch areas are affected first.

You may gather that this is not the easiest bonsai subject. In fact, you'll need to take great care when watering and to use light shade. A moisture-retentive, loam-based soil is helpful. However, the end result is very rewarding as the foliage in this species is striking. This is especially true of the cultivar *Chamaecyparis pisifera* 'Boulevard', which has soft, silvery-blue new growth. Containing the width of this tree is important because new growth shoots typically extend too far if you overfeed the tree or if you allow it to become waterlogged. If you aren't careful, the inner branches are quickly shaded out by the leaves if not managed properly. You'll have a strange, empty skeleton of branches with just blue tip growth. To avoid this condition, carefully control the amount of watering and feeding to reduce or eliminate the need for new-shoot tip pruning. Frequent repotting will have the same effect. Encourage the branches to divide and ramify in a horizontal fan shape by repeatedly pinching and pruning, avoiding long, thin branches with foliage only at the tip. If the new shoots exceed ⅜ inch (1 cm) in length, use your fingers to pinch the growth back to one-third or one-half the length throughout the season as shoots appear. Some shade is advisable after you prune the new shoot tips.

Aim for an open, airy branch structure that encourages retention of inner dormant buds. These are necessary if the branches extend too far and need shortening. The bark soon looks gnarly and aged on these trees, and a more open and airy structure helps show off this feature.

Wire loosely early at repotting time (February or March) until April. Wire marks are very unsightly on this species, and they are slow to disappear. Do your heavy pruning at repotting time. Sawaras are fairly free from disease and insect problems and will enjoy occasional foliage misting.

Although they are generally hardy on benches in winter, they are better protected in a cold greenhouse or hoop tunnel, I find. Do not be alarmed at the winter foliage discoloration. This is one of the tree's attractions, and color returns next season. Consider also *Ch. pisifera* 'Squarrosa' and *Ch. pisifera* 'Squarrosa Sulphurea'.

Case History 1

Chamaecyparis pisifera 'Boulevard' from Garden-Center Stock

I purchased this 2-year-old plant in 1975. It was pot trained into an upright style for 17 years, and the design transformed it into an acceptable image, thanks to a nice straight trunk and compact branching.

7–2 ● A 19-year-old tree ready for training.

7–3 ● A 19-year-old tree after initial training.

Case History 2

Chamaecyparis obtusa 'Nana Gracilis' from Garden-Center Stock

Originally, this was a 10-year-old grafted tree from a garden center. The tree was grown in a container for 26 years until it reached its final shape. A short history follows.

❖ After purchase in 1973, this tree was repotted into a deep bonsai pot rather than into a growing bed to encourage trunk thickening while developing fine branching detail, a slow, but successful process.

❖ Tree was repotted every four or five years at this stage.

❖ Thick wire was loosely applied to bend down heavy branches into a cedar of Lebanon shape, although wire stayed on for several years to fix the desired shape.

❖ After ten years of growing in containers, the inner branching was woody enough for some of the inner foliage to be stripped off, but only on wood three years old or older.

❖ About every four years from then on, the tree was given a haircut in April or May, selectively removing up to 50 percent of the fronds to thin out the structure; no routine pinching was necessary at this stage.

❖ In its fifteenth year of training (April of 1988), the desired main trunk and branch skeleton shape had been achieved. (Allow a tree to recover from a haircut before repotting; do not combine the two.)

❖ By the middle of May 1997, 24 years after purchase, I exhibited this tree for the first time, free of training wire and looking at home in this lovely pot. Notice how many of the fronds are following a wavy horizontal pattern, especially those near the underside of the pads to create that "cedar of Lebanon" feel.

Careful management of the outer tree profile helps create and frame the desired image. It has taken many years to extend the top trunk mass leftward to canopy the left-hand low branch and to extend the foliage pad of this low branch rightward to cross the trunk line, adding a more three-dimensional feel to the image.

7–4 • This is a 25-year-old garden-center tree after I had owned it for ten years (1988).

7–5 • The tree after a spring foliage thinning.

7–6 • A year later, I repotted the tree in a pot that was too shallow. The foliage is growing back slowly (June 1993).

7–7 • Several months later, the foliage growth was much improved (October 1993).

7–8 • Three years later, I achieved the "cedar of Lebanon" look I had been chasing.

I confess to rarely soft-shoot pruning this already compact form, relying on good soil drainage to reduce new growth and frond haircutting every few years to do the rest. However, soft-shoot pruning is necessary whenever long new shoots break the line of a frond or foliage mass profile and jar the eye.

These final two pictures, taken in April of 1999, show a slightly fuller tree, 26 years in training, exhibited at the 1999 Joy of Bonsai Exhibition in Bath. The close-up of the trunk base shows that the characteristic bark-peeling process has started.

I leave you with the final thought that I now need to create more holes for the birds to fly through, thinning the foliage with another haircut to come even nearer to that haunting Lebanon look. Who was it that said, "Concentrate on the negatives"? Where are my bonsai scissors?

7–9 • A close-up of the trunk.

7–10 • In the spring, the foliage is fuller and will soon need thinning again (1999).

8

Pine—the Ancient King of Bonsai

8–1 ● Pines shrouded in cloud at 1,800 feet (550 m) above sea level, Pico Arieiro, Madeira.

8–2 ● Scotch pines in their winter homeland.

OVERVIEW

Is it because pines have existed for over 100 million years that they are so admired by Japanese bonsai growers? I am sure that part of the answer involves their rugged good looks combined with the time, knowledge, skill, and patience required to produce and maintain a good pine bonsai, unmistakable in the final image. If you will excuse this very British mixed metaphor, pines are probably the Rolls Royce of Japanese bonsai. I certainly think that of all the evergreen and deciduous trees I have grown, pines require the longest time to develop, and they demand a clear understanding of how to control needle length in order to attain a satisfactorily finished image. Once you understand and accept this, they reward you by being a very long-lived genus. Indeed the Bristle cone pine (*Pinus aristata*) has the distinction of being the world's oldest living thing; some specimens have survived for 4,000 years.

Pines love sunny, open, well-drained sites. However, they can survive in poor soil and cold, windswept situations. Some species survive at up to 12,000 feet (3,700 m) above sea level. They dislike shade. In general, the five-needle varieties grow better in acid soil, although damp acid soil greatly increases the risk of fungal infection. These tough evergreens can also be found stunted in boggy areas and fighting for survival in sulphur-rich geyser country, eventually succumbing to the rising acid water table but still beautiful in defeat.

In the British Isles, our only native pine is the Scotch pine (*Pinus sylvestris*), which we refer to as "Scots pine." It spreads coast to coast across Europe. Specimens over 300 years old have been found in what remains of Scotland's Caledonian Forest. This species is well suited for bonsai as are the Japanese black (*Pinus thunbergii*), Japanese white (*Pinus parviflora*), Japanese red (*Pinus densiflora*), and mugo pines

Every time I look at this tree I tell it,
"One day you'll be a cover tree."

(*Pinus mugo*). My favorites are the Scotch and the Japanese black pines. However, many other pines are suitable and should be selected for their short needle, needle color, mature bark, texture, and other qualities.

I use a loam-based compost for most two-needle pines. Sometimes, however, I substitute ericaceous compost for the loam when potting five-needle pines. Scotch, mugo, and dwarf Siberian pines (*Pinus pumila*) are fully hardy on my benches, but I protect all three of these Japanese species in a cold greenhouse or hoop tunnel.

You can easily grow pines from seed. More often, they are wildlings, bonsai imports, or garden-center stock. I get great satisfaction growing from seed, although you are looking at a twenty- to thirty-year time span.

The three key steps for success with growing pines from seed are adding mycorrhiza, using growing beds, and transplanting carefully from the growing bed. Mycorrhiza, free from honey fungus, etc., is found in well-rotted (black) pine needles. Add it to the soil to produce thick trunks when used in conjunction with the second key factor: growing beds or deep growing boxes. The third key is successfully removing the pine from the growing bed into a large box or container. This is the most likely time to lose a pine but not if you read the information in the From Growing Bed or Box to Finished Image section of Chapter 2. Timing, minimum foliage removal, no wiring, and good aftercare are some of the issues clarified specifically for pines.

You should encourage mycorrhiza in all forms of pine to promote growth and strength. If none exists, scrape some off the base of another bonsai pot or root ball and fork it into the soil.

I do not lift trees from my growing bed for root reduction until they are finally removed from the bed. Better management of the surface root detail is possible if you lift the trees from time to time. If you are using boxes or containers during the early stages of pine development, you should repot only every four or five years; pine roots typically take a year, sometimes two or longer, to settle and become vigorous. Thickening happens after this and is aided by the small, natural increase in loam-based soil acidity each year. Allowing this vigor to build is an essential part of pine training and development, as you will see in the case histories that follow.

Repotting must always be carefully managed with pines to avoid desiccation of foliage. Typically, no more than 20 percent of the roots are removed (see the Repotting section in Chapter 2 for details). If the tree looks weak or if there is not much foliage mass, you may be wise to delay repotting. I always retain all the old needles throughout the pine's development years until the pine reaches the final few needle-refining years. This maximizes growth vigor and also ensures survival each time you repot. Once trees reach the refinement stage, they have so much foliage mass that the risk of desiccation is automatically lowered.

Great care must be taken when digging up wildlings to increase your chance of success. Keep as much root and soil intact as possible. Protect newly collected pines from chilling winds because the needles dry out after their roots are disturbed, especially if the soil is frozen for long periods. To maximize your chance of success, you should wait until the buds are elongated before you dig up pines. A cool, humid, wind-free semi-shaded sheltered area is ideal. If you only collected a few roots or a small amount of foliage, apply bottom heat as discussed in the Tree Reviving section in Chapter 2. You may also want to look at the Collecting from the Wild section of the same chapter.

Radical pine restyling is best performed in April, or at the latest May, to give the tree the maximum time to develop new needles and to allow wounds to begin callusing. Heavy trunk and branch pruning, heavy and detailed wiring, and all other design changes can be done at this time to maximum effect. However, you should only do this if the tree has full vigor and it has been at least a year, preferably two, since the last repotting. You might want to wait even longer if the tree was a newly collected wildling (see the case histories of successful radical restyling later in this chapter). The energy stored in the undisturbed roots bursts through the tree throughout the rest of the season, creating major budding and strong new needles capable of carrying the tree through the long winter months. No remaining old needles should be deliberately removed during this radical restyling. Wiring over some old needles is inevitable but not serious. I prefer to retain vigor than to have a pretty, but dead, tree!

A pruning technique used to produce budding (and hence shortening) on long, bare pine branches during the early stages of development is to avoid pruning any new shoots or candles for a year or two.

This encourages vigor until the foliage at the branch tips is very strong, and normally the needles will also be very long. Cut through the branch to remove two-thirds of this foliage in April, and new buds will eventually appear further down the bare branch. Once these buds have sprouted new needles, you can shorten the branch back to these new shoots. Repeat the grow-and-chop regime once more after two or three years, and you will have a lovely, compact bonsai.

Be careful not to shade out the lower branches and shoots of pines in growing beds. Foliage soon becomes very dense, and you'll need to remove some upper foliage to retain the energy in the lower parts of the plant. Preferably combine it with strategic branch and trunk pruning for shape, best done in April or May.

To aid refinement, remove the needles that point downward. These detract from a clean underbranch line. Repeat this procedure under each discrete pad and in any other areas that disrupt the peripheral lines. Pay particular attention to the corners of foliage pads, removing any needles that obscure a clearer definition of the corner shape and sharpness.

Pines do not need a great deal of feeding. They prefer low-nitrogen or no-nitrogen feeds (see the Feeding section of Chapter 2). To maximize thickening, water well in July and August when the young trees are developing. In order to avoid long needles, you'll need to be more careful about controlling the watering as the trees reach the refining stage.

Other cultivation requirements differ among pine bonsai species. I will present an overview of the species with which I have had some experience.

Dwarf Siberian pine (*Pinus pumila*) is a hardy species that dislikes lime in water or soil. Therefore, use a three-part ericaceous to a two-part grit soil mix. Prune new spring growth as for red pines (discussed previously), avoiding any late-season new-shoot pruning. In other aspects, treat them the same as Japanese white pine.

Japanese black pine (*Pinus thunbergii*) is a very drought, disease, and insect resistant vigorous two-needle pine. It is capable of living happily in relatively well-drained soil. The needles are rather too long for bonsai, but their rich green color contrasting against the almost black, craggy bark produces a wonderfully masculine image, which demands action to reduce needle length.

The needle length can be significantly reduced by pruning new and, if required, old-season shoot tips late in the season. The dense budding formed the following May is the result of pruning in the middle of September. Typically, the pruning removes 3⅛ inches (8 cm) of new and old shoots the previous season. This eventually produces a much denser, much shorter needle more in scale for this species as bonsai.

Japanese black pine bonsai must not be left on benches during winter. They are not hardy in cool climates, and the roots are badly weakened in very cold winters, causing death the next spring or early summer. Cold greenhouse or hoop tunnel protection is necessary.

The lower and inner branches of Japanese black pine also suffer from too much shade. Thus, these bonsai must be in full sun during the growing season. Do not remove them from the cold greenhouse until the first of May. You must also leave a reasonable gap of air and light between the branch layers.

New black pine spring candles can be very slow to sprout in prolonged hot weather. In 1995, my black pine buds extended very slowly through the season, only bursting into needle in the middle of August. Clearly, under such freak conditions, you must carefully review new-shoot pruning. You'll probably want to abandon the idea for a season to keep from further weakening the tree.

Japanese red pine (*Pinus densiflora*) is another two-needle pine. In my opinion, it is the weakest of the three Japanese pines discussed. For this reason, this tree is not my favorite species. The needles are long and thin, but they are a lovely, fresh, vivid green in spring. Because this tree does not like to be waterlogged, fast drainage is vital. Hence, you'll need to use two parts loam to three parts grit soil mix.

In the spring, prune the new shoots back to one-half length but do not perform any late-season pruning or you will weaken the tree. Use the same winter protection as for Japanese black pine.

Japanese white pines (*Pinus parviflora*) are five-needle pines often grafted on black pine stock. As a result, you must protect them in the winter as you would black pine. Prune the new spring growth as you would red pine but avoid pruning late-season new shoots. Like red pine, this species dislikes being waterlogged, and it, too, needs good drainage. An equal portion of compost (loam-based or ericaceous) and grit mix is suitable.

Mugo pine (*Pinus mugo*) is a fully hardy pine that grows very slowly. At high altitudes, the needles are aged, crooked, and compact. In less austere climates, its foliage is naturally leggy. Unless you cheat a little by selecting the *pumilio* dwarf variety, the main task is to promote dense branching, best achieved with late-season pruning in September or October. Little feeding is given to avoid excessive shoot growth and needle length.

Mugo pine requires repotting less frequently than most pines; every five to seven years will suffice if the pot is a reasonable size.

Scotch pine (*Pinus sylvestris*) is a fully winter hardy, vigorous, two-needle pine. It responds well to bonsai training, such as wiring and leaf-size reduction and is easily developed from seed, seedling, or wildling. It is fairly disease free, but woolly aphis attacks are common. You can recognize them by the white fluff at the base of some needles, usually starting around the bud. Treat them promptly with a strong jet spray of normal strength liquid malathion on all affected areas. This literally washes off many of the beasties. Repeating this treatment at intervals of two weeks twice more will normally cure the problem for a few years, providing you treat all your affected pines at the same time. More environmentally-friendly solutions are detailed in Chapter 2 under the Pests and Diseases section.

I do not prune the new candles in my growing beds. However, typically, I reduce the new candles of bonsai grown in containers to one-third of their length as soon as they are ⅜ to ¾ inch (1 to 2 cm) long, sooner rather than later to keep the new-shoot diameter small. I prune as the new shoots emerge (see the Early Season New Shoot Pruning section of Chapter 2). I select some shoots for growing. In weaker areas, some are unpruned or maybe pruned to a lesser degree. Neglecting to prune new shoots often produces new candles as thick or thicker than the parent branch, and you may need to remove them completely because they will destroy the fine branching detail essential to a nicely refined pine.

Scotch pines respond well to late-season pruning. This is true of pruned or unpruned new shoots, which develop markedly smaller needles and more new buds the following spring. Late-season partial or total new-shoot removal must only be used every two or three years and only on vigorous trees. It is a good refinement tool, but it slows down tree growth.

Therefore, it is used more during the later stages of branch refinement.

Scotch pines fatten quickly. This means that wires may dig into the bark. Keep an eye on this and wire loosely, especially at branch bases. Use heavier wire, which will bite in less. I rarely use raffia to protect Scotch pine bark. However, if the diameter is over ¾ to 1¼ inches (2 to 3 cm) and radical bending is required, I suggest you use it, wetted, under your wire. Scotch pine responds quickly to wire shaping, healing quickly if marked by wire. The wire can remain on benched bonsai throughout the winter.

These plants are thirstier than many pines, and they need an adequate soil volume during development. On the other hand, a reduction of soil volume is useful in controlling needle length as the tree approaches the final image. You should also reduce the needles somewhat as the branch tips multiply toward the final image because the same root volume has to supply more and more needles.

Shore pine (*Pinus contorta* var. *contorta*) is another two-needle pine. It is less vigorous than Scotch pine, but it responds to the same treatment. This tree prefers moist, acid soil. Hence, three parts ericaceous compost and two parts grit is ideal. It does have rather a long needle length, and the branches do not naturally ramify as well as Scotch pine, but they respond very well to late-season pruning in September and October.

Shore pines are not quite fully hardy on benches and need some winter protection. They also need full sun to produce good needle color and to avoid weakened branches.

8–3 • The denser and significantly shorter needles in this photo are the result of removing about 3¼ inches (8 cm) of new and old-season shoot tips the previous October (May).

Case History 1

Scotch Pine—Mother and Daughter from Seed

This tree was originally trained to be 8 to 12 inches (20 to 30 cm) tall. It has been grown in a container throughout its life. It grew a sacrificial branch on the left-hand side of the lower trunk. Eventually, the branch reached almost 10 feet (3 m) and was used to thicken up the trunk base. It worked too well. I missed the optimum time to remove the sacrificial branch, and the lower trunk of my small tree became far too thick, compared with the upper part of the trunk. In addition, the tree had a very noticeable step change in girth. I had to decide what to do next, remove the sacrificial branch or use the sacrificial branch and discard the original tree.

Eventually, I chose a British compromise: keep both of them. This was a bold step, but by drastically reducing the height of the sacrificial branch, the result, while ugly in the short term, eventually matured into a most unusual mother and daughter form. This required just nine years from the workshop. The tree was 28 years old from seed. The main training steps were as follows:

❧   Cones were collected, steamed to access the seeds, and then planted on April 16, 1969; seeds were lightly covered with soil mix, watered, and left outdoors in 3½-inch (9 cm) plastic pots.

❧   In July of that year, three of the eight seeds germinated.

❧   For approximately nine years, the seedlings were left in small-diameter pots and grew very little.

❧   For a further ten years, this tree was grown in a large and deep pot to encourage trunk thickening.

❧   Tree had been in the same pot for over two years and was very vigorous, ready for a makeover.

8–4 • At a workshop, I drastically reduced the height of the tree from 6½ feet (2 m) to 28 inches (72 cm) (1988).

8–5 • Here's my Scotch pine trunk getting the chop.

8–6 • The trunk cut was very ugly at this time, and the change in trunk diameter was equally so.

8–7 • I wired the future branches into position, and the end result was still pretty primitive.

8–8 • By early September of the same year, look at the vigorous new needle growth, plenty strong enough to survive the coming winter on benches.

8–9 • Note also the budding produced at the same time.

8–10 • In early June the following year, I scissor-pruned the new candles, removing two-thirds of the length. Some needles had grown a little too long and should have been pruned when only ¾ or 1¼ inches (2 or 3 cm) long.

8–11 • This is the result immediately after the pruning. Perhaps a few too many candles were left, making for an over-crowded tree.

8–12 ● By the end of July, I removed the wire to give the tree a rest. The foliage mass was building up well, helped by the large pot, the mycorrhiza fungus, and the lack of root disturbance that lasted for at least two years (1989).

8–13 ● Several months later, I rewired the tree and did a heavy late-summer pruning. Retaining too many candles improved the effectiveness of this late pruning.

8–14 ● Here's a close-up of the pruned trunk, showing the rewired trunk and the branches necessitated by the rapid branch regrowth (1989).

8–15 ● The Scotch pine's shape was developing (1991).

❖ On two occasions in early training years, all wire was removed from the tree for about two months in the early part of the growing season to give the tree a rest from the rigors of training; then, it was totally rewired and pruned. (This may not be absolutely necessary, but it forces you to remove all the wire, stopping any severe wire marks forming and preventing sap restriction, which might go unnoticed. Very occasionally, I have lost pine branches because of wire constriction at the base of a branch.)

❖ I made a simple notebook sketch of proposed final image requiring a great deal of additional branch mass;

three main design negatives overcome by this design were main trunk chop, rigid straight look of lower portion of trunk, and lack of integration of mother and daughter; first two problems were masked, and third solved in part by echoing shape of branches and tree between both; part by developing an overall profile and part by canopying the child with the mother, suggestive of protective parent.

❖ Tree continued to have early-season new-candle pruning annually combined with

❖ ...late-season new-shoot pruning every two or three years. Rewiring was occasionally needed to sharpen the image.

8–16 ● This is a schematic of the proposed future shape.

8–17 ●
I rewired and pruned the tree to sharpen up the lines (May 1993).

8–18 ● This photo shows the vigorous regrowth by late summer (1994).

8–19 ● The trunk scar was healing nicely (1997).

8-20 ● This is the image of the Scotch pine, just nine years after the workshop (September 1997).

8-21 ● A close-up of the Scotch pine's trunk.

Case History 2

Scotch Pine—Informal Style from Seed

Pot-grown from seed for eleven years, this pine was not progressing. I transferred it to a growing bed for seven years. The result was a lovely, fat, bent lower trunk and a sprawly mass of leggy foliage and long needle. Rather than settle for a less than optimal design based on the leggy branches, I began a program of branch reduction. It took four years to build up sufficient vigor before radically tip-pruning the branches. The process was repeated once more two years later, and the tree was well on the road to a more compact form, which was reached over the next six years.

Had I immediately planted this tree in the growing bed, I would have saved eight or ten years. Had I left it in the bed for two more years and done the branch reduction in the bed, I could have saved two or three years. This 30-year-old image could have been completed in less than twenty years. Hindsight is a wonderful thing.

❧ Cones were collected, steamed to access the seeds, and then planted on April 16, 1969; seeds were lightly covered with soil mix, watered, and left outdoors in 3½-inch (9 cm) plastic pots.

❧ In July of 1969, three of the eight seeds germinated.

❧ Seedling left in small-diameter pots for eleven years and grew very little.

❧ In May of 1980, it was transferred to an open sunny, growing bed.

❧ On March 21, 1987, tree was removed from garden bed and trunk radically pruned in two places; first sawed, then ground to shape with power tool; wounds were then sealed to encourage callusing.

❧ As always with first transfer from growing bed, pine foliage was reduced by no more than 30 percent and no wiring was performed.

❧ Needles depressingly long, and branches far too leggy.

❧ Following year, tree was looking stronger.

❧ By end of May of 1990, tree was strong enough to apply thick wire to upper trunk to encourage more acceptable curve.

❧ By end of March of 1991, trunk and all major branches were ready for major branch reduction; two-thirds of foliage mass was removed from all leggy branches, then whole tree was wired and any branches not required removed.

❧ Process repeated in 1993; by July 1994, tree was far more compact.

❧ By July of 1999, image was maturing.

8–22 • I removed the Scotch pine from the growing bed and potted it. It is very leggy at this stage (April 1988).

8–23 • A close-up of the shortened trunk I removed at repotting time.

8–24 • The "before" schematic for the Scotch pine.

8–25 • The "after" schematic for the Scotch pine. It needed considerable branch compaction and wire shaping.

8–26 • The tree is slowly regaining vigor (June 1989).

8–27 • The branches are not ready for wiring but are getting stronger.

8–28 • The needles are still too long.

8–29 • Some budding has emerged as new growth. The tree was almost vigorous enough to perform heavy branch-tip reduction, but some foliage had to be left on the branch to encourage sap flow (end of May).

8–30 • I performed heavy branch-tip removal and wired the tree at the same time (April 1991).

8–31 • The inner budding is beginning to ramify (July 1994).

8–32 • Eleven years after the growing bed, the current image is within two years of a good final image. This is a fine example of applying patience to create foliage over time rather than compromising the initial design (July 1999).

Case History 3

Japanese Black Pine—Cascade Style from Seed

This pine was left in small-diameter pots for ten years before I transferred it to my growing bed. Black pines fatten quickly in the open ground. You need heavy branch pruning several times to ensure that good taper and structure are achieved and to avoid the loss of vigor in the lower branches. This tree needs further foliage refinement to complete the image. Nevertheless, I am pleased with its progress to date. Here are the steps I took:

❧ Purchased seed was planted on April 3, 1970, after a soaking for 48 hours; seeds were lightly covered with soil mix, watered, and left outdoors in plastic seed trays.

❧ On May 19, 1970, seed germinated.

❧ Seedling left in small-diameter pots for ten years and grew little.

❧ Seedling transferred in May of 1980 to a sunny garden growing bed.

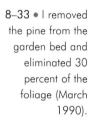

8–33 • I removed the pine from the garden bed and eliminated 30 percent of the foliage (March 1990).

8–34 • Three years later, after the tree was well established in the large plastic bucket, I settled on a cascade design, sawing off the upper trunk (February 1993).

8–35 • Notice how well the wound contour is merged to the trunk bend.

8–36 • I sealed the wound to encourage healing.

8–37 • Here the wound is starting to callus.

8–38 • The plan view shows the spreading branches of this cascade bonsai (October 1995).

8–39 • Late-season shoot-pruning was performed to promote tight new budding next spring (October 1995).

8–40 • Here's the resulting cluster budding the next spring. By the end of the spring, the new needle length was drastically reduced (end of May 1996).

8–41 • I removed all the old needles for the first time and wired the tree. The design was now emerging, nine years after I removed it from the growing bed (August 1999).

9

Maple—Spectacular Autumn Color

9–1 • These are the typical autumn hues of this magnificent maple leaf.

OVERVIEW

No other deciduous genus offers such a spectacular range of autumn color. Some maples also display colorful peeling or a striped bark. Understandably, the most popular maple bonsai subjects are Japanese due to their smaller stature and the prolific range of colorful variants and cultivars. Of course, there are many other interesting Asian, American, and European candidates, too.

Maple bonsai are generally very tolerant of soil types, accommodating acid or alkaline conditions. However, if given a choice, *Acer campestre* (field maple), *Acer cappadocicum* (Cappadocian maple), and *Acer pseudoplatanus* (sycamore) prefer alkaline. *Acer rubrum* (red or Canadian maple) prefers acid. I find loam-based compost works well for most types.

Maple bonsai are at home in wet or dry soils, but you should not let the soil dry out completely because the leaves can be damaged. Do not allow them to become waterlogged for long, especially in winter, because root damage is possible. Loam-based soils offer that extra security against drought and, combined with grit, avoid the risk of waterlogging.

Maples are relatively free of diseases and insects if you keep them healthy. Verticillium wilt, black or tar spot, aphids (causing sooty mold), and galls are probably the most common problems. Generally, they are happy city dwellers, able to survive polluted air (see the Pests and Diseases section in Chapter 2 for suggested treatments for these conditions). Clean up all diseased fallen leaves to reduce reinfection. More delicate early spring leaves, such as *Acer buergerianum* (trident maple), can be burned by some sprays, so test on a small area of a leaf first. Take care not to wet the leaves in full sun as they are susceptible to sun scorch through the water droplets. I have found bifenthrin (Bio Sprayday) to be a very gentle and effective insecticide for delicate-leaved maple, as well as most bonsai species. Cut off and burn any galls, which are fairly harmless and are usually caused by tiny mites, and seal all wounds. Drying spring winds will cause major windburn damage to some of the finer-leaved maple forms.

In the bonsai world, if pines are king, maples are queen.

Do not wire prior to bud burst because the shoots are too brittle. Apply wire during the early growing season, around May or June, a few weeks after bud burst. Try to remove wire on fine twigs before the cold winter chills the delicate branches or else give the tree extra protection (see Appendix 1 for more details by species).

Prune new shoots back to two or three leaves or buds once the shoots are 1¼ to 2¼ inches (3 to 6 cm) long. Some species, such as *Acer palmatum* (Japanese maple), *Acer ginnala* (Amur maple), *Acer griseum* (paperbark maple), and *Acer pseudoplatanus* (sycamore maple), have very leggy first growth. After a few weeks, you may have to completely remove some of this growth to encourage a second, shorter growth. Because maples have opposite buds, you need to remove the occasional bud to avoid the monotony of regular branch divisions and to introduce interesting branch direction changes.

Acers respond well to a little trimming of the previous year's shoot tips prior to bud burst in February or March. Trim back to the appropriate buds, thus ensuring that all of the currrent year's new growth will be in the proper places and that the ramification is improved.

Some maples, such as trident and Amur maples and, to a lesser extent, Japanese maples, love to send vigorous new shoots, similar in looks to suckers, out from the base of a branch. If you don't remove these shoots, the whole branch, with all of its detailed branchlets, may die. Similar vigorous shoots can emerge from trunks and branch tips. In order to balance the vigor of the tree, you should remove them quickly if they are not required. Some species, such as Amur maples, produce many suckers from the trunk base. By selectively keeping one or two of these suckers, you can improve the local trunk thickening and the wound scar healing.

I perform any heavy trunk and branch pruning only on vigorous maples in April at bud burst (see the case histories that follow). While I cannot confirm that this works well on all maple species, including variants and cultivars, it certainly works on the following, which I have grown: *A. buergerianum* (trident maple), *A. capillipes* (red snakebark), *A. cappadocicum*, *A. davidii* (snakebark, including cultivar 'Ernest Wilson'), *A. ginnala* (Amur maple), *A. griseum* (paperbark maple), *A. pseudoplatanus* (sycamore, including

the cultivar 'Brilliantissimum'), *A. palmatum* (Japanese maple, including 'Osakazuki' and 'Matsumurae') and *A. rufinerve* (snakebark, including the lovely leaved 'Albo-limbatum' cultivar).

Some cultivars, such as *A. davidii* 'Ernest Wilson' and *A. rufinerve* 'Albo-limbatum' are only authentic from grafts. This makes them less suitable for bonsai but still possible. Try using seeds or cuttings from these grafts to grow bonsai; you may be pleasantly surprised. The former is a wonderfully vigorous plant, but the leaf size is challenging; the latter has fabulously variegated leaf, bark, and autumn color, but it is also rather vigorous. *A. palmatum* var. *Dissectum* and variegated cultivars of *A. palmatum* are usually weak trees on their own roots. Grafted forms, while much stronger, must be selected carefully to avoid ugly trunk scars or shapes.

A favorite technique for leaf reduction on maples is total leaf removal. This should only be practiced on healthy trees and only every other year at most. Remove all leaves, leaving some of the leaf stalk and the dormant bud in the stem axil. This total leaf removal stimulates dormant buds in the axils to burst in four to five weeks, producing a smaller leaf that will produce even better autumn colors. Leaf removal must be performed several weeks after the first leaf but not so late in the season that new shoots either do not appear or are too soft to withstand winter weather. Early June is the latest time for total leaf removal, which is best done as soon as the first leaves have hardened.

When winter protection is recommended, don't return maples back to open benches too soon. None of my overwintering maples return to open garden benches before the first of May. When returning them to benches, wean delicate leaves slowly back to the sun and wind, either of which can wipe out your first leaves. New spring maple shoots are often leggy in low-light winter storage. New shoots are like watercress. Prune these shoots two or three weeks after you move the trees outdoors and the leggy new shoots are a little hardened. The tree is then stable and happy to grow new shoots. Trident maple is particularly prone to these shoots.

Always allow maples to experience cold temperatures to help trap leaf sugars and produce that autumn display for which they are famous. Because frost falls downward, overhead protection will reduce autumn coloration for some tree types. However, *A. palmatum* seems to perform without hard frosts, providing October temperatures fall to around 41°F (5°C). I once had a bonsai *Cotoneaster horizontalis* that mysteriously turned half red overnight. The other side remained green because the tree was directly beneath a half-open sliding roof light, and only half received frost. If you lift up any frost-reddened maple leaf, you'll see a stencil-like green leaf image on the leaf below it. The lower leaf was protected by the shadow of the higher leaf.

Winter cold hardiness varies greatly across the genus and is dealt with individually below, along with any other special comments for the maple species I have grown.

Amur maple *(Acer ginnala)* is my favorite maple for bonsai. It is fully winter hardy on benches, lives cheerfully in the most polluted environments, yet has striking autumn leaf color, albeit short-lived. The bark texture is good, the species grows fairly quickly, and it grows well from cuttings. While leaves of this Chinese species are not as compact or delicate as many Japanese maples, they respond well to total leaf removal, which will reduce leaf size. These leaves are small when compared to most of their American, Canadian, and European cousins.

Quickly remove vigorous new, sucker-like shoots growing at the base of established branches to avoid branch dieback. Prune off or wire any leggy new shoots. *A. ginnala* branches want to grow lanky at the expense of inner buds. Late-summer branch pruning is required every few years to encourage branch division and compactness.

Rapid trunk thickening occurs in garden beds. You can avoid root rot during the first transplant by placing just grit under large root wounds. I recommend using deep growing pots rather than garden beds for *A. ginnala* as this vigorous species can lose its marvelous trunk bumps and bends if it grows too fast. *A. ginnala* is an ideal species for raft group plantings.

Downy Japanese maple *(Acer japonicum* including 'Aureum'). This is a very slow-growing species best known for the 'Aureum' clone. These trees have very tender leaves, quickly burned by wind, cold, and sometimes by sun, especially if water is on the leaves.

Japanese or mountain maple *(Acer palmatum)* is an excellent subject for bonsai, easily propagated from cuttings, air layers, grafts, and seeds. It responds well to light and heavy pruning and grows well from seed, even though variability is possible.

Never assume that *A. palmatum* is fully winter hardy. People often consider that it is fully hardy because it is a common garden plant and survives for several winters in bonsai pots without protection. However, wait for a really cold winter or for a warm spring followed by sudden cold, and you'll learn a bitter lesson. One of the problems in diagnosing cause is the delayed death of an *A. palmatum* that appears to leaf quite normally for a week or two in the spring and then collapses due to lack of viable root. At best, the tree will experience twig dieback, possibly partial trunk loss (always from the outside branch tips inward, usually from the trunk apex downward); at worst, the tree will die.

Although root damage in a very cold winter spell is the prime cause, a cavalier repot in the middle of the summer can catch up with you. The leaves apparently survive the remaining season, but they collapse shortly after spring leafing. Planted in open ground, *A. palmatum* can withstand temperatures below -5°F (-20°C) without damage, but in bonsai pots, temperatures below 15°F (-10°C) are damaging. My policy is to give winter protection to all of my *A. palmatum* except 'Osakazuki', which I find hardy. I only bring 'Osakazuki' into a cold greenhouse during the coldest of spells, such as 5° to -5°F (-15° to -20°C). Winter protection means moving *A. palmatum* into a cold greenhouse after it has experienced a few light frosts to color the leaves. Normally, I don't move the tree until it has shed its leaves (see the Winter Protection section of Chapter 2).

Japanese maple 'Osakazuki' *(Acer palmatum* 'Osakazuki') is a cultivar I've singled out as a very good potential bonsai subject. In addition to its winter hardiness and vigor, it is the reddest of all maples in autumn and often has reddish tints during the summer months, too. The first shoots tend to be long and straight and may need pruning or wiring for shape. If you prune the tree, new shoots will appear in four to six weeks. This rigid, straight new growth is similar to *A. griseum* and is hard to train into a bonsai. Wiring new shoots in their first or second year before they get too stiff is helpful, as is training plants while still young seedlings. The leaves are fairly large and respond well to total leaf removal.

Japanese maple 'Matsumurae' (*Acer palmatum* 'Matsumurae') is a subspecies that also makes a very good bonsai. It is famous for its habit of forming a solid layer of root spreading out from the trunk base and for its lovely blood-red autumn leaf color. The care and cultivation is the same as for *A. palmatum*. Pay special attention to removing stiff, long, new growth and to pruning the early shoots to encourage compact new growth. Regular repotting and root pruning will encourage root ramification and a spreading trunk base.

Paperbark maple (*Acer griseum*) has beautiful orange flaking bark and lovely autumn color. A vigorous growing plant, its long, straight first shoots and leggy leaves do not make it an obvious bonsai candidate. Only tenacious first-shoot removal can produce sensibly sized secondary shoots, and this is a slow job.

A. griseum is not hardy and will suffer branch dieback if not winter protected. Remove all wire before the winter months. Wire sparingly and only wire young new shoots in order to avoid damaging the future bark texture. More rigid and linear in shape as a tree in nature than *A. ginnala,* this tree makes a challenging bonsai. It is notoriously difficult to grow from seed (see Growing from Seed section in Chapter 2). I recommend *A. griseum* to you as a bonsai because the end result will be wonderful.

9–3 • These are the typical autumn hues of the magnificent *Acer griseum.*

9–4 • Here's a good photo of the fascinating orange peeling bark of the paperbark maple.

9–2 • I grew this 29-year-old *Acer griseum* from a 6-year-old seedling. It still requires further branch ramification and leaf reduction, but the trunk shape is satisfactory due to careful initial trunk training and wiring.

✤ *Acer griseum* from 6-year-old seedling (**9–2**) still requires further branch ramification and leaf reduction, but trunk shape is satisfactory due to careful initial trunk training and wiring; typical autumn hues are appearing.

✤ Close-up of early autumnal leaf color (**9–3**); leaves later turn rich red before falling.

✤ Close-up of lower trunk showing beginnings of bark flaking, the most outstanding characteristic of this notable species (**9–4**).

Sycamore (*Acer pseudoplatanus*) is commonly found by the side of the road and in cities in the British Isles. It is the largest and most common *Acer* in Europe. As bonsai potential, it is often passed over in favor of some of its more ornamental Asian and American relatives. Anyone with a sycamore in or near the garden knows how prolific and tenacious the seedlings are; they fall and germinate ceaselessly. In its favor are its vigor, hardiness, and its ability to live in highly polluted or salty air. Repeated leaf pruning of this species (like its fellow European *A. campestre*) produces markedly smaller new leaves. Both species make excellent bonsai subjects.

An additional technique I have found helpful is preseason bud removal (see the case history below). However, you should only do this with vigorous sycamores and then only once every three years at most.

Sycamores are fairly hardy in Britain and cool climates and require protection only in the coldest winters.

Trident maple (*Acer buergerianum*) is one of the most popular and fastest growing bonsai subjects. Its wonderful small leaves and aged trunk are well suited, although it is one of the most vulnerable maples during winter months. It requires careful attention to this aspect. Store trident maples in a cold greenhouse or equivalent and, as always, do not return them to benches until the first of May. Then, you need to wean them for several weeks to avoid windburn and sunburn. The leaves are prone to burn with some insecticide or fungicidal sprays, so test such sprays on a small area and always protect newly sprayed trees from direct sunlight until the spray droplets disappear.

As trident maple branches love to grow long and leggy, a spring branch-tip prune is very helpful just prior to bud break. If you suspect that watercress-type weak growth will develop, leave this trimming until a few weeks after the first of May, once the tree has hardened. Do it at the same time that you remove weak new shoots.

Trident needs plenty of water and benefits from a deep pot. It needs more drainage than most other maples. Apply a liquid low-nitrogen feed regularly and prune continuously as soon as new shoots appear. You must provide some shade in the height of the summer. Trident responds well to total leaf removal.

You can wire new shoots early in the season with very light wire, once they have fully emerged. They should be set before the end of the season. Removing wire from young shoots before winter helps reduce branch dieback. Never wire from December to February, prior to bud burst or young branches may die. Rewire any unset branches the following year.

Tridents are prone to branch dieback. Every few years, they benefit from branch pruning just after leaf fall to remove the excess branches and to improve the inner ramification and the inner-tree light levels. You should store them in high-light winter conditions, or they will grow weak, long spring shoots, which need removing after the first of May. Low winter light levels also increase the chances of greater branch dieback; a hoop tunnel or cold greenhouse protection is ideal.

Case History 1

Acer palmatum—Formal Upright from Cutting

In the cold winter of 1981-82, we had an overnight temperature of -9°F (-23°C) in Birmingham. At that stage, I still left *Acer palmatum* outside with overhead protection only, in the lee of a wall. My *A. palmatum* group had developed for two years from 4-year-old purchased cuttings. However, these trees still only had an average diameter of ¼ inch (0.7 cm) and an average height of 12 to 16 inches (30 to 40 cm), as you'll see in the group picture from June of 1978. Shortly after the spring leafing, the top third to half of the foliage in the group collapsed, and the corresponding branches soon died. I learned the hard way about winter protection. In the spring 1983, I dismantled the group and planted what was left of each maple in my garden beds to become ornamental garden plants.

This and the following two case histories cover the developments of these scattered maples, most of which I reharvested five years later. Since I repotted them as bonsai, proper winter protection has allowed these trees to thrive once more. Case 1 is the parent of all my air layers and was left in the garden an additional six years. Not the daintiest of my maples, I call it my elephant's foot.

My goal is to create a viable winter image; this will take several more years.

9–5 • This garden-bed maple has retained its bonsai potential remaining in the garden bed, thanks to ten years of selective branch pruning.

9–6 • Clearly, root pruning every few years would have produced a better root ramification. Digging it out took me several hours.

9–7 • I removed most of the soil and cut and sealed all the heavy roots. I used Styrofoam to fill the bottom third of the bucket.

9–8 • I retained a little soil to reduce the shock to the remaining fine root and all the branches that had been heavily pruned.

9–9 • Once I potted the tree and wired it securely, a pendulous drooping branch style emerged for the lower branches. These suggest aged boughs drooping under their own weight; yet at their tips, the younger branch shoots arch back up to enjoy the sunshine (February 1994).

9–10 • A notebook sketch of the tree shape at the time of potting.

9–11 • Notebook sketch of possible future shape. Although this is not a typical slim, light maple, it should make an acceptable and venerable hollowed-out maple.

9–12 • Three years later, it has been growing vigorously and receiving annual haircuts and selective new shoot removal.

9–13 • After each annual haircut, I selectively wire new and young shoots.

9–14 ● Five years after repotting, its spring image is acceptable (May 1999).

9–15 ● The tree in autumn.

Case History 2

Acer palmatum— Windswept Style from Cutting

This tree was also rescued from the garden after just six years. Now, it has a lovely reaching style reminiscent of maples stretching over paths or water. The key design elements involved echoing the initial upper trunk curves throughout the new branches and foliage masses and the use of repeating horizontal branch lines.

Again, my goal is to create a lovely viable winter image; this will also take a few more years.

9–16 ● I took the tree out of the garden bed the previous year. It was now firmly established in its pot and ready for styling. Note the lack of vigor in the lower branches (spring 1989).

9–17 ● I used heavy pruning on the main trunk and the only thick branch.

9–18 ● This is a close-up of pruning wounds. Unfortunately these were cut across flat rather than being concave around the periphery. The negative results of this kind of cut show up clearly in the following years (May 1989).

9–19 ● Here, leaves are emerging six weeks later.

9–20 ● Sucker-type shoots are left to aid wound healing (June 1989).

9–21 ● The wounds after sealing.

9–22 ● The wounds are callusing nicely, but they are sticking out too far from the bark line because of the incorrect initial pruning (April 1990).

9–23 ● A horizontal form is starting to appear in this bare image following leaf removal (May 1991).

9–24 ● A second set of leaves formed six weeks later.

9–25 ● The horizontal form is continuing to develop (December 1993).

9–26 ● The lower wound is almost callused over, but the flat wound is influencing the poor final contour (March 1996).

9–27 ● The upper wound is healing far more convincingly (March 1996).

9–28 • Eleven years after I dug it up, the indications of the form of a final image are visible (October 1997).

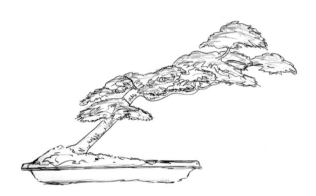

9–29 • A notebook sketch of the shape (1997).

9–30 • A notebook sketch of a possible future shape, showing areas where pads should be added or extended.

9–31 • The tree (rear view) in all its autumn splendor (early November 1997).

9–32 • The tree in full autumn glory (October 1999).

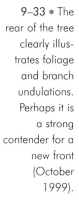

9–33 • The rear of the tree clearly illustrates foliage and branch undulations. Perhaps it is a strong contender for a new front (October 1999).

Case History 3

Acer palmatum—from Air Layer

Air layering offers a unique opportunity to copy leaf, flower, fruit, and other plant characteristics by vegetative propagation. At the same time, you can achieve instant trunk girth and flowering capability. *A. palmatum* is an ideal air layering subject. This case history explains my air layering technique for deciduous and evergreen trees. March is the ideal time to commence air layering, although August is another good month in cool climates.

Some species take two or three years to root when air layered, and some never do root. In general, deciduous trees are easier to layer than evergreens. *A. palmatum* normally root in a matter of months. If

started in March, they would be ready for removal by the middle of or the end of that season. Of course, you need to be sure that good roots have grown.

My *A. palmatum* layers were taken in March of 1992. I allowed them to stay on the tree until the next spring. The roots survived the winter cold admirably without a sack or plastic bubble-wrap protection. I would use such protection next time for more peace of mind, but I recommend spring air-layer removal because it fits well into the natural repotting cycle, and air layers removed just before bud break tolerate more root disturbance. The key steps are illustrated below.

9–34 ● I cut off a complete ring of bark about 1¼ inches (3 cm) long. Notice that I did not leave a bridge. I scraped off all traces of the green cambium layer carefully to ensure that the tree cannot callus back across the gap (March 1992).

9–35 ● Wet the wound surface and brush on hormone rooting powder. Handle this powder very carefully to avoid damaging your health. This is a discarded toothbrush.

9–36 ● Soak sphagnum moss in water to which you've added 50 to 100 drops of Superthrive or a similar reviver/transplanter. Drain the sphagnum moss and wrap it around the wound. Wrap clear plastic around the sphagnum moss and secure at the top and bottom with tape or wire.

9–37 • Using wire on the top seal can leave marks, as shown here three years after I removed this air layer from the parent tree. Instead of wire, use weatherproof tape or string to allow some stretch through the growing season.

9–38 • Wrap black plastic over the clear plastic to cut out light, assisting rooting. Secure loosely with tape so you can examine the root growth intermittently.

9–39 • Plenty of root is visible; the layer is ready. This example is certainly ready for removal (March 1993).

9–40 • When ready, sever the layer from the parent close to the bottom of the root ball and seal the wound.

9–41 • Normally, air-layer roots are considered very brittle, but after 11 months, I was able to tease at the roots gently with a root claw.

9–42 • A view of the underside of the root ball.

9–43 • Choose this first repotting time to perform heavy pruning on any excess trunk and branching. To avoid branch dieback, leave an extra ⅜-inch (1 cm) stub to die back naturally.

9–44 • The pruned layer is ready for repotting.

9–45 • The tree three months later.

9–46 • This is a typical air layer, six years after removal. The tree is allowed to grow unchecked in order to increase the diameter of the newly added trunk extensions. These will be cut back using the chop-and-grow technique to encourage short, well-tapered trunks (October 1999).

Case History 4

Acer palmatum 'Osakazuki'—Cascade from Seedling

I potted a 1-year-old seedling in a garden bed in 1978, then returned it to a container at the end of March of 1992. Eight years after I removed it from the growing bed, the tree has a very pleasing image.

9–47 ● This is a tree I dug up after thirteen years in a shady garden bed. The girth was slow to improve (March 1991).

9–48 ● The potted tree seems too long. Notice the crutch support until the roots take firm hold. This took several years.

9–49 ● I pruned the tree to a more appropriate length during this first repot.

9–50 ● During the first repot, I also wired the branches to a more suitable configuration before they became too rigid.

9–51 ● This species has long new shoots in the spring. They must be pruned quickly each year to minimize the extension. The leaves also need to be removed to encourage a second leaf crop from the leaf axils (March 1997).

9–52 • I performed an early-season total leaf removal (mid May 1997).

9–53 • In the latest picture, notice the lovely summer color of the 'Osakazuki', the earliest of the maples to begin their autumn show.

9–54 • Here's the full autumn color (September 1999).

Case History 5

Acer pseudoplatanus—Broom Style from Seed

If you want a challenge, this species is a good choice. Although this tree has large leaves, repeated total leaf removal over several years and the use of the pre-season bud removal technique work well. By repeated leaf pruning alone, I have seen credible sycamore bonsai between 4 and 8 inches (10 and 20 cm) tall.

9–55 • I removed all the tip buds (early May 1998).

9–56 • The masses of new leaves are smaller but still very large for bonsai use. I was moving house, hence the packing crate (mid June 1998).

Case History 6

Acer ginnala—Informal Style from Seed

This tree has been slow to develop. It has lived for 25 years in containers. Fortunately, *A. ginnala* are vigorous enough to still thicken while grown in a shallow container. I love the species for its hardiness and ruggedness. I used the following steps to grow this bonsai:

❖ Purchased seed planted March 5, 1973, in a seed tray with ⅜ inch (1 cm) of grit to cover drain holes, then a 2¼-inch (6 cm) layer of light peat compost, followed by a sprinkling of standard bonsai soil, the seeds, and then another sprinkling of bonsai soil; soil slightly firmed, then watered and placed outdoors to stratify seeds; ideally, should have been planted in early winter to maximize stratification.

❖ Eight seeds germinated April 7, 1974.

9–57 • The tree in training (April 1988).

9–58 • The tree base (April 1988).

9–59 ● I kept this sacrificial sucker-type branch to thicken the trunk base, heal the wound, and add some character.

9–60 ● Notice how the tree was developing (July 1994).

9–61 ● The tree was exhibiting autumn tints (September 1999).

9–62 ● The front view shows the lower trunk character.

9–63 ● A close-up of the rear shows that the scars were almost fully healed.

10

Juniper & Yew

OVERVIEW

I have paired these two quite different trees because in nature they share the ability to thrive on dry, poor, alkaline land exposed to sun all day. Most conifers, with the exception perhaps of pine and larch, would reject this soil in favor of moist, rich organic land. Both have forms capable of surviving at 8,000 feet (2,500 m). Apart from colonizing on sun-drenched, arid, southern slopes, they also share an uncanny number of other factors. They are both equally at home in shade and on moist acid land; both are dioecious with male and female flowers on different trees. They both have fleshy, berrylike fruit. They both grow relatively slowly and can live to great ages; yew can grow in excess of 1,500 years (Scotland); western junipers (*Juniperus occidentalis*) double this age have been found on the West Coast of the United States. Common yew (*Taxus baccata*) and common juniper (*Juniperus communis*) were also the only two evergreen conifers to exist in England in the Middle Ages.

Both make superb bonsai subjects as wildlings and as grown specimens. Driftwood styles (large areas of sun-bleached deadwood) are frequently found in wildlings collected from high altitude or from exposed sites. People often make the mistake of thinking that as bonsai, juniper and yew behave the same way that they do in their natural habitat. For juniper bonsai particularly, this is incorrect.

You should purchase a male and female plant to ensure that you'll have berries. Although females are preferred for bonsai, male yew flowers can also be very striking. Each genus is described in detail below.

Juniper

Juniper is a rugged tree and has many colorful garden derivatives not really suited to bonsai. The species that I have grown as bonsai and that I recommend are listed in the following two hardiness paragraphs (see Appendix 1 and the section on Winter Protection in Chapter 2 for further detail).

10–1 ● Trees survive at remarkable elevations. Weather-beaten spruce dominate the extremes up to 12,000 feet (3,700 m) above sea level, closely followed by the firs, then the larches, pines, and yews. Below 8,000 feet (2,500 m), junipers can colonize hot, southern slopes and in canyons such as those below the southwest rim of the Grand Canyon at 7,000 feet (2,200 m). Junipers lose the battle in moister, shadier lowlands to more vigorous deciduous trees, except in extremely alkaline soils.

A beautiful juniper showing the cascade style.

Bonsai species hardy on benches include:

Chinese juniper (*J. chinensis* 'San Jose')

Dahurian juniper (*J. davurica* 'Expansa')

Van Melle hybrids (*J. × media* 'Blaauw', 'Plumosa', 'Shimpaku', and 'Pfitzerana')

Sargent's juniper (*J. sargentii*)

Virginia juniper (*J. virginiana* and its cultivar 'Burkii').

Bonsai requiring cold greenhouse winter protection include:

Common juniper (*J. communis*)—especially newly collected, weak, and wired trees. Some of my developing trees (cuttings from a collected wildling) are perfectly hardy on benches but my collected *J. communis* needs and receives winter protection.

Hornibrook juniper (*J. communis* 'Hornibrookii')

Japanese needle juniper (*J. rigida*)—can suffer from shoot-tip browning and dieback in cool climates during cold winter months on benches.

Drooping juniper (*J. recurva*)—including its beautifully pendulous variant 'Coxii'.

Squamata juniper (*J. squamata* and its cultivar 'Meyeri').

Wiring is best done in April or May. Ideally, you should remove the wire before winter on nearly finished trees, although many of my developing trees sit wired all winter.

Needle **(10–2)** and non-needle (scalelike) **(10–3)** are two distinct foliage types of juniper. Some scale-

10–3 • This *Juniperus* x *media* 'Plumosa Aurea' shows the cloud formation and odd pointed growth typical of a scalelike juniper.

like species revert temporarily to juvenile needlelike foliage if heavily branch pruned or trunk pruned or if new scalelike shoots are too heavily pinched. (The tree will settle back to scalelike foliage over the next season or two once drastic pruning ceases.) Of the suitable trees I've listed above, *J. chinensis*, *J. davurica*, *J. sargentii* × *media*, and *J. virginiana* forms are scalelike. If I could recommend only one genus to a beginner, it would be juniper and particularly *Juniperus chinensis* 'sargentii', if available, otherwise the more readily available (although bluer) 'Blaauws' or the green or yellow 'Plumosa' forms or *J. virginiana* 'Burkii'. Each is robust, easy to wire, prune, and repot, drought resistant, and winter hardy in cool climates.

The new growth of *J. davurica* 'Expansa' (otherwise known as *J. chinensis* 'Expansa') is slightly coarser. The growth of *J. chinensis* 'San Jose' and 'Pfitzerana' and *J. squamata* 'Meyeri' growth is also slightly coarse, requiring more frequent new-shoot pinching and thinning, but this is compensated for to a degree because the trunk is quicker to fatten.

Finger-pinch new shoots as they emerge through the season. Wire early in the growing season when the sap is flowing well. You can finger-pinch scalelike foliage through the season as new growth appears, concentrating on reducing the terminal shoots, thus encouraging round cloudlike pads rather than spear shapes. Needlelike shoots extend greatly if you don't pinch them, and you must catch them early to encourage tight foliage. Heavy pruning and drastic restyling are best accomplished early in the growing season, but they can be done in the middle of the season.

10–2 • This is typical needle-juniper foliage.

Eventually, the growth of scalelike junipers (and *J. squamata* 'Meyeri') becomes too full and heavy. It must be thinned every few years to avoid branch dieback and to help lighten the bonsai image. Carefully select and scissor-prune small foliage areas, cutting the little woody base stem. Do not cut through the soft foliage or it will turn brown. Similar foliage thinning is usually required when you radically restyle these junipers.

Sun exposure is important for both needle and scaled types to avoid branch dieback. However, they will both benefit from slightly shadier conditions, which help darken the color of the foliage and avoid drying the foliage. Scalelike types are far more tolerant of the sun and wind and can sit all day in full sun; needle types are much happier in cooler, shadier spots but with adequate air flow and dappled sun or sunshine part of the day.

A good feeding regime is required for scalelike forms (more so than for most bonsai) to avoid loss of lower branch vigor. Needle junipers also require adequate feed for the same reason. Both love late summer low-nitrogen feeds.

Select a deeper than normal pot for needle-leaved junipers to avoid drought. To ensure that the surface roots of newly collected or transplanted trees do not dry out, mound extra soil on the surface and add a protective thick layer of surface moss. Both junipers like a well draining loam-based soil. In general, scalelike junipers grow faster, need repotting more frequently, and are stronger and more drought resistant than needle types. Do not neglect repotting or heat stress increases; negligence will cause the trees to weaken.

Both need to be watered well in the summer months. The needle varieties in particular must not be neglected. After pinching or restyling both types, select a cool, shady spot for a few weeks to avoid browning foliage tips.

Junipers are relatively free of disease and insects. The most common invaders are red spider mites, aphids, and scale insects; all are treatable (see the Pests and Disease section of Chapter 2).

For details on collecting common juniper, which require special care to ensure success, see the section on Collecting from the Wild in Chapter 2 and Case History 1 that follows.

Yew

Yew is unsurpassed as an ornamental hedging tree in cool climates, responding very well to foliage clipping to form a dense barrier or topiary subject. Its leaves are poisonous (particularly when rotting) as are the nuts inside the attractive fleshy red fruit arils. Along with the olive tree, it has the distinction of being the longest-lived genus in Europe.

This tree makes a very good bonsai, providing you take particular care to provide winter protection and good sun exposure. However, the slow growth means that garden-center or growing bed subjects are easier than starting from seed, allowing you to acquire a reasonable girth of trunk as a starting point.

Winter protection is needed to avoid damage to fleshy roots for common yew (*Taxus baccata*) and the Japanese yew (*Taxus cuspidata*). The leaves are resistant to wind damage. The hybrid between these (*Taxus × media*) also requires winter protection.

I leave yew bonsai in full sun all day. They are also happy in shade, but you must never move a yew from a long period in deep shade directly into full sun; the leaves will suffer sun scorch and the tree may die. Wean them into sunlight over a period of a few weeks.

Use well-drained loam soil. Heavy-prune and carve in April or early summer. This is also the time for heavy wiring and radical redesign. You should do light new-shoot wiring in the early to middle of the growing season. Be careful because the young shoot and branch bases are very brittle and break off easily.

I like to position drooping, structural yew branches well inside the desired edge profile line to allow new shoots to ramify outward to form the eventual outline (see Case History 4 that follows). New shoots are normally finger-pinched back to one-third their length once they are about ⅝ inch (15 mm) long. You may also leave them growing if you want to create a new or longer branch or trunk.

If left unpruned, yew branches tend to extend lengthwise. As they stretch out for new light, the terminal buds and side buds near the branch tip are more active than the inner buds. The end result would be a very wide, sprawly bonsai. To counter this tendency during development, you may need to shorten the branches late in the season, around September or October. Leave some foliage on the branch. This will encourage budding the following spring.

A useful alternative technique for encouraging budding is to pluck off selected old leaves, retaining only the narrow basal neck of the leaf and the bud in its leaf axil. Do this in May to allow these dormant buds to burst later the same season. If you do it in July, new buds will not emerge until following spring,

although masses of new buds will appear by September or October of the current year. Because they are evergreens, yews need to retain foliage to survive; hence, confine this treatment to small areas and apply it over several years.

Yews are fairly resistant to disease, but scale insect attacks must be arrested quickly (see the Pests and Disease section in Chapter 2).

Case History 1

Common Juniper Cascade from Wildling

This tree was collected in Scotland in 1976. It was about twenty years old, and it looked like a feature-less, small, round ball. Collected common juniper are notoriously difficult to settle down after collection. This tree's history describes a successful methodology, which has produced an individual cascade style.

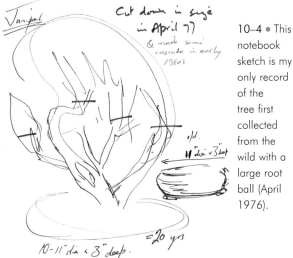

10–4 • This notebook sketch is my only record of the tree first collected from the wild with a large root ball (April 1976).

❧ After five years' care, it displayed little post-transplant tenderness. On the other hand, this tree will always need a little more winter care than its progeny of cuttings for reasons I cannot fully explain. Every tree must be considered on its merits and its habits and not completely generalized by species (see the Collecting from the Wild section in Chapter 2 for information about aftercare of wildling junipers).

❧ I believe the three most crucial factors for

collected *J. communis* wildlings are retaining soil moisture (especially for surface roots), providing winter protection, and using bottom heat to promote root growth for the first two months after collection. However, I did not use bottom heat in the following case history.

❧ I dug up the tree with the full root ball in the second week of April 1976 during a one-week vacation. The root ball measured 10 to 11 inches (25 to 28 cm) in diameter and was 3⅛ inches (8 cm) deep. I left the foliage ball unpruned.

❧ I wrapped the root ball in damp sphagnum moss and soaked the whole tree with water. Then, I transported it in a large plastic bag to my parents' home in Inverness. After discarding the plastic bag and carefully removing the sphagnum moss, I added local black loam soil to the root ball to supplement any gaps. I rewrapped the roots in damp sphagnum moss.

❧ I tied the root ball in a large piece of sacking, keeping the whole root mass firmly in place. I submerged the root ball in my parents' garden for the rest of the week. It was in a sheltered, shady spot where it was sprayed three times a day. Once I arrived back home, I planted the tree, complete with sacking, in a shady spot in my garden and sprayed it regularly for several weeks.

❧ In April of 1977, I reduced the foliage by half. I also removed or shortened some heavy branches. The tree was successfully transplanted into a pot with little root disturbance. In 1983, the planting angle was changed at repotting time to develop the tree as a cascade.

10–5 • The tree was well established in a cascade position and was very bushy (April 1988).

10–6 • The first heavy-wiring and pruning session establishes a basic design (May 1991).

10–9 • I used a wood hardener.

10–7 • I discovered some trunk rot (February 1994).

10–8 • I scraped all the rotten wood away.

10–10 ● I liberally painted the hardener on the affected area.

10–11 ● Here's the tree after the treatment. The tree had no recurrence of rot problem since this treatment.

10–12 ● A "before" notebook sketch.

10–13 ● An "after" notebook sketch.

10–14 ● This shows the typical upright growth of a common juniper.

10–15 ● This is the latest image, 23 years after I collected the tree (1999).

Case History 2

Virginia Juniper—Informal Upright from Garden Tree

This typical conifer, standing over 10 feet (3 m) tall, was transformed into a successful bonsai and incidentally produced a fabulous Christmas tree from the discarded top trunk. The root ball was so large I only escaped serious injury by drafting one of my strapping young sons to help me carry it to the car.

The following steps show how this giant conifer was turned into a bonsai in just six years:

10–16 • I chose this 10-foot (3 m) high, 30-year-old tree because of an interesting low branch (December 1990).

10–17 • I dug a substantial trench with a diameter of 3½ feet (1 m), leaving a giant root ball.

10–18 • I removed the top and potted the tree with as much of its original root ball as would fit into the largest bucket I had. Notice that the low branches, even though they are erect, offer an opportunity to design a bonsai.

10–19 • This is a sketch of the proposed design. Notice how the thicker, lowest-left branch will be discarded because it is too stiff, but the next branch up is flexible enough to wire so that it can become a new trunk.

10–20 • The tree was looking very vigorous. I heavy-wired the new leader into position (May 1991).

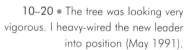

10–21 • I neatened up the top of the trunk a little at the same time.

10–22 • Once I established the leader-line, the whole tree was heavy-wired and heavy-pruned to develop the future image (May 1991).

10–23 • The foliage was growing back quickly (March 1992).

10–24 • I took the wires off to invigorate it (July 1994).

10–25 • Here's the tree, after my restyling at a demonstration (1996).

10–26 • This snow-clad image confirms that the tree will make a lovely bonsai one day.

Case History 3

'Shimpaku' Juniper from Young Bonsai Nursery Stock

I first met a wonderful bonsai enthusiast in April of 1993. She had bought a 2-year-old juniper bonsai import in 1970 in a pot measuring 4¾ inches (12 cm) by 3 inches (7.5 cm) by 1¾ inches (4.5 cm) high, and she did not know what to do next. She proudly showed me a picture of her tree. I volunteered to restyle it as a semicascade.

Four years later in November of 1997, she sold me the tree. She was then 85 years old, and arthritis had rendered her unable to continue tending her prize possession. I feel honored to continue the history of this tree, which received so much tender loving care that in the years since I have owned it, it is now even bigger and bushier than ever (see the Repotting section in Chapter 2 for the full story). I have purchased a beautiful pot and am hoping to transform this tree once more into a lovely semicascade bonsai. It was repotted and styled by a bonsai friend in 2001 following the author's sketch and wishes and is shown in **10–31**.

10–27 ● The picture shows how vigorous the tree was. Amazingly, it had only been repotted twice in 23 years (April 1993).

10–28 ● The initial low-branch placement was set (May 1993).

10–29 ● This stage of heavy wiring and pruning is complete. Many gaps remain where foliage needs to be developed.

10–30 ● This is what the tree looked like when I bought it. Note the rampant regrowth in 4½ years due to the feeding regime. Also notice how small the pot is relative to the foliage (November 1997).

10–31 ● The image in 2001, after being repotted and styled by Dan Barton according to the author's sketch and wishes. (Photo courtesy of Dan Barton.)

Case History 4

Common Yew from Hedging Stock

This yew reached an acceptable image eight years after I purchased it as a newly potted plant.

10–32 ● I purchased this tree as a newly collected tree and potted it (April 1988).

10–33 ● The foliage is discolored because the roots aren't established and because the tree was exposed to a cold winter.

10–34 ● I've identified the new trunk leader and wired it (May 1989).

10–35 ● Six weeks later, new, strong growth is establishing itself.

10–36 ● The preferred planting angle (April 1990).

10–37 ● Here's my rough notebook sketch of existing and proposed design. Note the attempts to reduce the dichotomy of two heavy trunks by masking the foliage and carving off the left-hand heavy branch.

10–38 • I've used heavy pruning and wiring to establish the future design (April 1990).

10–39 • This is the regrowth six months later (September 1990).

10–40 • I gave the tree another heavy pruning and wiring (September 1990).

10–41 • The tree gets a new pot (June 1991).

10–42 • This is a good show of male flowers (March 1996).

10–43 • Here's a close-up of the trunk base.

Larch—Graceful, Deciduous Beauties

11–1 ● This old, weather-beaten larch exhibits the rounded crowns only seen in very old specimens.

11–2 ● The female larch flowers sit like candles on spring branches.

OVERVIEW

The larch is native to cool mountainous areas, favoring the high valleys and slopes of the Northern Hemisphere. Larches thrive in dry, well-drained loam or mixed gravel and loam areas; most species dislike wet or boggy land. The European and Japanese varieties of these deciduous conifers can often be found at high altitudes, towering above pines and firs, where their bright spring greens and golden autumn hues uniquely light up the terrain. Their light crowns and fast growth have earned them a place as an invaluable shelter tree for developing hardwood plantations. Relatively short-lived trees, larches can tolerate very short growing seasons. Larches are not generally happy in wet, lowland frost pockets, though the North American larch, or Tamerack (*Larix laricina*) is a lowland bog dweller. Lovely gnarled forms are found at the extent of their range, which can be quite narrow and vary by species up to 11,000 feet (3,350 m) above sea level.

As bonsai, they are my favorite genus because of their speed of growth, hardiness, ease of wiring and shaping, and, most of all, for their beautiful foliage color in spring and autumn. Their lovely flowers, cones, and aged bark also deserve a mention. Their foliage rosettes and bark are reminiscent of the much longer-lived pines. Maybe it is the speed with which larch can be converted into mature pinelike images that makes them less attractive to some than the longer development cycle required for pines.

Like junipers, larch bonsai require conditions that do not always reflect their natural habitat, a result of the differences between container living and mountain living.

Above all, never let a larch dry out and never repot late in the season. If you avoid doing either of these things, larches are very easy to grow. Provide a cool, sunny, or semishady spot, and they will be very happy as long as you provide some shade in summer, particularly on days when the temperature is over 75°F (24°C). Larches love cool, shady garden areas, which help to avoid heat stress and darken foliage. If you have a tree that

A compact twin-trunk hybrid larch gives beautiful spring and autumn color.

is not happy, try this treatment. Trees in growing beds or deep growing boxes should be exposed to full sun at all times to ensure thickening.

Heat stress occurs when trees are so hot or the soil is so dry that they cease foliar growth, behaving almost like statues with their growth frozen until cooler conditions return. This hinders tree development, and, in severe cases, lower branches and those shaded out can die or be severely weakened. Developing trees in shallow pots can lose lower branches if all the new foliage has been retained. To aid the growth of such young trees, use very deep growing pots and keep the tree well watered; then you can expose it to more sun to encourage growth. Watch out for yellowing leaves. They are early signs of heat stress.

Larches love loam-based soil with sufficient grit to drain well. They are not tolerant of late repotting. You must repot before bud burst, before you see green leaves beginning to emerge, and while the swollen bud is still an unbroken sphere.

European larch (*Larix decidua*) and hybrid larch (*L. decidua × eurolepis*) are fully winter hardy on benches, even fully wired. Japanese larch (*Larix kaempferi,* formerly *Larix leptolepis)* needs some protection. I usually leave my Japanese larches out for a month after all other trees are in winter storage. I bring them in once they have had some extra cold and maybe some snow. Usually, I move them to the cold greenhouse early in December but always before the end of the year.

The hybrid larch is faster growing and has greater insect and disease resistance than its parents. This has justified the hybrid's marvelous reputation among foresters since its initial discovery in 1861 at Dunkeld, Scotland. It is a cross between *Larix deciduas* and *Larix kaempferi,* which I find excellent for bonsai. If I had to choose between the lovely textured bark, straw twigs, and medium-sized cones of the European larch; the orange/purple twigs and smaller cones of the hybrid; and the lusher foliage, interesting bark, and larger and fatter cones of the Japanese larch, the European has the slight edge. It looks a little more ancient and dignified in winter image.

Routine fine wiring is best done in early March before bud break to avoid foliage damage. Heavy pruning and wiring and radical restyling are best done in March or April. Larch trunks and branches can swell quickly in the spring and in August; there-

fore, take care to apply all heavy wire loosely.

Prune back new spring growth shoots to one-third their length once they are 1¼ to 2¼ inches (3 cm to 6 cm) long unless you need them long for design purposes. You can apply light wire to the shoots that were allowed to grow to help introduce interesting curves and character.

Branches heavily laden with cones will be weaker or die the following season. For this reason, you should consider whether to remove 50 percent of the young cones if a heavy crop appears. Old cones are no longer a drain, and it is lovely to see different generations of cones on a larch. European and hybrid larches seem to produce cones earlier and more freely than Japanese larch.

Larches are prone to mealybugs, which can be treated very effectively with pyrethrum or bifenthrin (Bio Flydown or Bio Sprayday) as soon as the bugs appear (see the Pests and Diseases section in Chapter 2 for alternative treatments). A little black dot in the center of each leaf is the first indication of mealybugs. Eventually, they produce a white fluff, and they mass around the bud at the heart of each foliage rosette. You may need to repeat the treatment once more after two weeks. The leaf usually bends at right angles in the middle. This is the easiest way to spot the early presence of mealybug; neglect leads to rampant infestation. European larch are susceptible to larch canker; hybrid and Japanese species are more resistant. Provided you keep the trees healthy, an attack is unlikely; I have never experienced an attack on my European larch. Cut out all the affected branches back to clear living wood and seal them with a protective paint. Cone-shaped galls can appear as a result of mite or similar damage. They should be removed and burned. Galls do not seriously weaken larches.

Water larches well but ensure adequate drainage to avoid causing the bark to swell too much and then split. Always select a deep pot for larch. You need one that provides a higher than normal soil volume to avoid the risk of drought and heat stress. Groups are particularly thirsty. Larch roots grow quickly, and once a larch is pot bound, it is more prone to heat stress and the loss of lower branches than normal. Do not forget to repot such trees the following spring. For the remainder of the year, double the water.

Developing larches fatten well when using Osmocote six- to-nine month granular feed, especially in conjunction with soil containing some rotted pine needle in the growing bed or box. This will encourage the growth of mycorrhizal fungus. Bonsai grown in containers need a low-nitrogen liquid feed at regular intervals through the growing season. On the other hand, you want to avoid heavy doses, which may split the bark. Only use Osmocote or alternative liquid feeds; never use both at the same time.

Late-season shoot pruning is a popular technique for larches. However, I do not recommend it because it produces prematurely old and arthritic-looking knuckles, and it prematurely thickens and weakens branches. True, in the short run, you get a denser tree, full of needlelike foliage, but this effect peaks and becomes ugly and disproportionate within a very few years. As a genus, larch can comfortably be made into a beautiful bonsai within ten years without this technique. In addition, larch can maintain an acceptable image for an additional fifty years with a combination of early-season shoot pruning and late-season tidying up and by avoiding large-scale late-shoot pruning. The thick old branches produced by late-summer pruning seem more vulnerable to heat stress and early dieback.

Like *Cedrus,* larches have two distinct leaf arrangements: rosettes, in which the leaves radiate around a dormant bud; and leaves, which grow along the length of new shoots, which were once dormant buds. Apart from their decorative quality, dormant buds are the lifeline for future branch replacement. Please leave some of them, particularly on inner branches, as an insurance policy.

When designing bonsai images, consider using a rounded crown to suggest age. You want to avoid the typical approach of arranging all your branches straight and having them come out at ninety-degree angles to a stiff, upright trunk pole, creating a stiff, regimental form. Even worse, don't place several such soldiers vertically in a totally uninspiring forest group. Do not be afraid to add angled lines and curved forms to branches and trunk. Look at larches in nature. By all means, create a group using straight, upright trunks, but why not add some flying or crossing branches or leaning trunks, typical of a young larch copse?

To aid refinement, pluck off all the needles that point downward. These detract from a clean under-branch (or pad) line. Remove any others that would spoil the outline at the periphery. Pay particular attention to the corners of foliage pads, removing any needles that obscure a clearer definition of the corner shape and sharpness.

11–3 ● A typical young larch copse.

Case History 1

Japanese Larch Pine Image from Garden-Center Stock

I bought this *Larix kaempferi* from a garden center on August 29, 1973. It was 35 inches (90 cm) tall. I was attracted to its good taper, particularly at the trunk base, which had a diameter of about 1¼ inch (3 cm). It had been grown in an outdoor bed and had been dug up at the end of August by the nursery. It had a very compact, good-sized root system. This was a month earlier than ideal, so I carefully planted it in a growing box and shaded it. I wired a forward-pointing branch to a vertical position to become the new leader after I shortened the trunk by two-thirds. I allowed the new leader to extend an additional 12 to 18 inches (30 to 45 cm) to thicken the base of the new leader. Now and again, I reduced the height of the new leader and chose another replacement leader to develop a taper in this new leader section.

By 1980, the original join was hardly visible from the front, and the trunk had a continuous taper from base to top. I returned the tree to a container on March 1, 1981, because the branches had started to become a little thick. At the same time, I undertook a radical untangling of the roots. They were all wired to produce a good radial spread. The trunk had fattened marvelously, thanks to the rotted pine needle combined with the Osmocote six- to nine month granular feed.

The main design criteria for this pinelike image revolved around the bottom right branch, which had an interesting curve. Despite suggestions that I straighten it, I continued to echo this pattern throughout the tree and to lean the trunk slightly toward the right as was its natural tendency. The other main requirement was to increase the number of pads and to place some to mask the two parallel branches on the left-hand side and any other heavy areas. Over time, the trunk has thickened more than the main branches due to a shallower pot and to the lack of any heavy late pruning, which would have created cluster budding and rapid branch thickening. The trunk base is now 3½ inches (9 cm) in diameter.

❖ August 29, 1973, tree was purchased as a 4-year-old grown in a garden-center plunging bed.

❖ Transferred without further root disturbance to a growing box that was 12 by 18 inches and 4 inches (30 cm by 45 cm and 10 cm) deep and placed tree in shade; soil was used around the edge of the root ball, but the roots were not disturbed further.

❖ August 29, 1973, height was reduced from 35 to 12 inches (90 to 30 cm) by making an angled cut downward from the front of the trunk just above a forward-pointing branch; branch was wired vertically. Over the next six or seven years, Osmocote six- to nine month granular feed was applied annually, and the new leader developed as described earlier.

❖ March 1, 1981, tree was transplanted into a container and roots wired radially.

11–4 ● This is my first styling of a Japanese larch. The branching is rather crude.

11–5 ● The tree was potted (March 1990).

11–6 • Notice the need for additional branch development (May 1990).

11–7 • The foliage pads were improving, especially the right-hand middle areas (April 1993).

11–8 • After twenty years, the tree has a mature, natural form (October 1993).

11–9 • This Japanese larch is enjoying the autumnal sun (October 1993).

11–10 • The light green spring image (May 1994).

11–11 • The frosted winter branches now show good branch ramification (December 1996).

Case History 2

Hybrid Larch Twin Trunk from Seedling

I developed this natural twin trunk from a batch of 3-year-old hybrid seedling culls purchased in early March of 1981. Trained as a rather formal and stiff version, it has a pleasant image, even if it isn't a hugely inspiring one. If you select such an upright style, it is important to straighten the trunk or trunks rather than have an awkward kink. This would detract from a smooth vertical eye movement.

✤ In 1981, purchased as a 3-year-old bare-rooted seedling.

✤ Plant grown in pot for seven years.

11–12 • Before the tree was repotted into a shallower container, a cane was used to aid in straightening the main trunks (spring 1988).

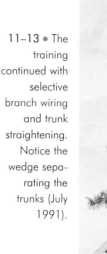

11–13 • The training continued with selective branch wiring and trunk straightening. Notice the wedge separating the trunks (July 1991).

11–14 • Summer image (July 1999).

11–15 • An image from autumn (October 1999).

Case History 3

Hybrid Larch Tall Twin Trunk from Seedling

This is another natural twin-trunk cull purchased at the same time as Case History 2. A lankier specimen, this tree was trained into a tall twin trunk. Inspired by a famous twin larch bonsai, this tree has a few years to go to match it.

❖ In 1981, purchased as a 3-year-old bare-rooted seedling.

❖ First trained and wired in 1982; note the mounded soil, which avoids removing too many roots until more compact fibrous roots are formed.

❖ Plant grown in pot for six more years.

11–16 ● Before I repotted the tree, I wired and straightened the main trunks again. Notice that the lower trunks are still rather kinked (spring 1988).

11–17 ● The tree was in need of pruning (June 1990).

11–18 ● After I wired and pruned, the growth was more balanced, but the upper half of the left trunk is short of branches (June 1990).

11–19 ● I eventually realized that exposing this tree to full sun in such a shallow pot was giving it heat stress, causing it to stop growing.

11–20 ● The foliage pads have gained height and vigor and are more balanced, but the new growth has not been pruned (July 1999).

Case History 4

European Larch Informal Style from a Friend

This tree was grown by good friends in the windswept style, but they were very unhappy with its progress and offered me the 19-year-old tree in 1992. There were only four small branches at the time plus a not-very-convincing apical deadwood stump. I love the windswept style, but frankly I think it rarely works without at least one branch on the windward side. This trunk is very awkward because of the ugly right-angled bend in the lower trunk.

When I turned this tree around, one viewing angle offered the promise of a lovely dynamic and rhythmical curved shape. I ignored all branching problems and potted the tree at the required angle. This meant that the vertical trunk section was now toward the back of the pot, adding depth to the composition.

Over the next four years, these four small branches were wired and encouraged to grow until a new tree image was born. The foliage areas now all hang off just four branches. I confess to really liking this new image, particularly after I was able to remove the top deadwood.

Future plans are to improve the all-round image of the tree, particularly the side view, looking directly at the right-angled trunk bend. This can be achieved by developing the foliage at this side, which will be hidden from the main front view by the existing foliage.

11–22 • This is the proposed new viewing angle. Notice how one-sided the remaining four branches are.

11–23 • The new growth is wired and a handkerchief hides the distracting top of the trunk deadwood (June 1992).

11–21 • The tree is bare-rooted and propped up at the angle at which it was previously potted as a windswept bonsai (February 1992).

11–24 • The growth is even on all four branches (August 1992).

11–25 • The tree foliage areas are developing. The wire will remain on through the winter months (September 1993).

11–26 • The new tree image is almost complete (August 1996).

11–27 • I can remove that unconvincing deadwood top (April 1998).

11–28 • A dusting of snow highlights the tree's winter form (April 1998).

11–29 • The latest image (September 1999).

12

Some Common Deciduous Trees as Bonsai

12–1 ● Common hawthorn, *Crataegus monogyna* foliage.

12–2 ● *Aesculus hippocastanum.*

CHAPTER OVERVIEW

This chapter includes a few trees that are not always common as bonsai. In some cases, such as horse chestnut or linden (called lime in Great Britain), the large leaf size may have been an obstacle; for others such as the Guelder rose, lack of exposure as a potential bonsai subject is the case.

OVERVIEW

Horse chestnut

These hardy, spreading ornamentals are very happy in cities and towns and are very tolerant of air pollution. Horse chestnuts are one of the first trees to signal the onset of autumn in cool climates; their leaves turn a handsome mix of yellow, green, and brown. The sight of strong early-morning sunlight streaming through an avenue of autumnal horse chest-nuts, with maybe an added touch of fog or mist, is so memorable that it demands we try and produce good bonsai subjects to recreate that magic.

While the common horse chestnut (*Aesculus hippocastanum)* has the slightly better autumn foliage color, its hybrid red horse chestnut (*A. carnea)* has the more decorative red, rather than white flowers. It also has somewhat smaller leaves and stature. The bark of the common horse chestnut is gray; its hybrid is a redder color; both are easily grown from seed, or should I say conker. As bonsai, both are hardy on benches and vigorous and easy to grow. They need no winter protection and are fairly free of disease. They enjoy moist, well-drained soil. It is helpful to reduce the soil volume as these trees mature to encourage smaller leaves and a slower growth. I recommend both for bonsai. Although the large, 12-inch (30 cm) vertical flowers are not this tree's best feature for bonsai, I would select the common tree for its leaf and bark color. Its

A European hornbeam showing the merged-trunk style in development.

extra vigor makes for quicker chop-and-grow trunk-taper development. If you don't mind protecting your horse chestnut over the winter, try the equally attractive Indian (*Aesculus indica*). This is a stout form with a twisted bark. The leaves are rather large, like common horse chestnut, with white flowers tinged with yellow or pink

At first, horse chestnut's spring growth seems unpredictable and unmanageable with little or no side-shoot or side-bud growth and unacceptably long new shoots and big leaves emerging from terminal buds. This is due to the dominance of the huge (and sticky) terminal bud whose hormones stop side-bud growth and suppress side-shoot development. If such bonsai terminal new-shoot growth is left uncorrected, the tree will grow ever taller and wider without any ramification or bonsai form. New horse chestnut shoots harden in a couple of seasons and become stiff and difficult to bend with wire after that time.

The standard answer is to prune off all the lanky first shoots and to wait for the shorter second growth that season, perhaps leaving the occasional shorter new shoot for wiring loosely into a bend or a new direction. This will eventually work, but it is a very slow and frustrating method that does not encourage dormant side-bud and small, side-shoot growth very efficiently.

The secret to ramifying and shaping them lies in forcing buds to shoot. These will be shorter in length, angled from the existing branch line, and more in number. To achieve this, I have found that a preseason dormant-tip bud removal technique works remarkably well. It produces masses of new buds in six to eight weeks. You may need to reduce the number of new shoots if too many emerge. This technique weakens the tree significantly. Therefore, you should use it only on healthy trees and then only with at least three years between repeat pruning episodes. It is best not to use it until after the main trunk form has been thickened and developed (and maybe also some initial major branches) because it is chiefly a branch-ramification tool. The technique also reduces leaf size and is applicable, with care, to other species with a vigorous spreading habit typically associated with dominant terminal buds such as sycamore maple.

Case History 1

Common Horse Chestnut from Garden-Center Stock

This common horse chestnut started life as a purchased ornamental container-grown tree in 1978. Before repotting it in the spring of 1979, I reduced it to one-sixth its height. However, I was looking to develop a fairly tall tree capable of keeping these huge leaves in scale. Eighteen years later, I have an acceptable image, although not the stereotypical upright tree form. After I used the preseason bud removal technique, the tree has produced leaves whose size is acceptable. In strong sunlight, these leaves display that magical translucent quality at leaf burst and in the autumn.

❖ Spring of 1979, the tree's height was reduced from 6½ feet (2 m) down to 14 inches (35 cm). The prune was angled from above a forward-facing dormant bud steeply downward and backward.

❖ April of 1983, new leader, which grew from the 1979 pruning, was reduced in length to 4 inches (10 cm) above first scar.

❖ April of 1986, new leader, from 1983 terminal pruning wound, was reduced in length.

12–3 ● The tree had thickened nicely. The top taper was acceptable, but the tree looked very stiff and erect (April 1988).

12–4 ● The initial and secondary trunk reduction scars were healing nicely (April 1988).

12–5 ● The tree is leafing out (May 1988).

12–6 ● I repotted the tree at a much better angle to suit the trunk shape, but the tree still lacked any branch detail (April 1990).

12–7 ● The lower right branch was extending well, but the leaves are still very large (April 1991).

12-8 • The buds were ready for preseason tip-bud removal (early March 1996).

12-9 • The tip removal in process (early March 1996).

12-10 • Here's the tree after I removed every tip bud (March 1996).

12-11 • New buds bursting into leaf at the branch tips (June 1996).

12-12 • Look at all those buds emerging from dormancy (June 1996).

12–13 ● This much-ramified tree was the result of many years of toil. The preseason tip-bud removal technique proved highly successful (April 1997).

12–14 ● This is the rear of the tree showing the latest scar healing.

OVERVIEW

Hawthorn

A traditional hedgerow tree in Britain, the tree forms an excellent barrier against wind and salty air. Like yew and hornbeam, hawthorns adapt very well to clipping, producing a dense, impenetrable hedge. When exposed to solitary moorlands and coastlines, the trees bend away from the prevailing winds. In extreme conditions, they even hug the contours of

12–15 ● Moorland style of *Crataegus monogyna*.

nearby rocks or soil to survive where many less rugged or flexible trees cannot. Typically, such weather-beaten branches are twisted and matted, curving like waves on the leeward side.

There are two common species: *Crataegus monogyna* (common hawthorn) and *Crataegus oxyacantha* (English hawthorn). The former has a profusion of flowers in April or May; the latter flowers at a similar time. Although it has fewer blossoms, the flowers have a wider variety of color. The English hawthorn also colors well in autumn. Both fruit well. The 'Paul's Scarlet' cultivar of *Crataegus oxyacantha* is, unfortunately, sterile; hence, it produces no fruit. It does, however, have a fabulous and prolific show of double red flowers, making it a beautiful subject for bonsai.

In fact, all hawthorn types make wonderful bonsai, but they are very susceptible to drought. Water well, use a water-retentive soil, and select a deeper than average container. Never (or rarely) water or spray the leaves or you may encourage mildew (see the Watering section of Chapter 2).

Hawthorns like full sun, but this means you must pay close attention to watering and to pot and soil selection; hawthorns also tolerate shade. Feed regularly in the growing season with a low-nitrogen liquid feed and apply a light surface dressing of bonemeal in November or December. Apply a trace element Frit in January or February to encourage flowering. Flowers form at the end of short shoots between September and March.

Heavily prune the trunk or branches in April or May. Wire trees from the early season to the middle of the season (April to July); these wires can remain on the tree during the winter months. After flowering, lightly prune all soft new shoots back to two or three leaves in spring. During the season, prune them once they are 1¼ to 2¼ inches (3 to 6 cm) long. Encourage and retain short shoots from which the flowers will emerge. Remove long sacrificial branches in February or March. Typically, hawthorns take 25 years to flower from seed.

Apart from mildew (see the Watering section and the Pests and Diseases sections in Chapter 2), hawthorns are relatively free of disease and insects. A small blister mite can cause an ugly leaf deformity. At first, this site looks like peach leaf curl. The leaf surfaces become a blotchy yellow, and the leaf margins become wavy and distorted. This mite attacks plants under stress from dry soil. You can control it with by permethrin, bifenthrin, or with more beneficial insect-friendly treatments (see Chapter 2).

The bonsai tree in Case History 2 is a classic moorland *Crataegus monogyna* (common hawthorn). I found it on a north England moor in 1976. This wildling had grown in the crevice of a limestone rock area for about 28 years. Its foliage and new shoots had been nibbled by sheep. The stone was being quarried, and the tree would have been excavated and lost. Thus, to date, I have extended its life by 24 years.

I always protect this tree in winter in a cold greenhouse or hoop tunnel following a near-death experience (see the Tree Reviving section in Chapter 2). I know people who leave hawthorn on benches, but this one is certainly tender, probably more so than most due to its shallow pot. Some winter cold improves the prospect of flowering for hawthorns, but be careful, particularly if the tree shows signs of tenderness, such as reddening of new spring buds or leaves.

Case History 2

Common Hawthorn Moorland Style from Wildling

❧ October 9, 1976, I carefully removed this wildling with very little soil or root volume, just a v-shaped wedge 8 inches (20 cm) long by 2¾ inches (7 cm) wide (at the top) and 3⅛ inches (8 cm) deep; managed to retain 80 percent of its root; no large taproots had formed due to its confinement in the limestone crevice. I collected some small pieces of limestone from the same area and eventually placed these pieces beneath the tree's canopy to try to recreate its original landscape.

❧ Tree was sprayed and bagged in a large plastic bag after I wrapped the root in plastic and taped the bag securely to avoid further root disturbance.

❧ No root or branches were removed, but the tree was well watered, wired securely into the pot, and sprayed daily for two weeks. I protected it all winter in a cold frame with the lid closed. No lime was added to the soil then or since; soil mix had a lower drainage content (grit or sand) than I would normally choose, but it was right for this particular situation where the tree was planted directly into a fairly shallow container, and the small root ball had to receive adequate moisture.

12–16 ● I had selected this side to be the front and removed one or two awkward jutting branches that spoiled the windswept movement of the tree (April 1988).

12-17 • The tree was filling out. The single root near the trunk base still needed to merge into the trunk to improve the image slightly (June 1990).

12-18 • I turned the tree around to show off the beautiful trunk and branch undulations (June 1994).

Actual May 96

12–19 • The tree was too evenly balanced around the trunk. A windswept tree would stretch out much farther on one side. So I drew this "before" image (May 1966).

Rejected possible May 96

12–20 • Keeping the present image as a dotted outline, I started redesigning it. This version lacks impact.

Proposed May 96

12–21 • I preferred this second redesign, and I decided to use it.

12–22 • After radically shortening the left-hand side and slightly shortening the right, the tree looked more balanced, but it needed to become more undulating and natural again (June 1996).

12–23 • A close-up of the trunk (June 1996).

12–24 • This is a more relaxed image, featuring more of an undulating top profile and showing off those undulating underbranches (August 1999).

OVERVIEW

Hornbeam

The hornbeams, often mistaken for beech trees, can be recognized by their distinctive and decorative vertical trunk fluting. In addition, their leaves are coarser and more deeply veined, compared to the round, smooth, parallel boles and silkier, flimsier, and often greener leaves of the beeches. Hornbeams are among the first large, mature trees to succumb to long periods of drought (typically two or more consecutive dry years), closely followed by the beeches. The British heat wave of 1990, preceded by a similar year of drought, caused many such mature trees to die.

Like the beeches, hornbeams are often used for hedging; they both respond well to pruning, and they retain many of their brown winter leaves. Hornbeams make a denser hedge, responding better to clipping. They thrive in any soil, are fairly wind hardy, and can withstand moderate levels of pollution.

As bonsai, European hornbeams (*Carpinus betulus*) and Japanese hornbeams (*Carpinus japonica*) are fully hardy on benches, are easy to grow from seed, cuttings, or layers, and are generally free of disease. Chinese or Korean hornbeams (*Carpinus turczaninowii*) only need protection from severe cold. They respond well to total leaf removal in order to reduce leaf size, and they make good bonsai subjects.

A slow-growing tree in a container, the hornbeam thickens quickly in growing beds. You can use heavy pruning on the trunk or branches in April or May. While they should be exposed to full sun when in a growing a bed or box, container-grown bonsai prefer some shade. In addition to avoiding drought, shade keeps the leaf color a more attractive dark green.

Bonsai branches with diameters below ⅛ inch (3 mm) remain flexible for many years before thickening and turning into the tough ironwood used in the past for machinery axles, spindles, etc. Wiring branches with small diameters is quite easy; on the other hand, you'll need very thick wire for larger diameters. You can leave wire on over the winter, although you should remove it from the fine-twigged *Carpinus turczaninowii*.

New-shoot growth is generally compact, and the shoots naturally bend from side to side in an angular fashion. Prune these new shoots back to two or three buds to encourage budding and to make use of the angular position of the buds to direct new growth angles.

One weakness with hornbeams is their lack of drought hardiness. Always water them well and keep the surface roots cool. Use a soil mix that is high in loam to retain moisture. In addition, select a pot that is deeper than normal. Sudden drying or browning of the leaf tips is a warning sign that the bonsai is too dry; total leaf drying is more serious, and trees showing evidence of drought will need special winter protection until they regain full vigor (see the Tree Reviving section of Chapter 2).

12–25 ● Sudden drying or browning of leaf tips was a warning sign that this European hornbeam had been drying out.

Case History 3

European Hornbeam from Cuttings

The following case history involves a simple pair of hornbeam cuttings now 25 years old. The trees are only 8 inches (20 cm) high, testimony to their slow growth and small leaves when confined for 25 years in a small container.

❧ In 1974, cuttings taken as described in the Cuttings section of Chapter 2.

12–26 • Two *mame* trees (October 1990).

12–27 • European hornbeam 25 years after cuttings were taken (July 1999)

Case History 4

European Hornbeam Merged-Trunk Style from Cuttings

The bonsai featured in this case history is my prize rule-breaker. It features crossing branches, opposite branches, generally knotted and winding branches, and an inverse trunk taper in order to emphasize the wonderful branch and trunk merging habit of this genus. This unusual bonsai has been artificially created by planting several cuttings close together in a bed until they were fully merged together. This is a quicker way to get thick trunks (often seen on some young maples consisting of several thin cuttings plaited together), and the end result can be fascinating. I hope you like it and will try the technique.

❧ In 1974, cuttings were taken.

❧ October of 1980, cuttings were transferred to garden growing bed.

❧ Eventually, I am hoping to remove the heavy diagonal trunk that straddles the two outer ones. In order to retain the disorderly look, I cannot do this until the area has more mature tangled branches.

12–28 • The large root ball under-lines the good growth of roots achieved in a garden bed during nine growing seasons (March 1990).

12–30 • The following spring, I reduced the root ball, again a little too late.

12–29 • The few leaves already opening indicate it was a little late for transplanting.

12–31 • A close-up of the trunks.

12–32 • I reduced the height of the trunks, wired them preliminarily, and planted the tree in a shallower pot.

12–33 • The tree was developing. I removed the bottom left-hand short branch.

12–34 • This is the image nine years after I removed the tree from the garden bed (July 1999).

12–35 • A close-up of the trunks.

12–36 • A close-up of some tangled branches.

Case History 5

European Hornbeam from Seed

The case history of this European hornbeam shows how interesting trunk and branch detail can slowly be achieved in a container by being patient for 28 years.

❖ April 3, 1970, seed soaked for 24 hours, then planted outdoors in a plastic seed tray containing loam-based compost. Watered seeds and left outdoors exposed to remaining frosts.

❖ April 1, 1971, seed germinated, requiring a winter's stratification, because it was a year since planting seed.

❖ Summer of 1977, all hornbeam seedlings were still very small due to leaving them in individual pots with a 4-inch (10 cm) diameter.

12–37 • I wired the branches and the top of the trunk. Notice that the movement in the trunk and branches is achieved by continually pruning back (July 1991).

12–38 • Here's the latest image (July 1999).

12–39 • In this close-up of the trunk, notice how the typical fluting character of the hornbeam is developing (July 1999).

Case History 6

European Hornbeam from Bonsai Nursery Growing-Bed Stock

This tree was created from growing-bed stock in eight years. I selected the tree for its trunk fluting, which was just developing, and for the nice taper of its lower trunk. Although too tall and parallel when purchased, it is beginning to have an acceptable shape. The trunk top taper has been developed for most of the eight years, leaving the branches in need of further ramification and refinement.

❖ Purchased in February of 1991 from a bonsai nursery growing bed; tree was twelve years old; the root volume was reduced by half; and the tree was potted the same day; at 30 inches (75 cm), tree was far too tall and had a crudely chopped off top.

❖ In February of 1991, I placed the tree outside one very cold night. When the tree was frozen solid in the pot, I marked a saw line ready to reduce the trunk height.

❖ Used a domestic jigsaw to shorten the trunk to 16 inches (40 cm), angling the cut steeply upward at a sideways angle. This is a great way of carving or pruning trees to avoid any root damage caused by rocking the tree sideways in the pot. Better still, prune as you transplant, just before potting.

❖ Effectively, we have a trunk with just one little branch. The next task is to grow a new leader. The trunk top is now fairly well tapered. In two or three years, it will be credible. The branches have been tidied up. Now it's time now to concentrate on developing the branch detail further and to develop a foliage outline that echoes and emphasizes the twists in the trunk.

12–40 ● I dug up this 12-year-old tree from a bonsai nursery growing bed and repotted it (March 1991).

12–41 ● I forgot to cut through the trunk before potting it, but one very cold night, the soil ball was frozen solid. I marked a saw line with a pen (April 1991).

12–42 ● Because the soil was frozen solid, I was able to saw through the trunk without damaging the fine roots.

12–43 ● This is the tree after cutting (April 1991).

12–44 ● Notice the regrowth within six weeks.

12–45 ● Here's a close-up of the wound three months after I pruned it.

12–46 ● The new leader is rewired.

12–47 ● This is the growth four weeks later.

12–48 ● I created a rapid new leader by allowing it to grow unchecked (December 1993).

12–49 • A close-up from December 1993.

12–50 • I selected the point to remove the thickened leader, leaving a much better taper between the trunk and the new leader (April 1995).

12–51 • Notice how the first scar is healing nicely and the second cut is as steeply angled as the first was (April 1995).

12–52 • This is a front view showing the new alignment of the trunk leader to continue the bend rhythm while retaining a new vertical leader.

12–53 • The branches need pruning (July 1999).

12–54 • This shot was taken after branch pruning (July 1999).

OVERVIEW

Linden (Lime)

Lindens (also known as limes in Great Britain), like horse chestnuts, are ideal avenue trees: both are early harbingers of winter. Linden trees turn colors even before horse chestnuts do. Both have fresh green foliage in spring and turn a striking yellow in autumn. The linden is the taller of the two trees. In fact, the common linden (*Tilia europaea*) is the tallest broad-leaved tree in the British Isles, but it suffers from heavy suckering at the base of the trunk and severe aphid attacks. The small-leaved linden (*Tilia cordata*) is not prone to suckering, which, combined with its smaller leaves, makes it an ideal bonsai candidate. Lindens are long-lived, hardy trees that thrive on polluted city life.

Linden bonsai are fully winter hardy on benches and can be exposed to full sun during the summer, provided the soil is never allowed to dry. This means a deeper than normal pot and a loam-rich compost.

If you allow lindens to dry out, the leaves droop and don't regain their former glory that season. Because these trees are prone to leaf scorch in hot weather, you should give them some shade.

Use heavy pruning in March or April, and wire early in the season after leaf burst. The wire can remain during the winter on benches. Prune back new shoots to two leaves or buds as soon as possible. Remove excessively long shoots to encourage shorter growth later on that season. Occasional dieback of thin shoots occurs, so avoid exposing very thin or weak wired shoots to excessively strong sun or severe cold. Most new shoots, however, are unaffected by such problems.

Apart from aphid attacks, lindens are fairly free of disease. Trees growing in beds or boxes love high-nitrogen feeds, such as Miracid or Miracle-Gro to help fatten trunks. However, you need to replace them with a low-nitrogen or no-nitrogen feed in late August and early September. More established trees grown in containers do better on mid- to low-nitrogen feeds (10:10:27) to avoid excessive shoot length.

Case History 7

Small-Leaf Linden from Seedling

The case history below is a tree given to me in 1975 by a friend. Although just a 5-year-old sapling, it already exhibited amazing basal trunk taper. Grown in a bed for seven seasons, this tree was then repotted and styled as a field tree image in eleven years. During this time, new straight growth was often removed to await the neater late growth. This was a slow process, but, hopefully, you'll agree it was worthwhile.

❖   Given to me in 1975 as a 5-year-old sapling grown in a pot.

❖   Transferred to a growing bed in October of 1990.

❖   Removed from growing bed early in April of 1987 and planted in a container.

The bonsai form is now satisfactory, but my aim is to ramify the branches further. Also in nature, the upper branches of lindens tend to point markedly upward, and the lower branches significantly downward. In addition, specimen trees in nature tend to have a more barreled foliage profile, meaning that they are wider in the middle. I will try to add these subtleties to the tree.

12–55 ● The new leader is establishing itself, but you'll see that a very big step in trunk diameter requires attention (1988).

12–56 • Here you see how much healing the scars need.

12–57 • Notice how well the trunk base flares; this is a characteristic feature of linden trees.

12–58 • The tree in leaf (August 1989).

12–59 • The leaf damage was caused by strong sun on newly sprayed leaves.

12–60 • The scar is healing slowly (October 1994).

12–62 ● This shows the trunk flare (July 1999).

12–61 ● The tree image is developing (July 1999).

12–63 ● Notice the autumn colors (September 1999).

OVERVIEW

Guelder rose (*Viburnum opulus*)

12–64 • *Mame Guelder rose after leaf trimming at the end of June.*

One day in the autumn of 1974, I was walking in Sutton Park, a local semi-wild area. I discovered a fabulous little deciduous bush with vivid, translucent red berries and leaves nestled in a mixed birch and holly copse. The twigs reminded me of elder but, upon gathering some seeds and a sample of twig and leaf, I discovered later that it was a Guelder rose. I was hooked, and the following spring I was rewarded by germinating Guelder rose seeds from the collected berries.

In the wild, Guelder roses love wet and boggy places. They are found in sunny and shady locations. The leaves, fruit, and bark of the Guelder rose tree are poisonous.

This tree produces multiple suckers freely and displays white flowers on the tips of this year's growth in May or June. The red fruits mature by August or September and persist into the winter. The leaves of Guelder rose trees, rather like Acer *palmatum* 'Osakazuki', have a redness that can start in the middle of the summer and persist and improve until the leaves fall in September or October. Comparing the autumn leaf color of Guelder rose to that of a maple is a compliment shared by only a few other families such as *Amelanchier*, *Liquidambar*, *Parrotia*, *Prunus* (cherry), Tupelo (*Nyssa sylvatica* or black gum), *Euonymus,* and some varieties or cultivars of *Malus,* oak, and ash.

Bonsai Guelder roses are fully hardy on benches and are happy in a well-drained loam mix. If you are growing them in a deep pot (to ensure that the soil does not completely dry out), their fairly robust leaves will survive happily in full sun, and, in fact, this will improve their summer reddening.

Remove all suckers except perhaps one or two basal ones. You can use these as sacrificial branches to enhance the thickening of the trunk base and the way the trunk scar heals.

New shoots tend to grow long and vertically. For this reason, most or all of the first growth is commonly removed on developing trees. However, this also removes the flowering tip buds. To minimize the potential length of new shoots, prune the developing new shoots back to two buds when they are 1¼ inch (3 cm) long. Total leaf removal is also very effective on this naturally vigorous plant, but this must be completed by the middle of May. Delaying into June may mean no new leaves until next spring, particularly if there is insufficient sunshine to encourage new leaf formation. You may repeat this every other year on healthy plants until the leaves become smaller, but only use total leaf removal on bonsai as they approach your final image stage.

For mature plants displaying flowers, prune the new shoots selectively after flowering, leaving some to bear fruit. Retain some long or lanky new shoots to encourage other short (flowering) shoots to form. Remove long sacrificial branches next February or March.

You can wire Guelder rose through the growing season, and you can leave the wire on during the winter. The growth habit of this tree, like elder (*Sambucus nigra),* is vertical; hence, to develop a good bonsai form, you have to wire new shoots down regularly, allowing new shoots to grow upward. You should wire the trunk and new shoots in the first season of growth.

Use heavy pruning on developing bonsai trees in April or May. Routinely remove any branch basal suckers during the growing season to avoid weakening the branches. Pruning scars are fairly slow to heal, but using suckers or shoots on the edge of the scar aids the healing process.

This delightful species is one of my favorites for bonsai. It is fairly disease-free, except for aphid attacks in the early spring. Spray them according to the directions in the Pests and Diseases section of Chapter 2.

Guelder rose makes an excellent bonsai subject. It has the look of old bark and lovely small, colorful leaves (often turning red in late summer before the lovely deep autumn reds), flowers, and fruit. Additionally, it propagates readily from seed, cuttings, or ground layering.

Case History 8

Guelder Rose from Seed

This 24-year-old bonsai was raised from seed and always grown in a container. The case history traces the slow development of the branch shape and ramification, which in its winter form is reminiscent of trees in a fairy tale.

Training Steps and Special Care

❖ Planted seed in 1974.
❖ Germinated in April of 1975.
❖ Grew in deep pot for next thirteen years; encouraged sacrificial basal suckering to aid thickening of lower trunk.
❖ Removed suckers after four or five years.

12–65 ● I've roughly wired the branches and placed the tree in a shallow container.

12–66 ● Here winter branching is developing along the lines of a tree in a fairy tale.

12–67 ● The tree is in leaf, but the leaves are smaller following a total leaf removal in June.

12–68 ● This is the latest front view (July 1999).

12–69 ● This is the latest side view showing a typical mid-summer reddening (July 1999).

12–70 ● A close-up of the trunk (July 1999).

12–71 ● The tree in all its autumn glory (1999).

13

Hopeless Cases

13–1 • Scotch pine, scrub style from seed.
(Discussed in Case History 2)

OVERVIEW

I am sure most bonsai enthusiasts have hopeless cases: trees they have grown or acquired that seem impossible to transform into good bonsai. Sentiment stops us from discarding them. This chapter features three of my hopeless cases that have been transformed by a sudden new design thought.

Case History 1

Scotch Pine Cascade Style from Wildling

Although I collected this 8-year-old pine at the wrong time of year, it survived. However, it had an uninspiring, tall, and spindly shape. Eleven years later, having extended the trunk in a most uninteresting fashion, I decided to turn it into a cascade. Because of the inflexibility of the bottom quarter of the trunk, I tried a risky double-longitudinal trunk-splitting technique to bend the rigid trunk.

My crude notebook sketch **(13–2)** shows how cutting one split along the length of the trunk would result in an eye-shaped bulge. Repeating the operation crossways effectively creates four longitudinal quadrant strands that bend far more sympathetically once wired. I didn't use raffia under the wire. I took great care to keep the cutting lines straight, avoiding cutting through any of the four quadrant-shaped strands.

The tree was radically transformed. With a little more branch refinement, it will make a good image.

❖ June 16, 1979, tree (together with three others) was dug up from the wild, far too late in the year (see Collecting from the Wild section of Chapter 2). A good root ball was obtained for this, and one other tree and each tree's roots were wrapped in plastic. An hour after being dug up, the 3⅛-inch (8 cm) long new candles were drooping badly; All trees were

Pyracantha 'Beauty of Bath' grown from seed and classed as a hopeless case, but "I'm improving with age." (This tree is discussed in Case History 3.)

potted; to increase survival chances, all top growth was drastically pruned back; trees were put under a fine misting unit, which sprayed every time the probe sensed the surface had dried out. All pines except the smallest one survived this ordeal, but, as often happens, growth was suppressed in subsequent years.

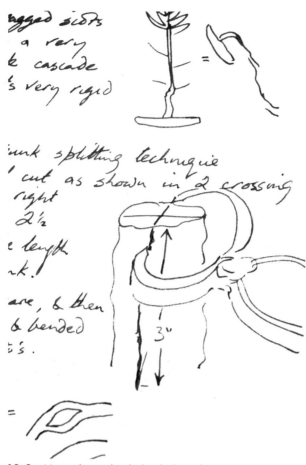

13–2 • My crude notebook sketch shows how cutting one split along the length of the trunk would result in an eye-shaped bulge. Repeating the operation crossways effectively creates four longitudinal quadrant strands that bend far more sympathetically once wired.

13–3 • Here, you see the rigid, stunted, lowest quarter of the trunk together with a new, straight, uninteresting trunk (August 1989).

13–4 • I cut through the trunk longitudinally twice, for a length of 4¾ inches (12 cm). Then I wired the whole trunk length three times in the rigid area to be bent (July 1990).

13–5 • This is a close-up of a cut made using a side-by-side branch pruner, which cuts straight through the trunk.

13–6 • Plan view showing spread of branches that will produce a good line and 3-D perspective.

13–7 • The tree is now wired completely (July 1990).

13–8 • I've replanted the tree in a deeper pot (March 1991).

13–9 • The tree is covered in snow (Christmas 1993).

13–10 • This is the latest view.

Case History 2

Scotch Pine Scrub Style from Seed

This pine was grown in a pot and rather neglected. It reached a stage where it was a short stump from which two small-diameter trunks emerged in alignment with the base trunk. By wiring the two trunks in a downward direction, the tree took on a windswept, weather-beaten look. Notice how important the diagonal lines are to the final image. The rear view shows the bland result without the strong diagonal lines.

❖　Cones were collected, steamed to access the seeds, and then planted on April 16, 1969, in a mixture of loam-based compost and 6 mm gravel. Seeds were lightly covered with soil mix, watered, and left outdoors in 3½-inch (9 cm) pots.

❖　Seed germinated in July of 1969.

❖　Seedling was left in small pot and grew slowly for fifteen years; then, reduced by two-thirds of its height; now measuring only 7 inches (18 cm).

❖　August of 1993, tree vigorous enough to perform late-season shoot pruning to encourage back budding in the subsequentt spring.

13–11 ● Four years after I reduced the trunk height, two equally long, thin, new trunks have emerged (April 1988).

13–12 ● This is the rear view (September 1988).

13–13 ● I've re-angled the bottom trunk and wired the two top new trunks as windswept branches (September 1988).

13–14 ● I rewired the branches and positioned them into a better orientation as two distinct lines. The branches are starting to thicken (spring 1990).

13–15 • I performed some additional branch layering and arranging. The tree still has too little foliage and not much budding (June 1991).

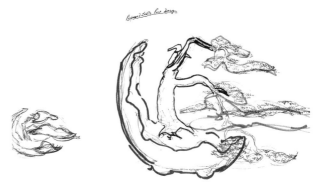

13–16 • This is a rough sketch of a proposed design. Budding had occurred by this year (1994).

13–17 • This is the latest image. Notice how important the diagonal branch line and the branch character are to this otherwise fairly plain design (July 1999).

OVERVIEW

Pyracantha

Pyracantha is a very versatile, hardy, garden shrub used as hedging, wall covering, and ground cover or as a single bush. It is a dense, vigorous, thorny plant with lovely small cream or white spring flowers and masses of colorful red yellow or orange fruits throughout winter. The plants thrive in sun or partial shade in any soil, but they grow better in chalky soil. Hedges are trimmed between May and July. These plants are readily available at garden centers in containers, and they make ideal bonsai.

Pyracantha bonsai are not fully hardy on benches in winter. I overwinter them in a cold greenhouse or similar environment. They are happy when placed in full sun during the growing season. They are a slow-growing plant in a pot, but they grow vigorously in the ground; hence, they are ideal material for thickening up. Because the trunks do not readily taper, you should repeatedly grow and chop these plants in growing beds to encourage taper.

They do best when propagated from seed or from cuttings taken in July or August. They are also often grafted. Pyracanthas require adequate moisture, although they are also fairly drought resistant. I grow them very successfully in a loam-based compost.

Apply plenty of low-nitrogen feed to encourage flowering; give the soil a bonemeal dressing in November or December.

You can prune the new shoots at any time because they flower prolifically from wood that is one, two, three, or more years old. Flowers form on the short shoots; therefore, when you are pruning, retain all the short shoots or spines.

Heavy design pruning is best done in the spring when the plant is vigorous and healing rapidly. Pyracantha are slow to heal, so be sure you prune in the spring. Make the cut as smooth as possible and use a nondrying sealant.

Old wood becomes very stiff; hence, you should wire new or young shoots to obtain maximum flexibility of shape. You can leave the wire on during the winter.

Case History 3

Pyracantha 'Beauty of Bath' from Seed

Before training in 1988, this plant had a typical container-grown garden-center shape, although it was actually grown from seed. It spent six years in a growing bed to thicken the trunk. The trunk ended up with a very parallel one with some taper near the top, thanks to a late application of grow and chop. Once reestablished in a pot, it was radically restyled. I removed most of the branches in order to regrow it from the trunk outward. Ten years from the first styling, this 23-year-old tree now has a pleasing image.

❧ December 7, 1976, seeds were extracted from dried fruits and allowed to dry on a tissue for two weeks, then sown in loam-based soil compost.

❧ March 1, 1977, 36 seeds germinated.

❧ March of 1981, seedling was planted in a growing bed to thicken up.

❧ Spring of 1985, top trunk was pruned back a little.

13–18 ● I dug up this pyracantha bush and potted it. I only pruned it slightly when I potted it (April 1988).

13–19 ● I radically pruned and wired the top two branches and a new leader, but this radical branch reduction produced a pretty meager-looking bonsai (December 1988).

13–20 ● This is a side view of the tree after the pruning and wiring (1988).

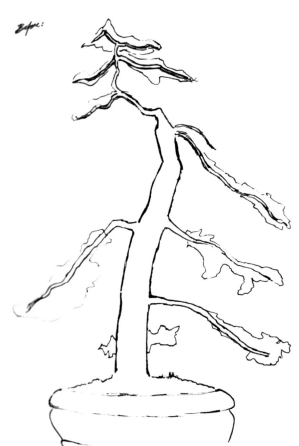

13–21 ● The "before" sketch of the existing tree shows these faults: too little trunk base visible; lowest rear branch is far too low; lowest right and rear branches are irrelevant; too rapid a change in trunk diameter two-thirds of the way up the trunk; too large a gap on the left-hand side between the lowest and next-lowest branches; no basal trunk flare; and no rear branches.

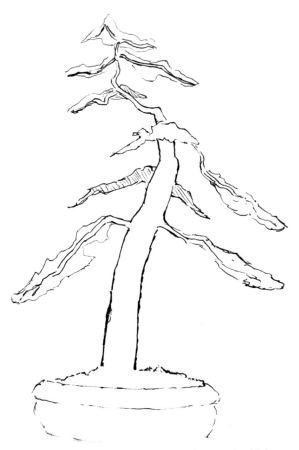

13–22 ● The "after" sketch shows these changes: third left-hand branch extended to fill a large gap on the left and extend slightly to the right; a front branch formed to hide the sudden change in trunk diameter; the higher of the two right-hand parallel branches has been removed, as has the lower right-hand branch; the underbranch lines of the lowest retained right-hand branch has been retained along with the lowest left one; the branchlets on the lowest have been thinned to reduce branch weight; and the lowest rear branch has been removed.

13–23 • The foliage and branches are growing back vigorously, but most of the growth is unwanted (August 1989).

13–24 • I removed the unnecessary foliage and branches (April 1990).

13–25 • The tree produced more rampant growth, requiring a repeat spring trimming (July 1990).

13–26 ● Here's another example of vigorous regrowth (August 1992).

13–27 ● The tree is taking shape in a new pot. The front view is now a slightly different angle (March 1996).

13–28 ● Here's the latest image, eleven years after the initial styling (July 1999).

14

Grouping Bonsai

OVERVIEW

Groups, whether a small copse or a large forest, provide a chance for a bonsai artist to go beyond a solitary tree image to encompass a mini-landscape. They also enable the use of younger material or of material lacking the potential for a single specimen, perhaps due to a lack of branches on one side or an unbalanced or stiff trunk. For me, the main criteria that produce a successful group image are

❖ Overall harmony—use of trees that are similar in vigor, shape, and color and an appropriate container.

❖ Good trunk rhythms—movement in trunks and major branches, each blending with the other and forming a credible overall pattern and interesting shapes between the trunks.

❖ Good foliage outline—having an interesting overall form, especially the skyline and the line below the foliage where it meets the trunks.

The first two criteria are of great importance early in the formation of a group. The third is normally developed over time. Each tree must be selected to fit the above criteria, then the group is assembled and shaped as if it were a single bonsai. That way the group is harmonious and homogeneous.

Try to avoid stiff parallel trunks because they lack perspective. However, straight trunks in a subtle fan shape, such as the Korean hornbeam featured in this chapter, are delightful. Greatly differing length, size, color, or strength of the foliage is another weakness in a group design. You can easily overcome any of these by using a root-connected (raft) design in which all trees are, in fact, one tree or by using cuttings taken from the same parent.

14–1 ● This is a display of bonsai at the National Bonsai Collection, Birmingham, England.

Two small European larches and a larger Japanese larch growing happily as a group planting. They were donated to The National Collection, in Birmingham, England.

Many bonsai books give typical trunk placements in a plan view. The most important element is to vary the distances between the trunks (in the front and side planes). Consider having all the trunks emanate from an imaginary point below ground. Avoid a straight line of trees. This is an easy trap with groups that have connected roots and branches wired up from a trunk that is lying on the soil. Contour the soil level, planting some trees higher than others. Place the trees so that the tallest is near the middle (preferably offset from the middle) rather than at the edge. Another key factor is creating an interesting foliage profile above and below the foliage masses (see also Chapter 3 on bonsai design).

If one of the plants in a group dies, be sure to remove the tree and its roots to avoid the risk of disease, which otherwise can spread through the soil.

Case History 1

Juniperus × media 'Plumosa Aurea' Raft from Cutting

This group started out in 1969 as a cutting from a neighbor's conifer. It developed a few long, sprawly branches low on the trunk, and this strange habit lends itself to a raft design. After many abortive attempts at designing sensible trunk angles and foliage shapes, I finally arrived at a form that worked.

This was a slow-growing conifer when potted. It took 28 years to create the final image (see Chapter 10 for a detailed overview of this juniper species). Its foliage tends to grow in a spearlike or pointed shape rather than a rounded, cloud shape. Hence, the main shaping is the reduction of the terminal pointed growth to return it to a rounded formation. By keeping the tree in a shallow pot and avoiding hard pruning, this species will naturally develop these lovely clouds.

14-3 • Winter color of *J. × media* 'Plumosa Aurea'.

If you expose it to full sun, you'll get an extreme contrast between the summer and winter colors. The species is fully winter hardy on benches, giving rise to this marked winter discoloration.

❧ December of 1969, took 6-inch (15 cm) cuttings of *J. × media* 'Plumosa Aurea', stripped foliage below soil level, dipped fresh, angular, cut base of heel cutting in water, then hormone rooting powder before planting into pots using loam-based compost.

❧ Sprayed cuttings occasionally and placed in a cold frame outdoors. Continued to winter protect in cold frames for two more years.

❧ Allowed tree to develop untrained in shallow pots for twenty years.

In the future, I would like to increase the merge of the top row of foliage areas slightly into one mass.

14-2 • Summer color of *J. × media* 'Plumosa Aurea' in full sun.

14-4 • This is an untrained group in a fairly shallow pot (June 1989).

14-5 • This is also an untrained tree, but it has more growth and vigor.

14-6 • This was my initial attempt to wire the five trunks before I transplanted the tree into a shallow pot (April 1991).

14-7 • I reshaped the three substantial and two spindly trunks again in May 1994.

14-8 • Notice how the old, natural clouds contrast with the new plume-shaped foliage (June 1995).

14-9 • I reduced the number of trunks to three prior to the latest shaping and refining (May 1997).

14–10 • Here's a shot after I've refined the tree. Notice the skyline and underfoliage lines.

14–11 • This is the final image for now. Note the improved underfoliage line and the echoing of foliage area shapes.

Case History 2

Hybrid Larch from Seedlings

I purchased these in the early spring of 1981 as 3-year-old seedlings. I immediately arranged them into a group on a slate with rocks secured through the slate with screws like bookends. Then, I was able to mound soil between the rocks, encouraging trunk thickening. The group grew well and was pruned and wired when required in the spring from 1982 onward. In March 1990, once trunk diameters were sufficient, the group was transferred to a shallower pot to reduce shoot growth and improve the composition. Early-season new-shoot pruning was applied rigorously from then on to encourage ramification. The present image, eighteen years after purchase, is fine but needs further branch ramification and consolidation of the foliage masses. Once each tree is well ramified, the foliage mass can be opened up a little to reveal the character and branching of each tree within an overall foliage envelope.

14–12 • I rewired and pruned the tree to shape it (April 1988).

❖   March 5, 1981, purchased as 3-year-old bare-rooted seedlings. Roots were trimmed and branches tip-trimmed before planting in deep soil on a slate. Then allowed to grow unpruned and unwired for a season.

14–13 ● This is a view of the tree repotted two months earlier into a shallower pot (May 1990).

14–14 ● Notice the tie between the two trees to correct the trunk angle of the tree on the left (June 1991).

14–15 ● This shows ample foliage growth and additional thickening of the trunks (June 1997).

14–16 ● This is the latest group image (October 1999).

Case History 3

Japanese and European Larch Group from Nursery Stock

The tallest tree in this group is a Japanese larch, and in 1991, it had lost the lowest left branch and had a fairly stiff and parallel trunk. I decided it might look better grouped with two smaller European larches.

I planted the group in the spring of 1993. Thereafter, the main task was wiring the branches as a unit, echoing branch angles and foliage pad shapes. In addition, I wanted to raise the trunk height of the middle tree. I began these two tasks in the middle of the summer of 1993. Over the next six years, the group has formed a very nice planting.

14–17 ● The lowest left branch on my 22-year-old Japanese larch died because of heat stress. The tree survived by starving the lowest branch (June 1991).

14–18 ● These are two 14-year-old European larches (April 1988).

14–19 ● I extended the height of the middle trunk by wiring a leader (October 1993).

14–20 • The toadstools add an autumnal feel (October).

14–21 • The snow mounded on each pad shows the future shape once I build up the pad height (Christmas 1993).

14–22 • Summer (July 1999).

14–23 • The autumn colors are just starting with yellow and green hues (October 1999).

OVERVIEW

Cryptomeria japonica (Japanese Cedar or Sugi)

This beautiful, hardy evergreen tree is the most important timber conifer in Japan, planted widely as both a forest tree and an ornamental. Specimens over 1,000 years old survive today. The tree loves cool, damp areas with rich, deep, alluvial soil. It survives even in shade and under other large trees. Reportedly, it grows better in Japan than in the United States or Europe.

Cryptomeria japonica has many forms of bark and foliage. Select a tree with a compact foliage form and good bark color and texture. Coarser foliage forms such as *Cryptomeria japonica* 'Elegans' do not make easy bonsai. They need constant new-shoot pinching to counter their vigorous growth and their tendency to droop. I once grew some *Cryptomeria japonica* from seed. They were very coarse and of inferior quality to the finer foliage of imported bonsai forms. I prefer cuttings with finer foliage, seedlings, or air layers rather than growing from seed unless I know the source of the seed is good.

The most vigorous and coarse foliage forms, as well as old, mature bonsai, require very gritty, well-drained shallow soil to suppress their fast growth. On the other hand, the finer forms such as 'Bandai-sugi' (see case history on next page) need a well-drained soil but with a higher loam content in order to keep the soil damp even at the end of a hot summer's day. This residual dampness is a key factor in the health of all *Cryptomeria*.

The pot should not be so deep that the tree remains waterlogged, nor should it be so shallow that its roots dry out by the end of the day. *Cryptomeria* are not big drinkers, so a pot with a medium depth (see the case history on next page) is ideal. Once you've selected the pot, manipulate your compost mix to achieve the required soil moisture.

Vigorous forms need full sun to encourage compact bonsai foliage. Finer forms such as 'Bandai-sugi' are able to survive in full sun, but they prefer a slightly cooler, shadier place. They still need good sun exposure to avoid branch dieback.

Cryptomeria always have some foliage dieback in autumn. Usually this includes areas that are shaded or underbranch areas. Occasionally, whole branches die. Excessive dieback can be frustrating. It is best countered by keeping the tree compact rather than sprawly and by removing all unwanted excess foliage. *Cryptomeria* are very apically dominant; only by repeated prunings of the upper branches can you keep the lower branches vigorous. Ironically, I once found that if too much dieback occurs, removing large areas of the upper tree arrested the problem by rebalancing its vigor. Such an action is simply a last resort and would need to be done carefully to retain a useful future shape. Cool yet sunny conditions for the foliage (and soil, as stated above) help to avoid drastic foliage loss as does winter protection. Daily foliar spray with a watering can help, although I manage to avoid excess *Cryptomeria* foliage loss without spraying the foliage.

You'll find it easy to keep the new shoots of 'Bandai-sugi' pinched. They need little intervention. However, the more vigorous forms such as *Cryptomeria japonica* or *Cryptomeria japonica* 'Elegans' need continuous pinching of new growth. You should remove two-thirds of the shoot. Use your fingertips, not a pair of scissors to avoid browning the cut foliage. With young, vigorous seedlings, you need to pinch leaders more carefully to avoid long parallel trunks and apical dominance at the expense of low branch vigor.

Branches soon become brittle and are easily broken. Hence, you should wire in the early spring and confine wiring to younger branches. Heavy pruning is best done in early spring also; any cut leaves will turn brown.

Cryptomeria do not need quite as much feed as most bonsai. Use a low-nitrogen liquid feed regularly from March to October. These trees are virtually free of disease and pests, although excessively damp or wet conditions can give rise to needle blight, requiring a copper compound spray. I have never experienced this in thirty years because I provide reasonable sun exposure combined with constantly damp but well-drained non-waterlogged soil. I have seen charcoal bits buried in peat-based 'Bandai-sugi' soil used to help keep them sweet, but I have never followed the practice in my loam-based soil mix.

Cryptomeria are borderline winter hardy in the British Isles and similar cool climates. If you move them to a cold greenhouse or similar environment, you must provide good levels of light to avoid foliage dieback. I can keep young bonsai perfectly healthy on sheltered benches in a normal winter, but I protect them if it becomes really cold, say below 5 to -4°F (-15 to -20°C). All my mature and valued *Cryptomeria* specimens are protected in a cold greenhouse with good light, but freezing to 23°F (-5°C) degrees or so is not harmful. Initial exposure to mild frost is also helpful before you move them to winter storage. The bronzing of the foliage is normal in winter; it will turn green again the following spring.

In summary, to avoid the commonest problem of excess foliage dieback in cool climates, *Cryptomeria* need adequate sun, residual soil moisture, initial frost exposure, winter protection in good light, a moderate feed program, and continuous pinching to control foliage and to avoid excessive growth or apical dominance.

Case History 4

Cryptomeria japonica 'Bandai-sugi' from Garden-Center Stock

August of 1977, purchased several *Cryptomeria japonica* 'Bandai-sugi' as 8-year-old garden-center stock.

14–24 ● I countered excessive branch dieback with drastic trunk pruning. Three years later, the tree's vigor was restored (spring 1991).

14–25 ● The latest group image (July 1999).

14–26 ● A close-up of the trunk (July 1999).

15

Handmade Rocks & Pots

15–1 ● This old Navajo Indian trail at 8,100 feet (2,500 m) runs by these limestone hoodoos in Bryce Canyon National Park.

OVERVIEW

Maybe it's winter, and you are feeling a little short on bonsai tasks? You are dreaming about repotting and which pot to use for a certain tree. Possibly you are playing musical chairs, mentally swapping a chain of containers. One answer is to use the winter to generate additional pots or rocks of your own.

We cannot always find or commission a pot with the right shape or look to fit our tree. Sometimes, we cannot afford a large ceramic pot, but we still want something special. Whatever your motivation, you can have a lot of fun and satisfaction making your own pots or rocks.

This chapter contains a step-by-step method for making realistic and natural-looking frost-proof pots and rocks. Although they probably cost less than ceramic pots you buy, these are not cheap because they are based on a blend of resin, fiberglass matting, and toughened mortar. All these strong materials combine to produce a highly durable result which, if made with care and patience, is difficult to distinguish from natural rock, especially when weathered.

I want to offer a few words of caution before you are overwhelmed with excitement. These creations can be heavy, and if you are thinking of something on a grand scale, consider substituting a light, fine aggregate such as perlite or vermiculite for grit. The outer skin of resin makes these creations rigid and impervious to water; therefore, unlike porous rocks, they do not hold any water reserves. For this reason, the soil pockets must be large enough to allow the tree to survive. Once the following steps are completed and the paint dries, the container or rock is immediately ready for planting or for presenting to someone as a gift.

Finally, follow all health and safety instructions carefully. Protect yourself against breathing in airborne fiberglass, resin fumes, or dust, and avoid fiberglass fragments. Keep resin and mortar from coming in contact with your skin. Work outdoors or in an airy place to avoid any buildup of fumes, naked flames, etc. Pay attention to all the health and safety aspects surrounding these materials.

A handmade fiberglass resin
and concrete rock planted with
Picea 'Nidiformis' spruce.

Case History 1

Fiberglass, Resin, and Concrete Crescent Pot

This crescent pot is 16 inches (40 cm) tall. I made it in the spring of 1990 without any particular tree in mind; it was my first experiment. After sitting on benches for ten years, it is still in perfect condition. The only slight change is that the surface finish has a duller, more natural look; the acrylic paint has survived without any aftercare. The Scotch pine shown in this crescent has lived happily in it for the last six years. I've discussed its early development in the following chapter.

15-3 • Types of filler and liquid resin.

15-2 • This is an assortment of the supplies you'll need to make fiberglass and concrete rocks.

Building Stages

Step 1

Acquire the necessary materials before you begin. These include fiberglass matting, liquid resin and hardener (do not use ordinary filler paste, which is too thick), old or disposable brushes, high performance (the brand shown is polymer blended) exterior masonry repairer, aluminum wire and galvanized steel mesh, an assortment of acrylic paints (I used light and dark brown plus yellow ochre), hand shears, power drill plus masonry drills, a plastic cover for your workbench, mixing bowl, and all the necessary health and safety equipment.

Step 2

The three products on the right are filler compounds highly suitable for building bases to steady collected rocks or to wrap around driftwood (see the next chapter), but for this application, a free-flowing liquid resin, such as the one on the right, is required along with the matching hardener.

Step 3

Build a frame by cutting a shape out of galvanized wire mesh. Use cuts the way you would use darts in dressmaking to help form the shapes, but tie the cut ends back into the mesh to create a rigid structure. Weave a few aluminum wires into the structure to add strength and to help form the feet.

Step 4

Three feet are ideal for building a stable structure. Here is a close-up of how to reinforce them **(15–5)**.

Step 5

Cut out some suitable-size pieces of fiberglass matting. Make them smaller if necessary for ease of use. You can layer them one above the other for increased strength. Mix a small quantity of resin and hardener as per instructions and paint it onto the matting you've placed on the outside of the mesh. Remember to vary the shape of the edge of the crescent, adding wavy and irregular shapes to give a natural feel. You can do this with the brush while the resin is still wet. Once the resin is dry, you won't be able to alter it. Apply more layers of resin and matting as desired, but all the layers must form a homogeneous crust that adheres to the mesh because of the resin. One or two layers will suffice, and you can cut off any poor edging and remake it at this stage.

Step 6
Once the skin is set with resin, you can mix exterior mortar and 2 to 4 mm grit (or a lighter weight substitute of similar size). The proportions of grit to mortar are not critical, but to achieve a good surface texture, you will need a substantial amount of grit. Add water to make a thickish mix.

Step 7
Paste the mortar and grit mix on the outer side of the crescent pot on top of the resin. Add texture by cutting into the surface of the mix with the knife and pressing the paste onto the skin to form a good bond. Check the feet for stability and for the correct pot angle, building each of them up as required.

Step 8
As you finish the outer mortar, ensure that the edges are thinner to lighten the final image. This will artificially reduce the apparent thickness of the crescent. Once the outer paste is dry enough (24 hours for this product is fine if you are working indoors), paste the inner surface, pushing the paste onto the mesh surface and again adding texture and thinning the edges.

Step 9
Drill holes for drainage unless you prefer to insert cork plugs to establish the holes in the pot from the beginning. If you are drilling holes, clamp the item firmly and then enlarge the hole in stages.

Step 10
Allow three full days for the mortar to harden completely (the exact time may vary from brand to brand). Mix some dry, coarse sand with some liquid resin and the hardener mix to form a gritty liquid that is runny enough to paint a finishing coat on the dry mortar layer. If you use too much sand, the mixture will be too sticky and awkward to use.

Some unsanded areas look like bone or ivory after painting, so do add some textural variety to the piece. Use unsanded mix near the edges and sparingly elsewhere.

Step 11
Paint this sand, resin, and hardener mix all over the inner and outer surfaces, creating a fine texture, which seals the mortar, adding an interesting surface texture. Work the mix into all the crevices to ensure a good weather seal. Clean the brush regularly with cellulose thinners. Do not forget to seal inside the drainage holes.

Step 12
Lightly mix different combinations of acrylic colors on the palette to produce a natural color variation over the crescent surface.

Step 13
Paint this mixed acrylic fairly thickly over the dry resin surface in small areas. It adheres much better on well-textured, sanded areas. Once it dries, the crescent pot is waterproof.

Step 14
Use a tightly balled rag to wipe off much of the wet acrylic to reveal some lighter resin highlights. In some areas these will look almost like bone through the paint. I used a rag soaked in cellulose thinners to assist in this task. Then, I used a dry, balled rag to remove or dry off more of the high points of the surface. This technique can take a while to perfect and is sometimes elusive to achieve. You may require plenty of patience to produce a good outcome.

Use dark browns and a little black as a base color deep in the crevices to accentuate texture. Build on lighter colors such as light brown, yellow, and red later.

Step 15
The finished surface should have a lovely ivory appearance where little or no sand is used. The pot is ready for use once the paint dries. This will take a day or so.

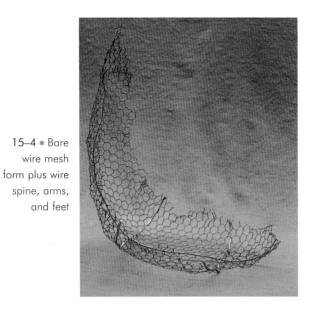

15–4 • Bare wire mesh form plus wire spine, arms, and feet

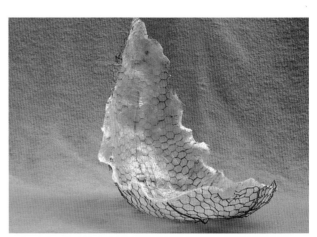

15–5 • This is a close-up of how to form feet.

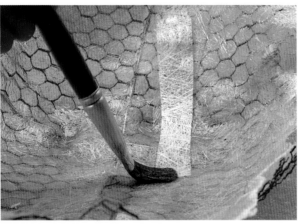

15–6 • Paint a mixture of resin and hardener onto the matting and onto the mesh, varying the edge line so that it is wavy.

15–7 • The inner fiberglass matting and the resin skin are completed.

15–8 • Mix grit or a lighter substitute, the mortar, and the water.

15–9 • Paste the mortar and grit mix onto the outer side, adding texture.

15–10 • The outer mortaring is complete. Notice how the edges are made thinner.

15–11 •
Once dry,
repeat the
process for
the inner skin,
ensuring thin
edges.

15–12 • Here, I've drilled the holes for drainage.

15–13 • The hole is enlarged.

15–14 • Mix dry, coarse sand with liquid resin and hardener for the outer surface resin coating.

5–15 ● Painting the entire surface creates a fine texture that is over-laid on a coarse grit/mortar texture to seal the mortar.

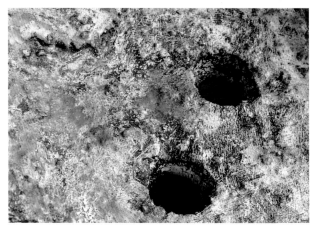

15–16 ● Paint the inside of the drain holes, too.

15–17 ● These acrylic colors are crudely mixed.

15–18 ● Paint the acrylic fairly thickly over the dry resin surface in small areas.

15–19 ● Using a tightly balled rag, wipe off much of the wet acrylic to reveal some lighter areas.

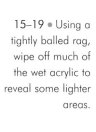

15–20 ● Here's a close-up of the finished surface.

15–21 ● This is the finished pot.

15–22 ● This is a Scotch pine in the crescent pot nine years later, showing the resilience of the surface treatment.

Case History 2

Fiberglass Resin and Concrete Small Rock

This little rock is 8¼-inches (21 cm) high. I made it in the spring of 1990. It has some top surface pockets built in. These help create the illusion of a very shallow planting. The method for building this pot closely follows the steps used in Case History 1.

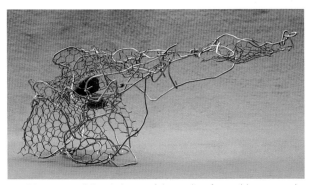

15–23 ● Most of the skeleton of the rock is formed by wire with some mesh to define soil pockets and large, empty spaces. Notice the stones for counterbalance.

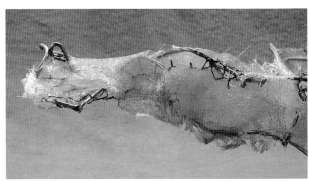

15–24 ● Apply fiberglass matting and paint with the resin and hardener.

15–25 ● Paste the mortar and grit onto the outside to form a rocklike shape.

15–26 ● Repeat this procedure in small sections across the rock. You can do this in several sessions, allowing the pot to dry between applications.

15–27 ● This is the completed mortaring.

15–28 ● Use masonry drills to create the drainage holes.

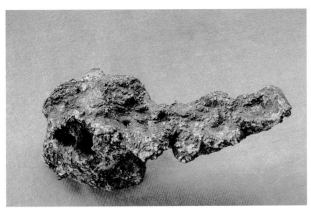

15–29 ● This is the acrylic painting method completed.

15–30 ● This rock is planted with two *Zelkova serrata,* a small Oriental spruce, and underplantings.

15–31 ● A winter image.

15–32 ● A spring image.

OVERVIEW

Spruce

15–33 • Though dwarfed and carved by the elements, these monumental Engelmann spruce cling to life at 12,000 feet (3,700 m) near Rainbow Curve, Rocky Mountain National Park, Colorado.

You can find some representatives of this evergreen conifer in hostile mountain areas, hanging on to life at 12,000 feet (3,700 m) above sea level in conditions that have defeated all other tree types. Other spruces are highly susceptible to late spring frosts, suffering trunk and branch-tip dieback and creating a conspicuously untidy dead crown. Their ideal habitat is deep, wet, and cold soil, preferably acidic, otherwise neutral. Spruces love a cool, humid, cloudy, or misty atmosphere. Waxy, leaved forms such as *Picea pungens* 'Glauca' (Colorado or blue spruce) can tolerate much drier soils, although the Colorado spruce dies back relentlessly in polluted city air. Because some spruce species will tolerate quite a bit of wind exposure, they are used as windbreaks, provided their roots are well established or in deep soil. Young *Picea*, however, generally have shallow roots and are soon uprooted in shallow soils when exposed to the wind.

Whether as trees or as bonsai, spruce generally dislike pollution. Serbian spruce (*Picea omorika*) is an exception. Many spruces are prone to aphis and to red spider mite attack in dry conditions and to rust, stem canker, and honey fungus. Pineapple galls are frequently formed from plant lice and adelgids, but although they are unsightly, they do little harm and can be cut off if required. You can treat gall pests on a dry, calm day with malathion or HCH in February or March. Treat spider mites and aphids early and repeatedly with malathion or dimethoate weekly until the attack ceases. Remove parts of a tree affected with rust and stem canker and burn them; the tree may well survive. Honey fungus frequently kills trees; burn all the dead matter and dispose of the soil, preferably after sterilizing it with a 2 percent formalin solution. The Pests and Diseases section in Chapter 2 discusses these problems and treatments in more detail.

Species such as Engelmann spruce (*Picea engelmannii*), white spruce (*P. glauca*), red spruce (*P. rubens*), black spruce (*P. mariana*) and Colorado spruce (*P. pungens*) are very hardy in the British Isles. They are happy on benches throughout the winter.

Norway spruce bonsai (*P. abies*) is not prone to late spring frosts in Britain. It can be grouped with trees such as Oriental spruce (*P. orientalis*), Serbian spruce (*P. omorika*), and Yezo spruce (*P. jezoensis*). It is classed as borderline winter hardy in Britain, able to survive on benches in all but the coldest winters.

Others such as Brewer's spruce (*P. breweriana*) or Sitka spruce (*P. sitchensis*) are not fully hardy and regularly suffer spring frost damage unless you give them protection in a cold greenhouse.

Most spruce bonsai prefer acid soil; Serbian spruce is an exception. Ericaceous soil mix is usually selected, although Serbian spruce will be happy in a loam-based mix. Like other acid lovers, spruce foliage will rapidly yellow without acid or ericaceous soil or if watered with hard (limey) water. You must address such yellowing in order to avoid a slow death over two or three seasons. Check the soil acidity and adjust to between 4.0 and 5.0 pH by adding chopped sphagnum moss or Flowers of Sulphur to acidify or ground limestone to increase the alkaline level. Allow a month for the adjustment to occur, then retest and continue adjusting as required (see the Soils section in Chapter 2 for further discussion on soil acidity/alkalinity).

In addition to the correct soil pH, spruces need moist and moisture-retentive soil. Mycorrhiza in the soil is also very important as is adequate but not excess sunshine. Foliage misting is beneficial, too. Provide these conditions and keep a careful watch on insect and disease prevention, and they are very rewarding trees.

There are many suitable spruce species. Select a short-needle variety like *P. orientalis* for small bonsai or smaller landscapes; try a more vigorous but still compact form such as *P. abies* 'Nidiformis' for medium to large bonsai. *P. albertiana* 'Conica', although small-needled, is too prone to red spider mite and frost damage and is perhaps too compact to be a suitable bonsai choice. Try also to avoid leggy specimens because spruce have a habit of growing too wide if you are not vigilant in plucking the new shoots early. Remove one-half to two-thirds of each new spring shoot once the shoot is ⅜ to ¾ inch (1 or 2 cm) long.

If you are heavily pruning bonsai foliage, always leave some green needles on each branch to avoid branch dieback. The branch needs greenery to sustain the sap flow until new buds form and emerge.

Wire early or in the middle of the growing season and prune heavily in the spring.

OVERVIEW

Zelkova serrata

Zelkova serrata, or Japanese gray bark elm, is a hardy species that makes very attractive wide-crowned deciduous specimens. When grown in good, well-drained, deep soil, *Zelkova* is capable of sending roots deep into the soil, making it highly resistant to drought. *Zelkova serrata* is a valuable lumber and ornamental tree in its native Japan and China. Its fine-

15–34 • *Zelkova serrata* in autumn colors.

grained, oily, and durable wood makes it ideal for construction. It is favored for use in temples. *Zelkova* is a genus in its own right, although it is a distant relative of the elms. It has lovely elmlike leaves capable of turning a beautiful spectrum of autumn colors ranging from yellow to gold to red to brown. The thin, smooth, gray bark is another outstanding feature.

As bonsai, *Zelkova* is best grown from seed or cuttings, avoiding any forced growth in deep containers or growing beds. Forced growth occasionally creates vertical splits in the trunk but almost inevitably requires a totally unacceptable chop and scar at the top of the trunk. Growing *Zelkova* is a real challenge if you want to obtain the shallow-rooted finely branched form so prized in Japan. It requires great skill and patience to develop interesting rootage, trunk, primary branching, and finely detailed branchlets that present a good winter image with a total absence of chops or stumps to jar the eye.

The nearest I have come to a decent *Zelkova* image from seed is shown in **15–11** in the winter of 1987 at thirteen years of age. Unfortunately, in my absence, the tree suffered a severe drought shortly after this picture was taken, and this caused most of the branchlets to die back. The tree has never recovered its form.

Zelkova must receive plenty of water. Even a mild drought is immediately punished by drooping leaves that remain drooped for the rest of the season. Attention to watering and use of a very moisture-retentive loam soil are essential. If the pot is shallow, I add even more loam. You should use shallow pots after the first five years in order to encourage good surface rootage and slower new-shoot growth.

Zelkova need some shade in the summer. Throughout the early to middle of the growing season, you must continuously prune back new shoots to two or three leaves as soon as they are ¾ to 1¼ inches (2 to 3 cm) long. Selecting the right direction for the new terminal bud is essential because most of the shaping is achieved by pruning new shoots, encouraging angular movement in primary branches and a smooth transition in taper from trunk to primary branches. The primary branches should not all emanate from the same height.

Zelkova have a habit of sprouting very vigorous (suckerlike) new shoots, which, if not removed, can spoil the shape of the tree. You should only retain such a shoot if it is to form a primary branch.

Total leaf removal in May or early June is necessary every few years with younger *Zelkova* to encourage smaller leaves and slower shoot growth.

Wiring should be loose and limited to young branches to avoid bark damage and only as a supplement to new-shoot pruning. Wire in the spring after new shoots are formed. Young seedlings should be staked and kept straight. If young trunks show any tendency to bend, correct this by using raffia tied to the stakes rather than risking trunk wiring, which may mark the delicate bark. Such wire marks would destroy the final image.

Although fairly winter hardy on benches, *Zelkova* cannot tolerate the coldest periods. I protect all fine-twigged specimens in a cold greenhouse environment to avoid branch and fine twig dieback. The species is fairly free of insects and disease, but red spider mite can be a problem. Treat it as described in the Pests and Diseases section of Chapter 2.

Case History 3

Fiberglass Resin and Tall, Concrete Rock

This 21-inch (53 cm) high, fairy-tale style rock was built in the spring of 1990. The main structural feature is two exceptionally deep side pockets to house two fairly vigorous spruce trees. Each has a long drainage hole. The top left pocket drains to the lower inside wall of the right-side pocket. The right pocket drains through to the base of the rock. The shallow pocket at the top of the rock drains into the inner wall of the top left pocket. Made with a grit and mortar mix with a solid mortar base that is one-third its height, this piece is quite a heavy unit. On such a large piece, the texturing over the whole surface must have a fairly common direction. The method of building follows very closely that used in Case History 1.

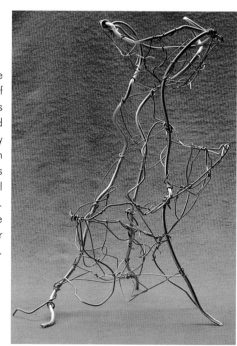

15–35 • The skeleton of this rock is formed entirely by wire with lighter wires defining soil pockets. Notice the thicker support wires.

Building Stages

The skeleton of the rock is formed entirely by wire with lighter wires defining the soil pockets. Notice how the top left pocket is fashioned so that once it is filled with soil and planted, the tree appears to be growing in purely surface soil. Use of thicker support wires is helpful in the overall rigidity of the completed rock.

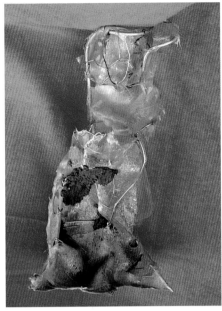

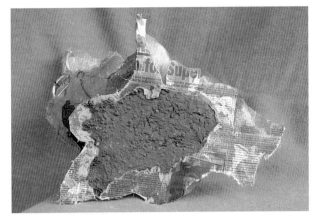

15-36 • Apply fiberglass matting and paint on resin mixed with hardener.

15-37 • Fill the base with mortar and grit mix for stability.

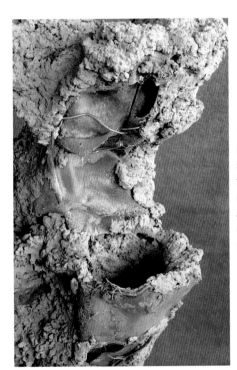

15-38 • Apply mortar and surface texture to the pot in small areas. Allow each to dry before you continue.

15-39 • Applying more mortar plus grit.

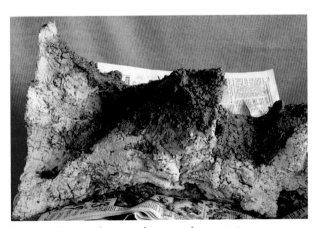

15-40 • This is a close-up of some surface texturing.

15–41 • The rock surfacing is almost finished.

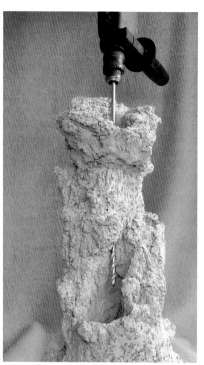

15–42 • Use masonry drills to create drainage holes, and paint on the outer resin and then the acrylic.

15–43 • *Picea* 'Nidiformis' for a rock planting.

15–44 • This is the initial planting (spring 1990).

15–45 • A shot taken one year later.

15–44 ● Here, I'm finger-pinching new spruce shoots.

15–46 ● This is a winter image less than three years after planting.

15–47 ● I took this four years after planting.

16

The Challenge of Deadwood

OVERVIEW

Deadwood usually results from exposure to extremes of weather, lightning strikes, old age, or disease. Frequent examples of beautiful deadwood abound in those areas of the world where trees live at higher altitudes, including the following wonderful examples. I hope you get some inspiration from them.

Recreating such detailed deadwood images is itself an art form that few bonsai artists seem to have the skill to reproduce realistically. This section examines two of my attempts at deadwood, or, what is more commonly termed in bonsai circles, driftwood styles. In bonsai parlance, small branch deadwood is known as "jin," and larger areas of trunk deadwood are called "shari." These case histories are not offered as shining examples of driftwood carving. Indeed, in the shadow of such a wonderful driftwood artist as Masahiko Kimura, I hesitate to include any such work.

16–1 • Statuesque lodgepole pines in Tioga Pass at 10,000 feet (3,000 m) above sea level at the eastern entrance to Yosemite National Park, California.

16–2 • These lodgepole pines at Firehole Pool in Yellowstone National Park are still beautiful, even in defeat.

Engelmann spruce defying the elements in
Rainbow Curve 12,000 ft (3,700 m) above
sea level in Rocky Mountain National Park.

Case History 1

Carving a Scotch Pine Grown from Seed

Pot-grown from seed for eleven years, this pine was not thickening much until I transferred it into a growing bed. After seven years, it had a lovely fat trunk and a sprawling mass of leggy foliage and long needles. The radical redesign of this tree began two years later, once the tree regained vigor. Based on an initial idea and a drawing from a friend, we proceeded to remove a substantial amount of bark and to create a lightning-struck image. After using fine carving tools, we burned the hardwood surface to create a more natural look and painted the exposed areas with lime sulphur. A year later, the tree was vigorous enough for me to bend the side branch down sufficiently to produce the new downward-pointing trunk. First, I undercut the inner bend area substantially to avoid having the new trunk break off. Ten years later, the tree has a new image, similar to my friend's original concept.

❖ Cones were collected, steamed to access the seeds, then planted on April 16, 1969, in a mixture of loam-based compost and 6 mm gravel. Seeds were lightly covered with soil mix, watered, and left outdoors in 3½-inch (9 cm) plastic pots.

❖ July of 1969, three of the eight seeds germinated. Seedling was left in small-diameter pots for eleven years and grew very little.

❖ May of 1980, was transferred to an open, sunny, growing bed that faces south.

16–3 • This is the tree one year after I removed it from a garden bed and potted it.

16–4 • This is a close-up of the scar from an earlier leader I removed (April 1988).

16–5 • Two years after I removed the tree from the growing bed, it is growing very vigorously (August 1989).

16–6 • I removed two-thirds of the foliage and all the bark from one side of the trunk.

16–7 • I painted lime sulphur to preserve and whiten the carved and exposed heartwood.

16–8 • I've completed the lime sulphuring.

16–9 • Now that the tree has regained its vigor, it is time to bend down the top right branch as the new leader (July 1991).

16–10 • I undercut this area with a trunk splitter.

Late March of 1992, the "big bend" or moment of truth. I used very thick wire wound loosely to hold the new trunk in position during and after gentle bending. Many people protect bark with wet raffia binding before wiring. I do this for very thick branch or trunk bending, but for small to medium, I prefer to use thicker wire and to wire loosely. Looking back at my radical foliage trimming, I cannot believe the shortage of needles on the lowered branch. However, in late March or April, provided you have a really vigorous tree and root system, the stored-up energy will burst into growth for the new season, providing some greenery remains on each branch. Take care to avoid late spring frosts or cold winds if you are tempted to be this extreme.

A close look at the trunk top shows the extent of undercut required to achieve the acute bend and again the use of thick wire. This time, it was used to tie down the newly bent trunk securely. I decided at the same time to remove the other potential leader, despite its value as an insurance policy against failure of the bent new trunk. I felt that if it remained, it would divert vigor from the lowered trunk foliage. The final step in this second phase of restyling was to make a concave wound cavity that would be level with the remaining bark when the wound healed. I used the same bit to undercut the trunk prior to the "big bend."

16–11 ● After gently bending it, I used very thick wire wound loosely to hold the trunk in its new position. I was concerned about the shortage of needles on the lowered branch (March 1992).

16–12 ● In this close-up of the top, you see the extent of undercut to achieve the bend and the use of thick wire to hold the bent trunk securely in its new position.

16–13 ● I decided it was necessary to remove the insurance leader to divert energy into the new, lowered trunk foliage.

16–14 ● I carved a concave wound to heal over. It is level with the remaining bark.

16–15 ● Here's the tree two months later, still low on foliage.

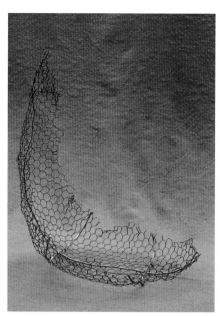

16–17 ● This is the wire frame of a home-made crescent pot.

16–16 ● Two years later, the tree foliage recovered well, thanks to the health of the roots prior to this radical foliage reduction (July 1994).

16–18 ● The finished pot.

16–19 ● This is the final image of this Scotch pine ten years after I lowered the trunk.

Case History 2

Wrap Around 'Blaauw' Juniper (*Juniperus* × *media* 'Blaauw')

One day I saw a pile of uprooted hawthorn hedgerow. I rescued one interesting piece of root. The following case history charts how I cleaned up, carved, and mounted this hawthorn stump and then wrapped a young juniper sapling around it. After several years of allowing the juniper to grow untrimmed, I drastically styled it in a first step toward the final image. Although

not completed, this tree is beginning to show good potential. A juvenile whip is beginning to look like a broad-based, old, weather-beaten tree in a relatively short time frame.

One essential component in the care regime of this juniper is providing sufficient feed to avoid the cascading branch losing vigor. In the following steps, I refer to the hawthorn root as "driftwood" and the juniper as a "wrap."

Always select durable wood such as hawthorn, juniper, yew, spruce, or cedar to have a long-lived driftwood. Durability is particularly important because some of the driftwood may end up buried below soil level. After carving, preserving, and mounting my hawthorn root on a base, I wrapped a young 'Blaauw' juniper sapling around it. For the best chance of success, choose a flexible whip and a species that naturally occurs in weather-beaten forms.

16–20 • I'm ready to carve the hawthorn driftwood (1990).

16–21 • Here the bark is cleaned off the driftwood.

16–22 • Remember to use appropriate safety measures for all your bonsai activities.

16–23 • Finishing off with a jeweler's flame gun.

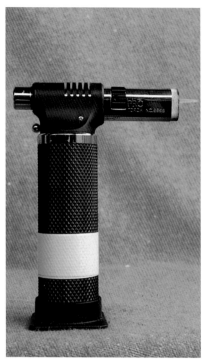

16–24 • Some guns are too fierce, but this little butane model is ideal.

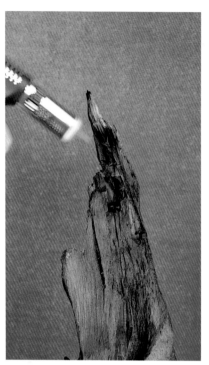

16–25 • Only apply the flame to dead-wood and use a small, concentrated, pointed flame.

16–26 • Occasionally the surface catches fire and needs extinguishing.

16–27 • Finish the effect by dressing the carved and burnt surface with a wire brush.

16–28 • Soak for two to three days in an exterior wood preserver that is safe for plants. Allow the preservative to dry in for four to six weeks before using.

16–29 • Wrap the wire around large screws secured in the drift-wood to form a shallow base frame (spring 1990).

16–30 • Mix epoxy filler compound in small quantities (Bondo plus hardener is used here) and paste it over the wire to form a stable foot for the driftwood.

16–31 • Apply lime sulphur over the surface of the driftwood to preserve and lighten it.

16–32 • I removed the unwanted secondary trunk of the wrap juniper.

16–33 • The wrap is ready for action.

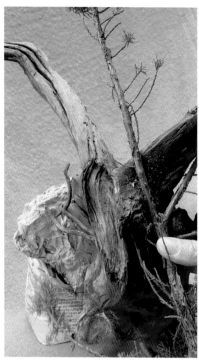

16–34 • The wrap is offered to the top of the driftwood.

16–35 • The wrap settled in the driftwood groove and planted.

16–36 • Two wrapped branches are anchored with electrical plastic straps.

16–37 • This picture was taken six months after I completed the initial planting.

16–38 • Here's a sketch of a current driftwood carving.

16–39 • This is the proposed future image.

16–40 • I allowed the tree to grow unchecked (April 1995).

16–41 • Here's the tree just before I restyled it (July 1996).

16–42 • Notice how the trunk is spreading over the driftwood (July 1996).

16–43 • The tree gets its first major restyle. Just one step on the way to the new image (July 1996).

17 Bonsai Garden Ideas

GARDEN EXAMPLES

Our bonsai spend the growing season and, for some hardy species, the winter on benches or displays. Your choice of location should take into account the various requirements of each species or subspecies as detailed in Appendix 1. Each area of our gardens differs in the amount of sun, shade, dryness, coolness, cold, wind, etc. No single location will have all the necessary attributes; therefore, you may need to select several. In some cases, you'll need to create shade artificially by adding overhead laths or netting; you may need to lessen the effects of cold winds with windbreaks such as fences or mesh screens. Sometimes, you'll use a display area for your specimens while the trees under development are housed on training benches.

Gardens may have many purposes; bonsai display is just one. It may be necessary to blend your bonsai into existing areas. Whatever your situation, this chapter is aimed at giving you some ideas to help design bonsai displays.

A plain background such as a wall or fence is good, but the background should not be too close to the trees, or it will reflect heat and reduce light. Dark foliage such as a hedge or holly bushes make a subtler backdrop.

17–1 ● Larches on benches in winter.

17–2 ● Dinmore Manor, Herefordshire, UK, in spectacular autumn color.

It's easy to gather garden ideas while
this beautiful, fragrant Wisteria enjoys a
midday soaking.

17–3 • Builder's hollow blocks create a marvelous base for podiums, but be sure you have the correct site as they are not easy to move.

17–4 • Layout of fence posting and hollow, showing how to assemble podiums.

17–5 • This is a sample podium. The concrete posts are set vertically into the square holes in the hollows.

17–6 • A close-up of a podium with a stone slab screwed securely into it.

17–7 • A tree on a podium.

17–8 ● Use of hollows as the top row of a block wall to cement the post and rail into.

17–9 ● Use of hollows to hold two vertical posts to hold a large long, high bench.

17–10 ● Here's an example of benches supported by this post system.

17–11 ● You can use a tree slice as a podium.

17–12 •
Empty
benches at
previous
home in
Sutton
Coldfield,
England.

17–13 • A new bonsai area on dismantled cold-frame foundations. The pedestals are made from earthenware drainage pipes.

Here are some additional examples of bonsai on display in a garden setting.

17–14 • I have used fence posts, small pebbles, stone paths, and rocks to create my bonsai display.

17–15 • Garden view at home.

17–16 • Bonsai with a natural backdrop.

17–17 • My garden display.

17–18 ● The author at work in the garden.

17–19 ● A *Zelkova* bonsai in a natural setting.

17–20 ● This is an alternative use of a bird bath.

17–21 ● Here are some alternative pedestal designs.

17–22 ● This is an 'Osakazuki' maple growing in the garden.

17–23 • Snow on garden benches makes a lovely Christmas scene.

Appendix 1
Cultivation, Care & Winter Protection

These guidelines for the growing and care of bonsai are for mature trees. Trees younger than four years should be given the special care noted in Chapter 2.

Unless otherwise noted, provide full sun early and late during the growing season. References in this text to sun conditions refer to sun requirements during the summer in the Midlands region of the British Isles.

Repotting is done before bud burst unless otherwise noted.

Feeding requirements are for healthy trees that have not been newly repotted.

Abies koreana (Korean fir)
Zone 6. Protect when really cold. During the winter and early spring protect from chilling winds. To repot, select a deep pot and add mycorrhiza. Prone to woolly aphis (adelgids) attack, rust, and air pollution. No preseason pruning; prune new shoots back early to one-third length; branches tend to grow long if new shoots are not pruned back consistently mid- and late season; prune heavily in the spring at repotting time when new buds are about to burst. Never remove all leaves. Wire in the spring and early summer. Provide partial cool shade. During growing season water normally to well; soil should remain moist. Attractive cones appear on young plants; compact foliage.

Abies veitchii (Veitch's silver fir)
Zone 3. Hardy on benches, hardy species. To repot, select a deep pot and add mycorrhiza. Prone to woolly aphis (adelgids) attack, rust and air pollution. No preseason pruning; prune new shoots back early to one-third length; branches tend to grow long if new shoots are not pruned back consistently mid- and late season; prune heavily in the spring at repotting time when new buds are about to burst.

Never remove all leaves. Wire in the spring and early summer. Provide partial sun and cool shade. During growing season water normally to well; soil should remain moist. Dislikes chalk. Smallest of the Japanese firs.

Acer buergerianum (Trident maple)
Zone 6. Protect from cold in a hoop tunnel or cold greenhouse. Keep soil dryish over winter, but never dry out. Avoid water on leaves as sun can burn them. Keep good winter light levels to avoid branch dieback. Buds open early in spring. When repotting, avoid windburn or sun scorch during spring or early summer. Wean from shade to sun slowly in spring to avoid sun scorch. Washing off all soil and encouraging spreading roots is highly beneficial every few years for trees under development. Aphid attacks, black spot, and borers on imported trees can be a problem. Young buergerianum leaves are easily burned by some chemical sprays. Trim back shoot tips to an appropriate dormant bud just prior to bud burst annually. Prune new shoots back early to two or three leaves as required through the growing season. New shoots tend to grow vertically and straight. Mid- and late-season pruning includes removing suckers or dormant buds at branch forks as they appear; trim back any remaining long shoots in October and provide reasonable gaps between branches to improve light levels; new shoots are very vigorous. Do heavy pruning in the spring at repotting time when new buds are about to burst; it is best done over two years leaving a stump the first year. Total leaf removal is done every three years or so to reduce leaf size. Wire new shoots in May, otherwise early in the season; remove fine, young branch wires before winter. Provide sun with some shade, especially when young branches are wired. Water well during growing season, avoid drought, and choose a deep pot to avoid branch dieback. Feed well using a low-nitrogen feed. A lovely bonsai subject, but needs more winter care than most

Acer buergerianum (Trident maple)

maples. Keep spring light levels high to avoid long (etiolated) new shoots. Remove such elongated shoots en masse if they occur.

Acer campestre (Field maple, hedge maple)

Zone 4. Hardy on benches. Avoid water on leaves as sun can burn them. Keep soil dryish over winter but avoid drought. Prone to aphid attacks and black spot. Prune back long shoots to an appropriate dormant bud just prior to bud burst annually. Prune new shoots back early to one-third their length (two leaves) as required through the growing season. Do heavy pruning in the spring at repotting time when new buds are about to burst. Total leaf removal is done every three years or so to reduce leaf size. Wire new shoots early to mid-season. Provide sun with some shade. Water well during growing season. Use a medium-nitrogen feed. The small leaf size, corky bark, and good response to total leaf removal makes this a good bonsai subject with good autumn color. Alkaline soils only.

Acer capillipes (Snake bark maple)

Zone 5. Protect when really cold. Fairly hardy, but protect roots from coldest temperatures. Prune new shoots early back to one-third length (two to three leaves) as required through the growing season. Do heavy pruning in the spring at repotting time when new buds are about to burst. Total leaf removal is done every three years or so to reduce leaf size. Wire in the spring and early summer; remove fine, young branch wires before winter. Provide sun with some shade. Water well during growing season. Use a medium-nitrogen feed. Superb autumn colors and one of the best snakebarks adaptable to bonsai. The white bark streaks, young red shoots, and swollen buds make a lovely winter image. Takes cuttings very readily.

Acer cappadocicum 'Aureum' (Cappadocian maple)

Zone 5. Protect when really cold. Protect leaves from sun scorch and from burn caused by water droplets. Every three to four years remove dormant buds as they swell but before they burst. Prune new shoots back early to one-third their length (two leaves) as required through the growing season. Do heavy pruning in the spring at repotting time when new buds are about to burst. Total leaf removal is done every three years or so to reduce leaf size but not in total-bud-removal years. Wire new shoots early to mid-season. Provide sun with some shade. Water well during growing season. Use a medium-nitrogen feed. Larger leaf size makes this a difficult bonsai subject, but by regular use of total leaf removal, a larger bonsai tree with a lovely mixture of autumn yellows and reds results. Likes alkaline soils but also is happy on acid soils.

Acer davidii
(Ernest Wilson snake bark maple)

Zone 6. Protect from cold in a hoop tunnel or cold greenhouse. Not fully hardy; branches and roots need protection from coldest temperatures. Prone to some branch dieback in winter on pruned branches. Prefers a well-drained soil to slow down growth; plant in a deep pot. Clean up branch dieback in February. Prune back long shoots to an appropriate dormant bud and thin out overly dense twigs just prior to bud burst annually. Prune new shoots back early to one-third their length (two leaves) or remove if too leggy, as required through the growing season. Avoid late-season pruning, which is subject to dieback. Do heavy pruning in the spring at repotting time when new buds are about to burst. Total leaf removal is done every

three years or so to reduce leaf size. Wire in the spring and early summer; watch out for rapid growth and wire marks; remove fine, young branch wires before winter. Provide sun with some shade. Water very well during the growing season. Use a medium-nitrogen feed. Very vigorous snake bark requiring a larger-scaled bonsai. However, by using shorter second growth and total leaf removal technique, it is a promising subject. Prefers acid soil. Willowlike growth habit.

Acer ginnala (Amur maple)

Zones 2 to 4. Hardy on benches. Fully hardy. Pollution tolerant. Prone to aphid attack. Prune back long shoots to an appropriate dormant bud just prior to bud burst annually. Prune new shoots back early to one-third their length and remove straight, leggy first growth as required through the growing season; remove suckers or dormant buds at branch forks as they appear, leaving reasonable gaps between branches to improve light levels; new shoots are very vigorous. Do heavy pruning in the spring at repotting time when new buds are about to burst. Total leaf removal is done every three years or so to reduce leaf size. Wire new retained long shoots early to mid-season. Provide sun with some shade. Water well during growing season. Use a medium-nitrogen feed. Very hardy bonsai subject and one of my favorites for its aged bark, good growth rate, and good (though brief) autumn color.

Acer ginnala (Amur maple)

Acer griseum (Mahogany bark maple)

Zone 5. Protect from cold in a hoop tunnel or cold greenhouse. Keep soil dryish over winter but never dry out. Keep spring light levels high. Remove any dead shoots that have died back over winter. Prune new shoots back early to one-third their length and remove leggy growth as required through the growing season. Do heavy pruning in the spring at repotting time when new buds are about to burst. Total leaf removal is done every three years or so to reduce leaf size. Wire long new shoots if retained for future design; avoid damaging bark; remove fine, young branch wires before winter. Provide sun with some shade to improve autumn color. Water normally during growing season, but do not allow to dry out. Use a medium-nitrogen feed. Needs great patience to control long, straight shoots. Often necessary to remove all first shoots and await second growth. Must be winter-protected. Keep spring light levels high to avoid etiolated shoots. Lovely autumn hues.

Acer griseum

Acer hersii (Snake bark maple)

Zone 5. Protect when really cold. Prune new shoots back early to one-third their length. Do heavy pruning in the spring at repotting time when new buds are about to burst. Total leaf removal is done every three years or so to reduce leaf size. Wire in the spring and early summer; remove fine, young branch wires before winter. Provide sun with some shade. Water well during the growing season. Use a medium-nitrogen feed. Snake bark has lovely autumn colors.

Acer japonicum (Shirasawanum or yellow moon maple)

Zone 5. Protect from cold in a hoop tunnel or cold greenhouse. Keep soil dryish over winter but never dry out. Avoid water on leaves as sun can burn them in spring and early summer. Protect from cold winds. Avoid windburn or sun scorch during spring or summer. Prone to aphid attack. Preseason tip pruning is not normally recommended, but remove any dead branches. Prune new shoots back early to one-third their length (two leaves) as required through the growing season. Do heavy pruning in the spring at repotting time when new buds are about to burst. Total leaf removal is done every three years or so to reduce leaf size. Wire in the spring and early summer; remove all wires before winter. Provide sun, partial shade, and cool, humid air. Water well during growing season. Choose a deep pot to avoid branch dieback. Use a medium-nitrogen feed. A slow-growing, rigid-looking tree worth persisting with as its beautiful yellow leaf color is excellent. Would do well as a cascade in the style of the 'Osakasuki' (see Chapter 9).

Acer negundo (Ash-leaf maple or box elder)

Zones 2 to 5. Hardy on benches. Fully hardy. When repotting, avoid windburn or sun scorch during spring or early summer; wean from shade to sun slowly in spring to avoid sun scorch. Prone to aphid attacks and canker. Canker may be due to bad soil drainage. Prune back long shoots to an appropriate dormant bud just prior to bud burst annually. Prune new shoots back early to one-third their length and as required through the growing season. Seal all wounds well during mid- to late-season pruning. Do heavy pruning in the spring at repotting time when new buds are about to burst. Total leaf removal is done every three years or so to reduce leaf size. Wire new shoots early to mid-season. Provide sun with some shade. Water well during growing season. Use a medium-nitrogen feed. A very vigorous, fast growing tree not very suitable for bonsai. Happy in alkaline soil.

Acer palmatum (Incl. *dissectum, matsumurae, senkaki*) (Japanese maple)

Zones 5 to 6. Protect from cold in a hoop tunnel or cold greenhouse. Keep soil dryish over winter but never dry out. Avoid water on leaves as sun can burn them in the spring and early summer. Protect emerging leaves from cold winds and air frosts. Roots die at temperatures below –14°F (–10°C). When repotting, avoid windburn or sun scorch during spring or early summer; wean from shade to sun slowly in spring to avoid sun scorch. Prone to aphid attacks, verticillium wilt, and coral spot. Prune back long shoots to an appropriate dormant bud just prior to bud burst annually. Prune off any twigs that have died back. Prune new shoots back early to one-third their length (two leaves) as required through the growing season. Remove suckers or dormant buds at branch forks as they appear, leaving reasonable gaps between branches to improve light levels. Seal all wounds well. Do heavy pruning in the spring at or prior to repotting time when new buds are about to burst. Total leaf removal is done every three years or so to reduce leaf size. Do not use copper wire on *senkaki*. Wire late spring and early summer. Do not wire prior to bud burst. Delicate bark. Remove fine, young branch wires before winter. Provide sun with some shade early and late in the growing season as well as during the summer. Water well during growing season. Use a medium-nitrogen feed. Beautiful bonsai species with fantastic autumn colors. Must be winter-protected.

Acer palmatum 'Osakasuki' (Japanese maple)

Zone 5. Protect when really cold. Keep soil dryish over winter but never dry out. Avoid water on leaves as sun can burn them in the spring and early summer. Air frosts can burn newly emerging leaves especially in the year the tree was repotted. When repotting, avoid windburn or sun scorch during spring or early summer. Prone to aphid attacks, verticillium wilt, and coral spot. Remove any dead shoots that have died back over winter. Prune new shoots back early to one-third their length (two leaves) as required through the growing season. Seal all wounds well. Do heavy pruning in the spring at or prior to repotting time when new buds are about to burst. Total leaf removal may be done every three years or so to reduce leaf size. Wire new spring shoots; remove fine, young branch wires before winter. Provide sun with some shade. Water normally during the growing season. Use a medium-nitrogen feed. Very good bonsai subject although shoots are a little thicker and stiffer than some *palmatums*. Best *palmatum* for summer reddening of leaves; good autumnal foliage color, too. Works well in a cascade style.

Acer palmatum 'Osakasuki' (Japanese maple)

Acer palmatum (Japanese maple, Shigitatsu sawa—"Snipe in a bog")

Zones 5 to 6. Protect when really cold. Keep soil dryish over winter but never dry out. Avoid water on leaves as sun can burn them in the spring and early summer. Protect from cold winds. Protect during repotting; be careful of very tender leaves. Avoid windburn or sun scorch during the spring or summer. Prone to aphid attacks, verticillium wilt, and coral spot. Prune new shoots back early to one-third their length (two leaves) as required through the growing season. Seal all wounds well. Do heavy pruning in the spring at repotting time when new buds are about to burst. Total leaf removal is done every three years or so to reduce leaf size. Wire new spring shoots. Delicate bark. Remove fine, young branch wires before winter. Provide semi-shade early and late in the growing season and partial shade in the summer. Water normally during the growing season. Use a medium-nitrogen feed. Needs winter protection. Fabulous pale summer foliage color.

Acer pensylvanicum (Snake bark maple)

Zones 4 to 5. Hardy on benches. Prefers a deep pot. Prune new shoots back early to one-third their length (two leaves) as required through the growing season. Do heavy pruning in the spring at repotting time when new buds are about to burst. Total leaf removal is done every three years or so to reduce leaf size. Wire in the spring or early summer; remove fine, young branch wires before winter. Provide sun with some shade. Water well during growing season. Use a medium-nitrogen feed. Lovely bark and red shoots in winter; leaves are a little large and require the use of the total-leaf-removal technique. Dislikes alkaline soil.

Acer platanoides (Norway maple)

Zones 4 to 5. Hardy on benches. Winter cold and frost hardy. Bark prone to squirrel attack. Pollution resistant but prone to aphid attacks and black spot. Chlorosis occurs in alkaline soils, so correct soil pH. Every 3–4 years remove dormant buds as they swell but before they burst. Prune new shoots back early to one-third their length or just selectively after total bud removal. Do heavy pruning in the spring at repotting time when new buds are about to burst. Total leaf removal is done every three years or so to reduce leaf size, but not in a total-bud-removal year. Wire in spring and early summer. Provide sun with some shade. Water well during growing season. Use a medium-nitrogen feed. Not a first choice due to the large and fairly plain leaves, but a challenge. A vigorous tree with good autumn hues. Likes alkaline soils but also grows in acid soils.

Acer pseudoplatanus (Sycamore maple)

Zone 4. Hardy on benches. Bark prone to squirrel attack. Choose a deep pot to avoid branch dieback. Very pollution resistant. Prone to aphid attacks and black spot (which is usually inhibited in polluted cities). Every 3–4 years remove dormant buds as they swell but before they burst. Prune new shoots back early to one-third their length or just selectively after total bud removal. Seal all wounds well mid- to late season. Do heavy pruning in the spring at repotting time when new buds are about to burst. Total leaf removal is done every three years or so to reduce leaf size, but not in a total-bud-removal year. Wire in the spring and early summer; remove fine, young branch wires before winter. Provide sun with some shade. Water well during growing season, and choose a deep pot to avoid branch dieback, but use high grit content as this tree dislikes waterlogging. Use a medium-nitrogen feed. You need a great deal of patience to style the stiff, long growth of this large-leaved tree. Likes alkaline soils.

Acer pseudoplatanus 'Brilliantissimum' (Sycamore)

Zone 4. Protect from cold in a hoop tunnel or cold greenhouse. Keep soil dryish in winter but do not dry out. Very pollution resistant but prone to severe aphid attacks. Prune back long shoots to an appropriate dormant bud just prior to bud burst annually. Prune new shoots back early to one-third their length (two to three leaves) as required through the growing season. Seal all wounds well mid- to late season. Do heavy pruning in the spring at repotting time when new buds are about to burst. Total leaf removal is done every three years or so to reduce leaf size. Wire in the spring and early summer; remove fine, young branch wires before winter. Provide sun with some shade. Water normally during growing season, but tree dislikes waterlogging. Use a medium-nitrogen feed. A lovely salmon pink in mid- to late May, this tree, although usually grafted, can be grown from seed (leaf color variable) and makes a delightful spectacle in spring. Likes alkaline soil.

Acer rufinerve 'Albo-limbatum' (Snake bark maple)

Zone 5. Protect when really cold. When repotting, keep an eye on the dogwood-like winter shoots and spring buds that emerge earlier than most maples (early February). Choose a deep pot to avoid branch dieback. Prone to aphid attack. Prune new shoots back early to one-third their length (two to three leaves) as required through the growing season. Long, vigorous first growth may need to be removed. Seal all wounds well. Heavy pruning is done in the early spring at repotting time when new buds are about to burst. Total leaf removal is done every three years or so to reduce leaf size. Wire in the early spring and early summer; remove fine, young branch wires before winter. Provide sun with some shade. Water normally during the growing season. Use a medium-nitrogen feed. Only true to form from grafted subjects, nevertheless worth growing if the graft is tidy for its prolific flowering, pale green-striped bark, lovely variegated (ivylike) leaves in summer, and beautiful autumn pinks and purples. Needs to be a larger-scale bonsai due to its vigorous growth.

Acer rubrum (Canadian or red maple)

Zone 4. Hardy on benches. Bark prone to squirrel

attack. Pollution resistant but prone to aphid attacks and black spot. Chlorosis occurs in alkaline soils, so correct soil pH. Prune new shoots back early to one-third their length (two leaves) as required through the growing season. Seal all wounds well mid- to late season. Do heavy pruning in the spring at repotting time when new buds are about to burst. Total leaf removal is done every three years or so to reduce leaf size. Wire in the spring and early summer. Provide sun with some shade. Water well during growing season. Likes moist acid soil and tolerates wet soil. Use a medium-nitrogen feed. Lovely autumn color. Alkaline soil reduces autumn color.

Aesculus hippocastanum (Common horse chestnut)

Zone 4. Hardy on benches. Tree needs cold winter in order to trigger bud burst subsequent spring. Fully winter hardy, but watch tender new shoots if air frosts occur after a repot. Prefers a deep pot. Withstands pollution well. Prone to leaf hopper infesta-

Aesculus hippocastanum (Common horse chestnut)

tions and coral spot. Do not let soil dry out as it weakens pest and disease resistance. Every 3–4 years during development remove all dormant buds as they swell but before they burst. See Chapter 12, Case History 1. Prune new shoots back early to one-third their length or just selectively after total bud removal. Only one growth push per year. Do heavy pruning in the spring at repotting time when new buds are about to burst. Total leaf removal is done every three years or so to reduce leaf size, but not in a total-bud-removal year. Wire in the spring and early summer; watch out for rapid growth and wire marks. Provide sun. Water normally during growing season or more sparingly if in a deep pot. Lovely subject for larger-scale bonsai. Very dominant terminal bud. Likes alkaline soils.

Aesculus carnea (Red horse chestnut)

Zone 4. Hardy on benches. Tree needs cold winter in order to trigger bud burst the following spring. Fully winter hardy but watch tender new shoots if air frosts occur after a repot. Prefers a deep pot. Withstands pollution well. Prone to leaf hopper infestations and coral spot. Do not let soil dry out as it weakens pest and disease resistance. Every 3–4 years during development remove all dormant buds as they swell but before they burst. See Chapter 12, Case History 1. Prune new shoots back early to one-third their length or just selectively after total bud removal. Only one growth push per year. Do heavy pruning in the spring at repotting time when new buds are about to burst. Total leaf removal is done every three years or so to reduce leaf size, but not in a total-bud-removal year. Wire in the spring and early summer; watch out for rapid growth and wire marks. Provide sun. Water normally during growing season or more sparingly if in a deep pot. Smaller leaf than *A. hippocastanum*. Very dominant terminal bud. Likes alkaline soils. Pink flowers.

Aesculus indica (India horse chestnut)

Zone 7. Protect from cold in a hoop tunnel or cold greenhouse. Withstands pollution well. Prone to leaf hopper infestations and coral spot. Do not let soil dry out as it weakens pest and disease resistance. Every 3–4 years during development remove all dormant buds as they swell but before they burst. See Chapter 12, Case History 1. Prune new shoots back early to one-third their length or just selectively after total bud removal. Only one growth push per year. Do heavy pruning in the spring at repotting time when new buds are about to burst. Total leaf removal is done every three years or so to reduce leaf size, but not in a total-bud-removal year. Wire in the spring and early summer; remove fine, young branch wires before winter. Provide sun. Water during the growing season. Needs wet soil. Good subject for larger-scale bonsai. Very dominant terminal bud. Likes alkaline soils. Pink flowers.

Alnus glutinosa (Common alder)

Zone 4. Hardy on benches. Winter hardy. Deep pot preferable. Tolerates pollution. Prone to aphid attack and a few fungal diseases such as bracket and leaf spot fungus. Cut off all affected areas back to healthy wood, seal, and burn affected parts. Prune new shoots back early to one-third their length (two leaves) as required through the growing season. Do heavy pruning in the spring at repotting time when new buds are about to burst. Total leaf removal is done every three years or so to reduce leaf size. Wire in the spring and early summer. Provide sun with some shade. Water very well during growing season and keep soil moist. Low-nitrogen feed. Underrated water-loving genus. Dislikes lime.

Arbutus andrachne or Arbutus unedo (Cypress strawberry tree, strawberry tree)

Zones 7 to 8. Protect from cold in a hoop tunnel or cold greenhouse. Keep soil dryish over winter period but never dry out. Protect from frost and rain during flowering and never expose to cold winds. Does not transplant easily, therefore remove no more than 15 to 20 percent of soil when repotting. Subject to whitefly. No preseason pruning. Prune new shoots back early to one-third their length (two leaves). Do heavy pruning in the spring at repotting time when new buds are about to burst. Never remove all leaves. Wire in the spring and early summer. Bark is delicate. Remove all wires before winter. Provide shade and cool during flowering (early and late in growing season); partial shade during the summer. Water very well during growing season. Beautiful bark and autumn flowers. Strawberrylike fruits form from the previous year's flowers. Prone to whitefly attack. Lime tolerant.

Azalea (satsuki) and Azalea (kurume)

Zones 4 to 6. Protect from cold in a hoop tunnel or cold greenhouse. Protect from frost and rain during flowering. Root-bound trees flower too much, and some flowers must be removed to avoid weakening tree. Repot before root bound. I prefer to repot before bud burst; many growers repot immediately after flowering. Remove galls. Prone to whitefly. Never allow soil to dry out, especially if using peat as it will take a long time to resaturate. Prone to fungal root attack, so seal all wounds and use pure grit under heavy wounds. No preseason pruning. Prune shoots late spring to early summer, then stop to avoid pruning new flower buds. Prefers acid soil, therefore use ericaceous mix. Do heavy pruning in the early spring at repotting time when new buds are about to burst; seal all wounds. Never remove all leaves. Only wire when soil is dry as new shoots are brittle. Wire carefully after flowering; bark is delicate. Remove all wires before winter. Provide sun. Water well during growing season using non-lime bearing water. Apply sequestered iron in February or March. Well drained soil is essential. Feed sparingly using a low/no-lime release fertilizer such as Miracid. Basally dominant, therefore prune lower branches more to avoid a weak top. Purchase plants on the basis of flower size and color.

Betula pendula (Common silver birch)

Zone 3. Protect when really cold. Avoid cold winter winds. Keep up winter light levels to reduce branch dieback. Dislikes repotting, so use a deep pot. Incinerate rust-affected leaves and branches; quarantine affected trees as some rusts are common to many other tree species. Birch is prone to aphids, honey fungus, and bracket fungus. Prune back long shoots to an appropriate dormant bud just prior to bud burst annually and trim to ensure all branches receive good light levels. Prune new shoots back early to one-third their length. Seal all wounds well mid- to late season. Do heavy pruning in the spring at or before repotting time when new buds are about to burst. Total leaf removal is done every 3–4 years to help reduce leaf size. Wire in the spring and early summer; remove fine, young branch wires before winter. Provide sun. Needs partial shade in the summer only on hot days. Requires good light and cool conditions. Water very well during growing season. Use a low-, or better still, no-nitrogen feed. Prone to branch dieback.

Betula papyrifera (Paper bark birch)

Zone 3. Protect when really cold. Avoid cold winter winds. Keep up winter light levels to reduce branch dieback. Dislikes repotting, so use a deep pot. Incinerate rust-affected leaves and branches; quarantine affected trees as some rusts are common to many other tree species. Birch is prone to aphids, honey fungus, and bracket fungus. Prune back long shoots to an appropriate dormant bud just prior to bud burst annually and trim to ensure all branches receive good light levels. Prune new shoots back early to one-third their length. Seal all wounds well mid- to late season. Do heavy pruning in the spring at or before repotting time when new buds are about to burst. Total leaf removal is done every 3–4 years to help reduce leaf size. Wire in the spring and early summer; remove fine, young branch wires before winter. Provide sun. Needs partial shade in the summer only on hot days. Requires good light and cool conditions. Water very well during growing season. Prone to branch dieback.

Betula utilis (Himalayan birch)

Zone 7. Protect from cold in a hoop tunnel or cold greenhouse. Not winter hardy. Avoid cold winter winds. Keep up winter light levels to reduce branch dieback. Dislikes repotting, so use a deep pot. Incinerate rust-affected leaves and branches; quarantine affected trees as some rusts are common to many other tree species. Birch is prone to aphids, honey fungus, and bracket fungus. Prune back long shoots to an appropriate dormant bud just prior to bud burst annually and trim to ensure all branches receive good light levels. Prune new shoots back early to one-third their length. Seal all wounds well mid- to late season. Do heavy pruning in the spring at or before repotting time when new buds are about to burst. Total leaf removal is done every 3–4 years to help reduce leaf size. Wire in the spring and early summer; remove fine, young branch wires before winter. Provide sun. Needs partial shade only on hot days. Requires good light and cool conditions. Water very well during growing season. Prone to branch dieback.

Camellia

Zone 7. Protect from cold in a hoop tunnel or cold greenhouse. Protect from air frost and rain while flowering and remove some flower buds if there are many to avoid weakening bonsai. Common pests include red spider mites. No preseason pruning. Prune new shoots sparingly, immediately after flowering. Never remove all leaves. Wire after flowering. Bark is delicate. Remove all wires before winter. Provide partial shade early and late in the growing season. Avoid early morning sun on frost-covered blooms. Provide cool shade in the summer. Water normally during growing season using non-lime bearing water; apply sequestered iron during February/March. Likes well drained soil. Use a low/no-lime release fertilizer such as Miracid. Prefers acid soil and needs cool roots. Dislikes lime.

Carpinus betulus (European hornbeam)

Zones 5 to 6. Hardy on benches. Avoid water on leaves as sun can burn them. High winds can also damage tender leaves. When repotting, avoid windburn or sun scorch during spring or early summer. Tolerates some pollution. Prone to leaf hopper infestations. Do not let soil dry out as it weakens pest and disease resistance. Prune back long shoots to an appropriate dormant bud just prior to bud burst annually. Prune new shoots back early to one-third their length and through the growing season. Do heavy pruning in the spring at repotting time when new buds are about to burst. Total leaf removal is done every 2–3 years to help reduce leaf size, with good response. Little wiring is required, most shaping is by pruning. Any wiring should be done in the spring or early summer. Provide partial shade to avoid leaf scorch and help darken leaves. Water well during the growing season and keep the soil moist and surface cool. Feed well. Very hardy bonsai subject, but do not dry out. Old leaves may remain attached through winter. Likes alkaline soil.

Carpinus japonica (Japanese hornbeam)

Zone 5. Hardy on benches. Avoid water on leaves as sun can burn them. High winds can also damage tender leaves. When repotting, avoid windburn or sun scorch during spring or early summer. Tolerates some pollution. Prone to leaf hopper infestations. Do not let soil dry out as it weakens pest and disease resist-

Carpinus betulus (European hornbeam)

and disease resistance. Prune back long shoots to an appropriate dormant bud just prior to bud burst annually. Prune new shoots back early to one-third their length and throughout the growing season. Do heavy pruning in the spring at repotting time when new buds are about to burst. Total leaf removal is done every 3–4 years to help reduce leaf size, with good response. Little wiring required; most shaping is by pruning. Any wiring should be done in the spring or early summer; remove fine, young branch wires before winter. Provide partial shade to avoid leaf scorch and help darken leaves. Water well during the growing season and keep the soil moist and surface cool. Feed well. Very hardy bonsai subject, but do not dry out.

Cedrus atlantica 'Glauca' (Blue atlas cedar)

Zones 6 to 7. Needs winter protection. Protect from cold in a hoop tunnel or cold greenhouse. Avoid strong, cold, desiccating winds in spring that dry out needles especially if soil is frozen or after a repot or warm spell. Keep soil a little drier over winter but never dry out and select a deeper than normal pot.

ance. Prune back long shoots to an appropriate dormant bud just prior to bud burst annually. Prune new shoots back early to one-third their length and through the growing season. Do heavy pruning in the spring at repotting time when new buds are about to burst. Total leaf removal is done every 3–4 years to help reduce leaf size, with good response. Little wiring is required; most shaping is by pruning. Any wiring should be done in the spring or early summer. Provide partial shade to avoid leaf scorch and help darken leaves. Water well during the growing season and keep the soil moist and surface cool. Feed well. Very hardy bonsai subject, but do not dry out. Old leaves may remain attached through winter. Likes alkaline soil.

Carpinus laxiflora (Japanese hornbeam)

Zones 5 to 9. Protect when really cold. Avoid water on leaves as sun can burn them. High winds can also damage tender leaves. When repotting, avoid wind-burn or sun scorch during the spring or early summer. Tolerates some pollution. Prone to leaf hopper infestations. Do not let soil dry out as it weakens pest

Cedrus atlantica 'Glauca' (Blue atlas cedar)

When repotting, do not remove more than 20 percent of the soil to avoid needle drop. Cedars are prone to honey fungus, which is best avoided by good soil hygiene and correctly fed plants. Prune new shoots back early to one-third their length selectively as required. Do heavy pruning in the spring at repotting time when new buds are about to burst. Never remove all leaves. Wiring is easiest in the spring when new shoots are just starting to open. Heavy wiring is best left until late spring when sap is flowing well. Full sun. Water normally during growing season, well in hot weather. Protect in winter to avoid wholesale needle drop.

Cedrus brevifolia (Cypriot cedar)

Zone 7. Needs winter protection. Protect from cold in a hoop tunnel or cold greenhouse. Avoid strong, cold, desiccating winds in spring that dry out needles, especially if soil is frozen or after a repot or warm spell. Keep soil a little drier over winter but never dry out and select a deeper than normal pot. When repotting, do not remove more than 20 percent of the soil to avoid needle drop. Cedars are prone to honey fungus, which is best avoided by good soil hygiene and correctly fed plants. Prune new shoots back early to one-third their length selectively as required. Do heavy pruning in the spring at repotting time when new buds are about to burst. Never remove all leaves. Wiring is easiest in the spring when new shoots are just starting to open. Heavy wiring is best left until late spring when sap is flowing well. Remove fine, young branch wires before winter. Full sun. Water normally during growing season, well in hot weather. Protect in winter to avoid wholesale needle drop.

Cedrus deodara (Deodar cedar)

Zone 8. Needs winter protection. Protect from cold in a hoop tunnel or cold greenhouse. Avoid strong, cold, desiccating winds in spring that dry out needles especially if soil is frozen or after a repot or warm spell. Keep soil a little drier over winter but never dry out and select a deeper than normal pot. When repotting, do not remove more than 20 percent of the soil to avoid needle drop. Cedars are prone to honey fungus, which is best avoided by good soil hygiene and correctly fed plants. Prune new shoots back early to one-third their length selectively as required. Do

heavy pruning in the spring at repotting time when new buds are about to burst. Never remove all leaves. Wiring is easiest in the spring when new shoots are just starting to open. Heavy wiring is best left until late spring when sap is flowing well. Remove fine, young branch wires before winter. Full sun. Water normally during growing season, well in hot weather. Protect in winter to avoid wholesale needle drop.

Cedrus libani (Lebanon cedar)

Zone 6. Needs winter protection. Protect from cold in a hoop tunnel or cold greenhouse. Avoid strong, cold, desiccating winds in spring that dry out needles especially if soil is frozen or after a repot or warm spell. Keep soil a little drier over winter but never dry out and select a deeper than normal pot. When repotting, do not remove more than 20 percent of the soil to avoid needle drop. Cedars are prone to honey fungus, which is best avoided by good soil hygiene and correctly fed plants. Prune new shoots back early to one-third their length selectively as required Do heavy pruning in the spring at repotting time when new buds are about to burst. Never remove all leaves. Wiring is easiest in the spring when new shoots are just starting to open. Heavy wiring is best left until late spring when sap is flowing well. Full sun. Water normally during growing season, well in hot weather. Protect in winter to avoid wholesale needle drop.

Chaenomeles japonica (Quince)

Zones 6 to 8. Hardy on benches in deep pots. When repotting, choose a deep pot to avoid branch dieback. Prone to leaf blight; seal wounds, then spray tree with bordeaux mixture or copper fungicide; also prone to mildew. No preseason pruning; plant flowers on old wood. Cut back after flowering and reduce new shoots to one-third, or leave shoots untrimmed until October. Remove suckers or dormant buds at branch forks as they appear, leaving reasonable gaps between branches to improve light levels. Seal all wounds well. Do heavy pruning in the spring at repotting time when new buds are about to burst. Wire present year's growth through the summer. Shape all shoots while young as they become very rigid. Full sun. Water very well during the growing season. Feed well using a low-nitrogen feed and don't feed during fruit set until half size. Beautiful flowers in February on this very hardy species.

Chamaecyparis obtusa (Hinoki cypress including 'Nana Gracilis')

Zone 3. Protect when really cold. When repotting, do not remove more than 20 percent of the soil and do not let tree get too root bound. Very insect and disease resistant. Selectively shorten long pointed new growth to one-third, or back-level with fan-shaped growth. Do heavy pruning in the spring at repotting time when new buds are about to burst. Never remove all leaves. Wire in the spring. Provide sun for vigorously growing plants or cool, partial shade. Water normally during growing season, retain some moisture at all times. Do not move rapidly from shade to full sun to avoid sun scorch. Ensure adequate light levels all around the tree to avoid branch dieback. Prefers slightly acid soils.

Chamaecyparis pisifera (Sawara cypress)

Zones 3 to 4. Protect when really cold. Prefers a deeper pot. Very insect and disease resistant. Finger-pinch early back to one-third length selectively throughout the season. Do heavy pruning in the spring at repotting time when new buds are about to burst. Never remove all leaves. Wire in the spring and early summer. Partial shade. Water very well during growing season. Avoid drying out the soil; use loam-rich soil. Dislikes lime.

Chamaecyparis pisifera 'Boulevard' (Sawara cypress)

Zones 3 to 4. Protect tree from cold in a hoop tunnel or cold greenhouse. Tender foliage needs cold greenhouse protection. When repotting, use a deeper pot; tree must not become pot-bound. Very insect and disease resistant. Finger-pinch early back to one-third their length selectively throughout the season. Prune to balance growth, especially upper growth, as tree is apically dominant, which can produce a lack of vigor and dieback in lower branches. Do heavy pruning in the spring at repotting time when new buds are about to burst. Never remove all leaves. Wire in the spring and early

Chamaecyparis obtusa (Hinoki cypress including 'Nana Gracilis')

Chamaecyparis pisifera 'Boulevard' (Sawara cypress)

summer; remove fine, young branch wires before winter. Partial shade but good light levels. Water very well during growing season, but do not dry out as lower and shaded branches will shrivel and die. Avoid drying out the soil, use loam-rich soil.

Cotoneaster cornubia

Zone 7. Protect from cold in a hoop tunnel or cold greenhouse. Keep soil a little drier over winter but never dry out. When repotting, avoid windburn or sun scorch during spring or early summer; repot before tree becomes pot-bound to avoid weakening tree. Pollution tolerant. Prone to silverleaf and scale insect attacks. Also prone to fireblight. Prune new shoots back early to one-third their length selectively as required. Seal all wounds well mid- to late season. Do heavy pruning in the spring at repotting time when new buds are about to burst. Wire new shoots as necessary; later shaping is clip and grow. Remove fine, young branch wires before winter.

Partial shade. Water well during growing season and choose a deep pot to avoid branch dieback. Feed well but stop during flowering until fruits are half their size. Ensure winter protection and avoid sun and frost scorch when moving from winter protection into sunlight.

Cotoneaster frigida (Himalayan tree)

Zone 7. Protect from cold in a hoop tunnel or cold greenhouse. Keep soil a little drier over winter but never dry out. When repotting, avoid windburn or sun scorch during spring or early summer. Repot before tree becomes pot-bound to avoid weakening tree. Pollution tolerant. Prone to silverleaf and scale insect attacks. Also prone to fireblight. Prune new shoots back early to one-third their length selectively as required. Seal all wounds well mid- to late season. Do heavy pruning in the spring at repotting time when new buds are about to burst. Wire new shoots as necessary; later shaping is clip and grow. Remove fine, young branch wires before winter. Partial shade. Water well during growing season and choose a deep pot to avoid branch dieback. Feed well but stop during flowering until fruits are half their size. Ensure winter protection and avoid sun and frost scorch when moving from winter protection into sunlight.

Cotoneaster horizontalis (Herringbone)

Zones 6 to 8. Protect from cold in a hoop tunnel or cold greenhouse. Keep soil a little drier over winter but never dry out. When repotting, avoid windburn or sun scorch during spring or early summer. Repot before tree is pot-bound to avoid weakening tree. Pollution tolerant. Prone to silverleaf and scale insect attacks. Also prone to fireblight. Design branch placement to ensure all branches receive good light levels as this species is prone to branch dieback. Prune new shoots back early to one-third their length selectively as required. Seal all wounds well mid- to late season. Do heavy pruning in the spring at repotting time when new buds are about to burst. Wire new shoots as necessary; later shaping is clip and grow. Remove fine, young branch wires before winter. Partial shade. Water well during growing season and choose a deep pot to avoid branch dieback. Feed well but stop during flowering until fruits are half size. Lovely bonsai subject. Ensure winter protection and avoid sun and frost scorch when moving from winter protection into sunlight.

Cotoneaster horizontalis (Herringbone)

Crataegus monogyna (Common hawthorn)

Zone 5. Protect from cold in a hoop tunnel or cold greenhouse. Protect from frost and rain during flowering. When repotting, use a deep pot or high-loam mix. Pollution tolerant. Prone to mildew, blister mite, rust, and fireblight. Quarantine rust-affected trees as some rusts are common to many other species. Preseason pruning should only involve removing sacrificial branches. Prune long shoots back to one-third as they emerge only after flowering. Seal all wounds well mid- to late season. Do heavy pruning in the spring at repotting time when new buds are about to burst. Total leaf removal is done every 2–3 years to help reduce leaf size. Wire new shoots in the spring after flowering and early summer as necessary; later shaping is clip and grow. Full sun or partial shade in hot spells. Water well during growing season and choose a deep pot to avoid branch dieback. Low-nitrogen feed. Winter-protect in shallow pots but allow some cold exposure to encourage flowering. Do not dry out or let get root bound even though root-bound trees flower better. Water soil, not leaves, to avoid mildew. Likes alkaline soil.

Crataegus monogyna (Common hawthorn)

Crataegus oxycantha (May hawthorn)

Zone 5. Protect from cold in a hoop tunnel or cold greenhouse. Protect from frost and rain during flowering. When repotting, use a deep pot or high-loam mix. Pollution tolerant. Prone to mildew, blister mite, rust, and fireblight. Quarantine rust-affected trees as some rusts are common to many other species. Preseason pruning should only involve removing sacrificial branches. Prune long shoots back to one-third as they emerge only after flowering. Seal all wounds well mid- to late season. Do heavy pruning in the spring at repotting time when new buds are about to burst. Total leaf removal is done every 2–3 years to help reduce leaf size. Wire new shoots in the spring after flowering and early summer as necessary; later shaping is clip and grow. Full sun or partial shade in hot spells. Water very well during growing season. Low-nitrogen feed. Winter-protect in shallow pots but allow some cold exposure to encourage flowering. Do not dry out or let get root bound even though root bound trees flower better. Water soil, not leaves, to avoid mildew. Likes alkaline soil.

Cryptomeria japonica 'Bandai-Sugi'

Zones 6 to 7. Can stay out in mild winters. Protect from cold in a hoop tunnel or cold greenhouse. Keep soil a little drier over winter but never dry out. Protect newly repotted trees from cold. Repot before tree is root bound. Needle blight may be treated with Benlate.

Finger-pinch leaving one-third of new growth as required. Bandai-sugi has such a compact growth it needs very little such treatment. Avoid apical dominance during mid- and late-season pruning by selective (and if necessary, heavy) pruning and by keeping generous gaps for light between branches. Remove dead foliage at year-end. Do heavy pruning in the spring at repotting time when new buds are about to burst. Never remove all leaves. Shoots and branches are very brittle and at the base; most wiring is done on young shoots and in late spring. Finger-pinching is then used on more mature branches. Remove all wires before winter. Good sunshine primarily, but in hot spells find a cool/humid sheltered place. Branches die back in insufficient sun. Water very well during growing season and keep soil moist. Use low-nitrogen feed (also darkens color). Always retain some residual soil moisture, and in winter store in high-light levels.

Escallonia 'Apple blossom'

Zones 8 to 9. Protect from cold in a hoop tunnel or cold greenhouse. Keep soil a little drier over winter but never dry out. Protect from frost and rain during flowering and from cold winds. Prune new growth to one-third its length throughout the season as growth occurs. Prune in June or July after flowering to thin out and shorten growth. Do heavy pruning in the spring at repotting time when new buds are about to burst. Never remove all leaves. Wire young shoots early in the summer after flowering. Remove fine, young branch wires before winter. Full sun. Water well during the growing season. Lovely flowers and aged bark on this fast growing bonsai.

Eucalyptus coccifera (Tasmanian snow gum)

Zone 6. Protect from cold in a hoop tunnel or cold greenhouse. Keep soil a little drier over winter but never dry out and protect from cold winds. Prune long shoots back to one-third their length as they emerge. Do heavy pruning in the spring at repotting time when new buds are about to burst. Never remove all leaves. Wire young shoots in the spring and early summer. Remove all wires before winter. Full sun. Water normally during the growing season.

Eucalyptus globulus (Blue gum)

Zone 9. Protect from cold in a hoop tunnel or cold greenhouse. Keep soil a little drier over winter but

Crytomeria japonica 'Bandai-Sugi'

never dry out and protect from cold winds. Prune long shoots back to one-third their length as they emerge. Do heavy pruning in the spring at repotting time when new buds are about to burst. Never remove all leaves. Wire young shoots in the spring and early summer. Remove all wires before winter. Full sun. Water normally during the growing season.

Eucalyptus gunnii (Cider gum)
Zone 7. Protect from cold in a hoop tunnel or cold greenhouse. Keep soil a little drier over winter but never dry out and protect from cold winds. Prune long shoots back to one-third their length as they emerge. Do heavy pruning in the spring at repotting time when new buds are about to burst. Never remove all leaves. Wire young shoots in the spring and early summer. Remove all wires before winter. Full sun. Water normally during the growing season. Dislikes lime.

Euonymus alatus (Winged spindle)
Zone 3. Protect when really cold. Tolerates pollution. Aphid-prone. Preseason, tidy up old wood. Finger-pinch new growth back to one-third its length throughout the season as growth occurs. Do heavy pruning in the spring at repotting time when new buds are about to burst. Total leaf removal is done every 3–4 years to help reduce leaf size and improve autumn color. Wire young shoots carefully in early summer; winged bark is delicate. Provide sun or partial shade but needs good light. Water well during the growing season and keep the soil moist and well drained. Normal feeding. Likes lime. Fabulous autumn hues. Hosts overwintering black aphids. Lovely corky and winged bark.

Euonymus europaeus (Spindle)
Zone 3. Protect when really cold. Tolerates pollution. Aphid-prone. Preseason, tidy up old wood. Finger-pinch new growth back to one-third its length throughout the season as growth occurs. Do heavy pruning in the spring at repotting time when new buds are about to burst. Total leaf removal is done every 3–4 years to help reduce leaf size and improve autumn color. Wire young shoots carefully in early summer; bark is delicate. Provide sun or partial shade but needs good light. Water well during the growing season and keep the soil moist and well drained.

Normal feeding. Likes lime. Fabulous autumn hues. Hosts overwintering black aphids.

Fagus crenata (Japanese white beech)
Zones 4 to 8. Protect from cold in a hoop tunnel or cold greenhouse. Keep soil a little drier over winter but never dry out. Do not expose emerging leaves to cold winds or frost. When repotting, avoid windburn or sun scorch during spring or early summer. Likes loam or lime soils and needs mycorrhiza in soil. Not pollution tolerant. Prone to leaf hopper infestations and woolly aphid attacks. Do not let soil dry out as it weakens pest and disease resistance. Prone to root rot so seal all cuts and use pure grit under large wounds. Prune back long shoots and any young shoots pointing too vertically upward to an appropriate dormant bud just prior to bud burst annually. Finger-pinch new emerging long shoots back to one-third their length as soon as they appear. No second growth mid- and late season. Do heavy pruning in the spring at repotting time when new buds are about to burst. Total leaf removal is done every 3–4 years to help reduce leaf size, with good response. Only wire young shoots (early summer) of this delicately barked species. Remove fine, young branch wires before winter. Provide sun, but with some shade due to thin bark and leaves. Take care to shade when young branches are wired. Water normally-to-well during growing season but avoid waterlogging. Moist soil helps retain dead leaves on shoots all winter. Use medium-nitrogen feed. Be vigilant with new-growth pinching; there is no second growth, but leaf size is highly dependent on early first-shoot pruning. Wide acid/alkaline soil tolerance.

Fagus sylvatica (European beech)
Zone 5. Protect when really cold. Keep soil a little drier over winter but never dry out. Do not expose emerging leaves to cold winds or frost. When repotting, avoid windburn or sun scorch during spring or early summer. Likes loam or lime soils and needs mycorrhiza in soil. Not pollution tolerant. Prone to leaf hopper infestations and woolly aphid attacks. Do not let soil dry out as it weakens pest and disease resistance. Prone to root rot so seal all cuts and use pure grit under large wounds. Prune back long shoots and any young

shoots pointing too vertically upward to an appropriate dormant bud just prior to bud burst annually. Finger-prune new emerging long shoots back to one-third their length as soon as they appear. No second growth mid- and late season. Do heavy pruning in the spring at repotting time when new buds are about to burst. Total leaf removal is done every 3–4 years to help reduce leaf size, with good response. Only wire young shoots (early summer) of this delicately barked species. Remove fine, young branch wires before winter. Provide sun, but with some shade due to thin bark and leaves. Take care to shade when young branches are wired. Water normally-to-well during growing season but avoid waterlogging. Moist soil helps retain dead leaves on shoots all winter. Use medium-nitrogen feed. Be vigilant with new-growth pinching; there is no second growth but leaf size is highly dependent on early first-shoot pruning. Wide acid/alkaline soil tolerance.

Fraxinus excelsior (European ash)
Zone 4. Hardy on benches. Fully winter hardy. Not pollution tolerant. Prone to leaf hopper infestation. Mildew and other fungal diseases can affect the ash. Remove and burn all affected material; cut back to healthy wood and seal wounds before burning infected debris. Leave or remove new shoots depending on their length. Do heavy pruning in the spring at repotting time when new buds are about to burst. Wire long new shoots if retained for future design. Partial shade. Water well during growing season. Use medium- to high-nitrogen feed until mid-summer. Prefers a lime soil.

Gingko biloba (Maidenhair tree)
Zone 5. Protect from cold in a hoop tunnel or cold greenhouse. Pollution tolerant. Keep soil a little drier over winter but never dry out. Shelter from winter cold. Prone to fungal infections. Prune sparingly and seal wounds. Not prone to insect attack. Leave or remove new shoots depending on their length. Do heavy pruning in the spring at repotting time when new buds are about to burst. Wire long new shoots in the late spring or early summer if they will be retained for future design. Remove all wires before winter. Full sun. Water normally during growing season. Feed well using a low-nitrogen feed. Avoid winter cold especially on roots.

Hamamelis mollis and Hamamelis japonica (Chinese and Japanese witch-hazel)
Zones 5 to 6. Protect when really cold. Prune new shoots after flowering. Do heavy pruning in the spring at repotting time when new buds are about to burst. Wire in the spring after flowering. Provide sun or partial shade. Water well during growing season; always keep soil moist. Flowers December onward. Chinese has better flowers; Japanese, better autumn colors. Use lime-free soil.

Ilex aquifolium (European holly)
Zones 5 to 6. Hardy on benches. Keep soil a little drier over winter but never dry out. Does not transplant easily (especially the first time from the wild), therefore when repotting remove no more than 15 to 20 percent of the soil. Pollution tolerant. A leaf miner causes galls; spray with pirimiphos-methyl. Prune long shoots back to one-third their length as they emerge. Do heavy pruning in the spring at repotting time when new buds are about to burst. Never remove all leaves from evergreens. Only wire young shoots (early summer) of this delicately barked and brittle branched species. Remove all wires before winter. Some shade, especially when young branches are wired. Water normally during the growing season. Dislikes wet or waterlogged soil. Wide acid/alkaline soil tolerance.

Jasminum nudiflorum (Winter jasmine)
Zones 6 to 9. Protect from cold in a hoop tunnel or cold greenhouse. Keep soil a little drier over winter but never dry out. Repot regularly to avoid weakening tree. Remove sacrificial shoots only; tree flowers on old wood. Prune long shoots back to one-third after flowering. Tidy up in September. Do heavy pruning in the spring at repotting time when new buds are about to burst. Wire in the spring after flowering. Partial shade. Water well during growing season; always keep soil moist although a little drier during flowering.

Juniperus chinensis (Chinese juniper)
Zones 3 to 5. Hardy on benches. Winter hardy. Repot before pot-bound. Incinerate rust-affected leaves and branches and quarantine affected trees as some rusts are common to many other tree species. Red spider mite infestations are common in warm

weather and must be treated early and repeatedly with malathion spray. Finger-pinch long, pointed new growth back to cloud profile during growing season up until the end of June; any later and die-back may result. Seal all wounds well. Do heavy pruning in the spring at repotting time when new buds are about to burst. Never remove all leaves. Wire in the spring and early summer. Provide full sun for compact growth, although species can tolerate shade. Water normally during the growing season. Needs more than average amounts of low-nitrogen feed starting February/March with low dose or foliar feed. Very hardy and drought-tolerant subject, ideal for bonsai. Compact foliage.

Juniperus chinensis 'San Jose' (Chinese juniper)

Zones 4 to 5. Hardy on benches. Winter hardy. Repot before pot-bound. Incinerate rust-affected leaves and branches and quarantine affected trees as some rusts are common to many other tree species. Red spider mite infestations are common in warm weather and must be treated early and repeatedly with malathion spray. Finger-pinch long, pointed new growth back to cloud profile during the growing season. Seal all wounds well. Do heavy pruning in the spring at repotting time when new buds are about to burst. Never remove all leaves. Wire in the spring and early summer. Provide full sun for compact growth, although species can tolerate shade. Water normally during the growing season. Needs more than average amounts of low-nitrogen feed starting February/March with low dose or foliar feed. Very hardy, fast-growing subject, ideal for bonsai; foliage coarser than *J. chinensis* 'Sargentii'.

Juniperus x *media plumosa* and *Juniperus plumosa* 'Aurea'

Zone 4. Hardy on benches. Winter hardy. Repot before pot-bound. Incinerate rust-affected leaves and branches and quarantine affected trees as some rusts are common to many other tree species. Red spider mite infestations are common in warm weather and must be treated early and repeatedly with malathion spray. Finger-pinch long, pointed new growth back to cloud profile during the growing season. Seal all wounds well. Do heavy pruning in the spring at repotting time when new buds are about to burst. Never remove all leaves. Wire in the spring and early

summer. Provide sun or partial shade. Water normally during the growing season. Needs more than average amounts of low-nitrogen feed starting February/March with low dose or foliar feed. Brown/golden winter discoloration is normal. Foliage is bright yellow in full summer sunlight. Good, hardy, and compact bonsai subject.

Juniperus x *media plumosa* 'Aurea'

Juniperus x *media* 'Shimpaku'

Zone 4. Hardy on benches. Winter hardy. Repot before pot-bound. Incinerate rust-affected leaves and branches and quarantine affected trees as some rusts are common to many other tree species. Red spider mite infestations are common in warm weather and must be treated early and repeatedly with malathion spray. Finger-pinch long, pointed new growth back to cloud profile during the growing season. Seal all wounds well. Do heavy pruning in the spring at repotting time when new buds are about to burst. Never remove all leaves. Wire in the spring and early summer. Provide sun or partial shade. Water normally during the growing season. Needs more than average amounts of low-nitrogen feed starting February/March with low dose or foliar feed. Lovely fine-foliaged form and scale. Not frequently found, but this exceptional juniper is worth tracking down. Good, hardy, and compact bonsai subject.

Juniperus x media
'Shimpaku'

Juniperus communis (Common needle juniper)

Zones 3 to 6. Protect from cold in a hoop tunnel or cold greenhouse. Keep soil a little drier over winter but never dry out. Maintain good winter light levels. Repot infrequently in a deep pot before tree becomes pot-bound. Keep surface roots well covered with soil and moss. Only remove 20 percent of soil. Incinerate rust-affected leaves and branches and quarantine affected trees as some rusts are common to many other tree species. Red spider mite infestations are common in warm weather and must be treated early and repeatedly with malathion spray. Susceptible to fungal attack. Finger-pinch shoots early back to one-third their length selectively throughout the season. Finger-pinch long, pointed new growth back to cloud profile during growing season. Seal all wounds well. Do heavy pruning in the spring at repotting time when new buds are about to burst. Never remove all leaves. Wire in the spring and early summer. Remove fine, young branch wires before winter. Provide partial sun, but it is important to keep surface roots cool and keep up good light levels. Water normally-to-well during the growing season.

Do not let the soil dry out, especially the surface soil. Needs average amounts of low-nitrogen feed starting March/April with low dose or foliar feed. Never dry out this tree. Grows well on lime or acid soils but requires more care and attention than non-needle juniper species. Lovely old gray bark.

Juniperus davurica 'Expansa'

Zone 6. Hardy on benches. Winter hardy. Repot before pot-bound. Incinerate rust-affected leaves and branches and quarantine affected trees as some rusts are common to many other tree species. Red spider mite infestations are common in warm weather and must be treated early and repeatedly with malathion spray. Finger-pinch long, pointed new growth back to cloud profile during the growing season. Seal all wounds well. Do heavy pruning in the spring at repotting time when new buds are about to burst. Never remove all leaves. Wire in the spring and early summer. Provide full sun. Water normally during the growing season. Needs more than average amounts of low-nitrogen feed starting February/March with low dose or foliar feed. Very hardy and drought-tolerant subject, good for bonsai; foliage is a little coarser than *J. chinensis* 'Sargentii'.

Juniperus communis (Common needle juniper)

Juniperus communis 'Hornbrookii' (Common juniper)

Zones 3 to 6. Protect when really cold. Winter hardy. Repot before pot-bound. Incinerate rust-affected leaves and branches and quarantine affected trees as some rusts are common to many other tree species. Red spider mite infestations are common in warm weather and must be treated early and repeatedly with malathion spray. Finger-pinch long, pointed new growth back to cloud profile during the growing season. Seal all wounds well. Do heavy pruning in the spring at repotting time when new buds are about to burst. Never remove all leaves. Wire in the spring and early summer. Provide full sun. Water normally during the growing season. Needs more than average amounts of low-nitrogen feed starting February/March with low dose or foliar feed. Very hardy species. Compact foliage and prostrate form.

Juniperus x *media* 'Blaauw'

Zone 4. Hardy on benches. Winter hardy. Repot before pot-bound. Incinerate rust-affected leaves and branches and quarantine affected trees as some rusts are common to many other tree species. Red spider

Juniperus x *media* 'Blaauw'

mite infestations are common in warm weather and must be treated early and repeatedly with malathion spray. Finger-pinch long, pointed new growth back to cloud profile during the growing season. Seal all wounds well. Do heavy pruning in the spring at repotting time when new buds are about to burst. Never remove all leaves. Wire in the spring and early summer. Provide full sun. Water normally during the growing season. Needs more than average amounts of low-nitrogen feed starting February/March with low dose or foliar feed. Ideal hardy bonsai subject more available than *J. Chinensis* 'Sargentii' and almost as fine a foliage; slightly bluer color.

Juniperus recurva 'Coxii' (Drooping juniper)

Zones 7 to 9. Protect from cold in a hoop tunnel or cold greenhouse. Very tender species in winter. Repot before pot-bound. Incinerate rust-affected leaves and branches and quarantine affected trees as some rusts are common to many other tree species. Red spider mite infestations are common in warm weather and must be treated early and repeatedly with malathion spray. Finger-pinch long, pointed new growth back to cloud profile during the growing season. Seal all wounds well. Do heavy pruning in the spring at repotting time when new buds are about to burst. Never remove all leaves. Wire in the spring and early summer. Remove all wires before winter. Provide full sun. Water normally during the growing season. Needs more than average amounts of low-nitrogen feed starting February/March with low dose or foliar feed. Prone to die in cold winters but beautiful weeping habit.

Juniperus rigida (Temple juniper)

Zone 6. Protect from cold in a hoop tunnel or cold must be treated early and repeatedly with malathion spray. Finger-pinch long, pointed new growth back to cloud profile during the growing season. Seal all wounds well. Do heavy pruning in the spring at repotting time when new buds are about to burst. Never remove all leaves. Wire in the spring and early summer. Remove fine, young branch wires before winter. Provide sun or partial shade. Water normally during growing season but must have fast-draining soil. Needs much more than average amounts of low-nitrogen feed starting February/March (to stop dieback) with low dose or foliar feed. Prone to tip dieback in cold winters if not

protected. More compact growth than *J. communis*; brighter needle color. Lovely old gray bark.

Juniperus 'Sargentii'

Zone 4. Hardy on benches. Winter hardy. Repot before pot-bound. Incinerate rust-affected leaves and branches and quarantine affected trees as some rusts are common to many other tree species. Red spider mite infestations are common in warm weather and must be treated early and repeatedly with malathion spray. Finger-pinch long, pointed new growth back to cloud profile during growing season up until the end of June, any later and dieback may result. Seal all wounds well. Do heavy pruning in the spring at repotting time when new buds are about to burst. Never remove all leaves. Wire in the spring and early summer. Provide full sun for compact growth although species can tolerate shade. Water normally during the growing season. Needs more than average amounts of low-nitrogen feed starting February/March with low dose or foliar feed. Hardy and drought-tolerant subject, ideal for bonsai. Compact foliage.

Juniperus squamata (Flaky juniper)

Zones 5 to 8. Protect when really cold. Do not repot late as this causes branch dieback. Repot before pot-bound. Incinerate rust-affected leaves and branches and quarantine affected trees as some rusts are common to many other tree species. Prone to small scale insects and to red spider mite; infestations are common in warm weather and must be treated early and repeatedly with malathion spray. Finger-pinch long, pointed new growth back to cloud profile during the growing season. Seal all wounds well. Do heavy pruning in the spring at repotting time when new buds are about to burst. Never remove all leaves. Wire in the spring and early summer. Remove fine, young branch wires before winter. Provide full sun for compact growth although species can tolerate shade. Water normally during the growing season. Needs more than average amounts of low-nitrogen feed starting February/March with low dose or foliar feed. Lovely, craggy species with equally nice peeling bark.

Juniperus squamata 'Meyeri' (Flaky juniper)

Zones 5 to 8. Protect when really cold. Do not repot late as this causes branch dieback. Repot before pot-bound. Incinerate rust-affected leaves and branches and quarantine affected trees as some rusts are common to many other tree species. Red spider mite infestations are common in warm weather and must be treated early and repeatedly with malathion spray. Finger-pinch long, pointed new growth back to cloud profile during the growing season. Seal all wounds well. Do heavy pruning in the spring at repotting time when new buds are about to burst. Never remove all leaves. Wire in the spring and early summer. Remove fine, young branch wires before winter. Provide full sun for compact growth although species can tolerate shade. Water normally during the growing season. Needs more than average amounts of low-nitrogen feed starting February/March with low dose or foliar feed. This vigorous blue cultivar is a good choice for bonsai. It does, however, form very dense foliage which demands a great deal of shoot plucking and thinning during the growing season.

Juniperus virginiana (including Juniperus burkii) (Pencil cedar)

Zones 3 to 9. Hardy on benches. Very hardy species. Repot before pot-bound. Very insect tolerant. Prone to rust. Quarantine affected trees as some rusts are common to many other tree species. Red spider mite infestations are common in warm weather and must be treated early and repeatedly with malathion spray. Finger-pinch long, pointed new growth back to cloud profile during the growing seasoon. Seal all wounds well. Do heavy pruning in the spring at repotting time when new buds are about to burst. Never remove all leaves. Wire in the spring and early summer. Provide full sun. Water less than normal during the growing season but do not dry out. Needs average amounts of low-nitrogen feed starting March/April with low dose or foliar feed. Very hardy and drought-tolerant subject, ideal for bonsai. Likes dryish, alkaline soil and tolerates extremes of moisture and temperature.

Laburnum anagyroides (Common golden chain laburnum)

Zone 5. Protect when really cold. Leaf miner attacks are treated by prompt spraying with pirimiphos–methyl or as per Chapter 2. Preseason, remove weak and dead shoots. Do heavy pruning in the spring at repotting time when new buds are about to burst. Total leaf removal is done every three years or so to reduce leaf size. Wire after flowering. Provide sun and

Juniperus virginiana (including Juniperus burkii)

some shade in the hottest weather. Water very well during growing season, but do not waterlog. Likes alkaline soil.

Larix decidua (European larch)

Zone 2. Hardy on benches. Do not repot late as this causes branch dieback or even death. Repot before pot-bound and use a deeper than normal pot. Prone to mealybugs; treat with bifenthrin spray at high pressure. If larch canker occurs, prune off infected shoots back to healthy tissue. Seal wounds and burn infected parts. Keep up feed regime to maintain good health, and avoid drying out. Prune most long shoots back to one-third as they emerge during the season; use scissors if left too late. Retaining too many long shoots risks low/shaded branch dieback on very hot days. Do not perform late season shoot pruning or buds will become too knobbly. Do heavy pruning in the spring at repotting time when new buds are about to burst. Never remove all leaves. Structural and heavy wiring may be done in February prior to bud burst or in April, if preferred. Wire all new shoots in place in May/June. Provide summer sun, but cool, partial shade if weather is hot or tree growth slows or stops due to heat stress. Keep up light levels. Water very well during the growing season. Remove 50 percent of cones on heavily laden branches to avoid branch dieback. Ensure soil has some mycorrhyza and never dry out a larch or repot late.

Larix eurolepis (hybrid dunkeld larch)

Zone 5. Hardy on benches. Do not repot late as this causes branch dieback or even death. Repot before pot-bound and use a deeper than normal pot. Prone

Larix eurolepis (hybrid dunkeld larch)

to mealybugs; treat as *Larix decidua,* above. Prune most long shoots back to one-third as they emerge during the season; use scissors if left too late. Retaining too many long shoots risks low/shaded branch dieback on very hot days. Do not perform late season shoot pruning or buds will become too knobbly. Do heavy pruning in the spring at repotting time when new buds are about to burst. Never remove all leaves. Structural and heavy wiring may be

done in February prior to bud burst or in April, if preferred. Wire all new shoots in place in May/June. Provide summer sun, but cool, partial shade if weather is hot or tree growth slows or stops due to heat stress. Keep up light levels. Water very well during the growing season. Remove 50 percent of cones on heavily laden branches to avoid branch dieback. Ensure soil has some mycorrhyza and never dry out a larch or repot late.

Larix kaempferi (*L. leptolepis*) (Japanese larch)

Zone 7. Protect from cold in a hoop tunnel or cold greenhouse. Do not repot late as this causes branch dieback or even death. Repot before pot-bound and use deeper than normal pot. Prone to mealybugs; treat as *Larix decidua*, above. Prune most long shoots back to one-third as they emerge during the season; use scissors if left too late. Retaining too many long shoots risks low/shaded branch dieback on very hot days. Do not perform late season shoot pruning or buds will become too knobbly. Do heavy pruning in the spring at repotting time when new buds are about to burst. Never remove all leaves. Structural and heavy wiring may be done in February prior to bud burst or in April, if preferred. Wire all new shoots in place in May/June. Provide summer sun, but cool, partial shade if weather is hot or tree growth slows or stops due to heat stress. Keep up light levels. Water very well during the growing season. Remove 50 percent of cones on heavily laden branches to avoid branch dieback. Ensure soil has some mycorrhyza and never dry out a larch or repot late.

Ligustrum lucidum (Glossy privet)

Zone 7. Protect when really cold to avoid winter leaf drop. Pollution tolerant. Spray thrips with dimethoate from June to August; treat as per Chapter 2. Prone to honey fungus. Prune long shoots back to one-third their length as they emerge. Do heavy pruning in the spring at repotting time when new buds are about to burst. Total leaf removal is not recommended. Wire in the spring and early summer. Remove fine, young branch wires before winter. Provide sun or partial shade. Water well during growing season.

Liquidamber styraciflua (Sweet gum)

Zones 5 or 6. Protect from cold in a hoop tunnel or cold greenhouse. Keep soil dryish over winter but do

Larix kaempferi (L. leptolepis)

not dry out. Avoid water on leaves as sun can burn them. Avoid cold winds and air frosts on emerging new leaves. When repotting, use a deep pot. Growing-on trees love rotted pine needle and hence mycorrhiza fungus. Prune back long shoots to an appropriate dormant bud just prior to bud burst annually. Prune long shoots back to one-third their length as they emerge. Do heavy pruning in the spring at repotting time when new buds are about to burst. Total leaf removal is done every 3–4 years to help reduce leaf size. Wire in the spring and early summer. Remove fine, young branch wires before winter. Partial shade. Water well during the growing season. Likes moderately wet soils. Needs winter protection. Dislikes lime.

Lonicera nitida (Honeysuckle)

Zones 4 to 10. Hardy on benches. Keep soil dryish over winter to reduce risk of fungal infection but do not dry out. Repot with well-drained soil. Silverleaf destroys leaves, stems and even the tree. Remove and burn all affected parts back to healthy wood. Seal and keep up a good feeding regime. Trim shoot tips to a satisfactory shape. Trim pads back to a profile line continuously through the growing season. Seal all branch and root wounds well as *Lonicera* is prone to fungal attacks. Total leaf removal is not required. Wire new shoots as necessary; later shaping is clip and grow. Remove fine, young branch wires before winter. Provide sun. Water well during growing season, but avoid waterlogging this species. Small leaves, rampant growth, lovely aged bark, and thick hedging materials make this a very good bonsai subject.

Magnolia

Zones 5 to 7. Protect when really cold. Protect from air frost, cold winds, and rain during flowering. Repot regularly. Pollution tolerant. Treat aphid attacks with permethrin spray in early spring. Any branches/trunk found with coral spot should be pruned back to healthy wood and sealed; burn infected wood. Prune long shoots back to one-third after flowering. Seal all wounds well mid- to late season. Do heavy pruning in the spring at repotting time when new buds are about to burst. Wire early in the summer after flowering; bark is delicate. Remove all wires before winter. Provide shade early and late in the growing season. Provide some shade in the summer, especially when young branches are wired. Water well during the growing season; keep soil moist. Flowers are a bit large for bonsai. Loves acid soil.

Malus spp. (Domestic apple)

Zones 2 to 5. Hardy on benches. Protect from frost and rain during flowering, but tree needs a cold winter to trigger bud burst in the spring. Remove all garden soil over several repots to discourage root rot; needs a deep pot. Prone to aphid, scale, insect attacks, canker, mildew, rust, and honey fungus. Preseason, remove sacrificial branches only. Prune long shoots back to one-third after flowering. Remove some fruits of overladen branches to avoid weakening. Remove basal suckers mid- and late season unless used for trunk thickening. Seal all wounds well. Do heavy pruning in the spring at repotting time when new buds are about to burst. Wire in the late spring and early summer after flowering. Provide sun normally, but partial shade in hot periods. Water very well during growing season, especially after fruit has formed. Use low-nitrogen feed and don't feed during fruit set until half size. Water soil, not leaves, to avoid mildew and apple scab. Apples are very prone to root rot after heavy root pruning; clean and seal all large root prunings and use neat grit under wounds to avoid damp.

Malus baccata (Siberian apple)

Zone 3. Hardy on benches. Protect from frost and rain during flowering, but tree needs a cold winter in order to trigger bud burst in the spring. Remove all garden soil over several repots to discourage root rot; needs a deep pot. Prone to aphid, scale, insect attacks, canker, mildew, rust, and honey fungus. Preseason, remove sacrificial branches only. Prune long shoots back to one-third after flowering. Remove some fruits of overladen branches to avoid weakening. Remove basal suckers mid- and late season unless used for trunk thickening. Seal all wounds well. Do heavy pruning in the spring at repotting time when new buds are about to burst. Wire in the late spring and early summer after flowering. Provide partial shade. Water very well during the growing season, especially after fruit has formed. Use low-nitrogen feed and don't feed during fruit set until half size. Water soil, not leaves, to avoid mildew and apple scab. Apples are very prone to root rot after heavy root pruning; clean and seal all large root prunings and use neat grit under wounds to avoid damp.

Malus cerasifera (Nagasaki crab apple)

Zones 3 to 4. Hardy on benches. Protect from frost and rain during flowering, but tree needs a cold winter in order to trigger bud burst in the spring. Remove all garden soil over several repots to discourage root rot; needs a deep pot. Prone to aphid, scale insect attacks, canker, mildew, rust, and honey fungus. Preseason, remove sacrificial branches only. Prune long shoots back to one-third after flowering. Remove some fruits of overladen branches to avoid weakening. Remove basal suckers mid- and late season unless used for trunk thickening. Seal all wounds well. Do heavy pruning in the spring at repotting time when new buds are about to burst. Wire in the late spring and early summer after flowering. Provide partial shade. Water very well during growing season especially after fruit has formed. Use low-nitrogen feed and don't feed during fruit set until half size. Water soil, not leaves, to avoid mildew and apple scab. Apples are very prone to root rot after heavy root pruning; clean and seal all large root prunings and use neat grit under wounds to avoid damp.

Malus cerasifera (Nagasaki crab)

Malus halliana (Hall's crab apple)

Zones 5 to 6. Protect from cold in a hoop tunnel or cold greenhouse. Protect from frost and rain during flowering, but tree needs a cold winter in order to trigger bud burst in the spring. Remove all garden soil over several repots to discourage root rot; needs a deep pot. Prone to aphid, scale insect attacks, canker, mildew, rust, and honey fungus. Preseason, remove sacrificial branches only. Prune long shoots back to one-third after flowering. Remove some fruits of overladen branches to avoid weakening. Remove basal suckers mid- and late season unless used for trunk thickening. Seal all wounds well. Do heavy pruning in the spring at repotting time when new buds are about to burst. Wire in the late spring and early summer after flowering. Provide partial shade. Water well during the growing season especially after fruit has formed. Use low-nitrogen feed and don't feed during fruit set until half size. Water soil, not leaves, to avoid mildew and apple scab. Apples are very prone to root rot after heavy root pruning; clean and seal all large root prunings and use neat grit under wounds to avoid damp.

Malus hupehensis (Japanese apple)

Zone 5. Hardy on benches. Protect from frost and rain during flowering, but tree needs a cold winter in order to trigger bud burst in the spring. Remove all garden soil over several repots to discourage root rot; needs a deep pot. Prone to aphid, scale insect attacks, canker, mildew, rust, and honey fungus. Preseason, remove sacrificial branches only. Prune long shoots back to one-third after flowering. Remove some fruits of overladen branches to avoid weakening. Remove basal suckers mid- and late season unless used for trunk thickening. Seal all wounds well. Do heavy pruning in the spring at repotting time when new buds are about to burst. Wire in the late spring and early summer after flowering. Provide partial shade. Water very well during growing season especially after fruit has formed. Use low-nitrogen feed and don't feed during fruit set until half size. Water soil, not leaves, to avoid mildew and apple scab. Apples are very prone to root rot after heavy root pruning; clean and seal all large root prunings and use neat grit under wounds to avoid damp. Fragrant species.

Morus alba (White mulberry)

Zone 5. Protect from cold in a hoop tunnel or cold greenhouse. Keep soil dryish over winter and spring but do not dry out. Protect from frost and rain during flowering. Prone to fungal attack, so seal all wounds. Prune new shoots back to one-third after flowering, throughout the season. Do heavy pruning early in the spring before repotting time while the tree is still dormant. Wire early in the summer after flowering. Remove fine, young branch wires before winter. Provide sun. Water very well during growing season in summer, but do not dry out. Feed sparingly using low-nitrogen feed. Do not feed during fruit set until half size. Likes alkaline soils.

Morus nigra (Black mulberry)

Zone 6. Protect from cold in a hoop tunnel or cold greenhouse. Keep soil dryish over winter and spring but do not dry out. Protect from frost and rain during flowering. Prone to fungal attack so seal all wounds. Prune new shoots back to one-third after flowering, throughout the season. Do heavy pruning early in the spring before repotting time while the tree is still dormant. Wire early in the summer after flowering. Remove all wires before winter. Provide sun. Water very well during growing season in summer but do not dry out. Feed sparingly using low-nitrogen feed. Do not feed during fruit set until half size. Likes alkaline soils.

Nothofagus antarctica (Antarctic beech)

Zone 7. Protect when really cold. Protect from cold winds. Prefers a deep pot. Prune long shoots back to one-third. Do heavy pruning in the spring at repotting time when new buds are about to burst. Wire in the spring or early summer. Remove fine, young branch wires before winter. Provide partial shade. Water during the growing season. Dislikes lime.

Nothofagus obliqua (Roble beech)

Zone 7. Protect when really cold. Protect from cold winds. Prefers a deep pot. Prune long shoots back to one-third. Do heavy pruning in the spring at repotting time when new buds are about to burst. Wire in the spring or early summer. Remove fine, young branch wires before winter. Provide partial shade. Water during the growing season. Fast growing. Dislikes lime.

Nothofagus procera (Southern beech)

Zone 7. Protect when really cold. Protect from cold winds. Prefers a deep pot. Prune long shoots back to one-third. Do heavy pruning in the spring at repotting time when new buds are about to burst. Wire in the spring or early summer. Remove fine, young branch wires before winter. Provide partial shade. Water during the growing season. Fast growing, with good autumn color. Dislikes lime.

Nyssa sylvatica (Tupelo or Black gum)

Zone 5. Protect from cold in a hoop tunnel or cold greenhouse. Keep soil dryish during winter but do not dry out. Protect from frost and rain during flowering. Does not like root disturbance so limit soil removal to 15 to 20 percent when repotting. Prune long shoots back to one-third. Do heavy pruning in the spring at repotting time when new buds are about to burst. Wire in the spring or early summer. Remove fine, young branch wires before winter. Provide partial shade. Water well during the growing season; likes moist/wet soil in the growing season. Spectacular autumn color.

Parrotia persica (Ironwood)

Zones 5 to 6. Protect from cold in a hoop tunnel or cold greenhouse. Keep soil dryish but do not dry out. Prune long shoots back to one-third. Do heavy pruning in the spring at repotting time when new buds are about to burst. Total leaf removal is done every 2–3 years. Wire in the spring or early summer. Remove fine, young branch wires before winter. Provide sun and good light. Water well during the growing season; needs moist soil. Feed well. Challenging, large leaves but lovely spring flowers and autumn color. Can tolerate lime.

Picea abies (Norway spruce)
(incl. 'Little Gem' and 'Nidiformis')

Zones 3 to 5. Hardy on benches. Winter hardy. Repot infrequently and remove no more than 20 percent of root. Prune pineapple gall (caused by a type of adelgid) back to healthy wood; seal and burn, then spray (e.g., malathion at bud burst and onward). Rust should be similarly removed and burned. Red spider mite infestations are possible in warm weather. Finger-pinch new growth when nearly ½ inch (1 cm) long back to one-third. Prefers acid soil, there-

Picea abies 'Nidiformis'

fore use ericaceous mix. Do heavy pruning in the spring at repotting time when new buds are about to burst. Never remove all leaves. Wire in the spring or early summer. Provide partial shade. Water well during the growing season. Apply sequestered iron in February/March. Needs an acid soil; avoid hard water and ensure some mycorrhiza in the soil. Remove and burn any galls caused by mite infestation. Small needle size of Little Gem makes it a lovely subject.

Picea engelmanni (Engelmann spruce)

Zone 3. Hardy on benches. Repot infrequently and remove no more than 20 percent of root. Prune pineapple gall (caused by a type of adelgid) back to healthy wood; seal and burn, then spray (e.g., malathion at bud burst and onward). Rust should be similarly removed and burned. Red spider mite infestations are possible in warm weather. Finger-pinch new growth when nearly ½ inch (1 cm) long back to one-third. Prefers acid soil, therefore use ericaceous mix. Do heavy pruning in the spring at repotting time when new buds are about to burst. Never remove all leaves. Wire in the spring or early summer. Provide partial shade. Water well during the growing season. Apply sequestered iron in February/March and keep the soil moist. Needs an acid soil; avoid hard water and ensure some mycorrhiza in the soil. Remove and burn any galls caused by mite infestation.

Picea glauca 'Conica' (also known as *Picea albertiana* 'Conica') (White spruce)

Zone 3. Protect from cold in a hoop tunnel or cold greenhouse. Dislikes cold and frost. Repot infrequently and remove no more than 20 percent of root. Prune pineapple gall back to healthy wood; seal and burn, then spray (e.g., malathion at bud burst and onward). Rust should be similarly removed and burned. Red spider mite infestations are very common and very serious in warm, dry weather, so treat early. Finger-pinch new growth when nearly ½ inch (1cm) long back to one-third. Prefers acid soil, therefore use ericaceous mix. Do heavy pruning in the spring at repotting time when new buds are about to burst. Never remove all leaves. Wire in the spring or early summer. Provide partial shade. Water well during the growing season. Apply sequestered iron in February/March and keep soil moist. Needs an acid soil; avoid hard water and ensure some mycorrhiza in the soil. Red spider mite will devastate the tree in hot, dry weather unless prompt action is taken. Not a good bonsai subject.

Picea jezoensis (Yezo spruce)

Zone 5. Protect when really cold. Needs some protection from cold. Repot infrequently and remove no more than 20 percent of root. Red spider mite infestations are common in warm weather and must be treated early and repeatedly. Finger-pinch new growth when nearly ½ inch (1cm) long back to one-third. Prefers acid soil, therefore use ericaceous mix. Do heavy pruning in the spring at repotting time when new buds are about to burst. Never remove all leaves. Wire in the spring or early summer. Provide partial shade. Water well during the growing season. Apply sequestered iron in February/March and always keep soil moist. Needs an acid soil; avoid hard water and ensure some mycorrhiza in the soil. Remove and burn any galls caused by mite infestation.

Picea orientalis (Oriental spruce)

Zone 5. Hardy on benches. Winter hardy. Repot infrequently and remove no more than 20 percent of root. Red spider mite infestations are common in warm weather and must be treated early and repeatedly. Finger-pinch new growth when nearly ½ inch (1 cm) long back to one-third. Prefers acid soil, therefore use ericaceous mix. Do heavy pruning in the spring at repotting time when new buds are about to burst. Never remove all leaves. Wire in the spring or early summer. Provide partial shade. Water well during the growing season. Apply sequestered iron in February/March. Needs an acid soil; avoid hard water and ensure some mycorrhiza in the soil. Remove and burn any galls caused by mite infestation.

Picea pungens (Colorado spruce)

Zone 3. Hardy on benches. Winter hardy. Repot infrequently and remove no more than 20 percent of root. Not pollution tolerant. Rust fungus should be removed back to healthy wood, sealed, and all affected material burned. Spray tree early (e.g., with zineb or maleb). Red spider mite infestations are possible in warm weather. Finger-pinch new growth when nearly ½ to 1 inch (1-2 cm) long back to one-third. Prefers acid soil, therefore use ericaceous mix. Do heavy pruning in the spring at repotting time when new buds are about to burst. Never remove all leaves. Wire in the spring or early summer. Full sun; tolerant of dry air. Water well during the growing season. Apply sequestered iron in February/March. Needs an acid soil; avoid hard water and ensure some mycorrhiza in the soil. Remove and burn any galls caused by mite infestation.

Picea sitchensis (Sitka spruce)

Zone 7. Protect when really cold. Prone to spring frost damage. Repot infrequently and remove no more than 20 percent of root. Red spider mite infestations are possible in warm weather. Prone to spruce aphid attack in dry weather. Finger-pinch new growth when nearly ½ inch (1 cm) long back to one-third. Prefers acid soil, therefore use ericaceous mix. Do heavy pruning in the spring at repotting time when new buds are about to burst. Never remove all leaves. Wire in the spring or early summer. Provide partial shade. Water well during the growing season. Apply sequestered iron in February/March. Needs an acid soil; avoid hard water and ensure some mycorrhiza in the soil. Remove and burn any galls caused by mite infestation.

Pieris floribunda (Mountain pieris) and Pieris 'Forrestii' (Chinese pieris)

Zones 6 to 8. Protect from cold in a hoop tunnel or cold greenhouse. Protect new leaves, then flowers, from air frost or cold wind burn in April/May. Prone to aphids. Remove half the new shoots early on to generate new, smaller red leaves in four weeks. Prefers acid soil, therefore use ericaceous mix. Do heavy pruning in the spring at repotting time when new buds are about to burst. Never remove all leaves. Wire early in the summer. Remove all wires before winter. Provide partial shade to avoid yellowing of old leaves. Water well during the growing season. Apply sequestered iron in February/March. New shoots are prone to frost damage if not protected; tree does, however, recover and reshoot if so affected.

Pinus genus (Pines)

All pines benefit from mycorrhiza in the soil to improve vigor. Pines grown on moister, waterlogged acid soils are far more prone to a variety of fungal attacks than on loam. Prone to honey fungus and needle cast. Watch out for woolly aphid from February onward on susceptible pines. Water during the growing season.

Pinus aristata (Bristlecone pine)

Zone 6. Hardy on benches. Protect from desiccating winds in the spring, especially if the soil is frozen, the tree has been repotted, or a warm spell preceded the hostile weather. Use mycorrhiza in the soil. Resin on needles is not to be mistaken for a fungus; it is perfectly normal. Leave old needles on during tree development. Reduce candles to one-third their length when they are 1 inch (2 to 3 cm) long. Do heavy pruning in the spring at repotting time when new buds are about to burst. Never remove all leaves. Wire in the spring or early summer. Full sun. Water normally during growing season; avoid waterlogging as it causes excess needle growth. Needs more than average amounts of low-nitrogen feed starting in February/March with low dose or foliar feed. The oldest living tree species with at least one example over 4,000 years old.

Pinus contorta 'Contorta' (Shore or beach pine)

Zone 7. Protect when really cold. Hardier than the zone number suggests. Protect from desiccating winds in the spring, especially if the soil is frozen, the tree has been repotted, or a warm spell preceded the hostile weather. Use mycorrhiza in the soil. Mildly

prone to woolly aphis (adelgids). Leave old needles on during tree development. Reduce candles to one-third their length when they are 1 inch (2 to 3 cm) long. Every three years, do not needle-prune in the spring, but remove old shoots in September to encourage smaller new-shoot growth. Do heavy pruning in the spring at repotting time when new buds are about to burst. Never remove all leaves. Wire in the spring or early summer. Provide full sun. Water normally during the growing season; avoid waterlogging as it causes excess needle growth. Needs more than average amounts of low-nitrogen feed starting in February/March with low dose or foliar feed. Needs adequate light and late-season pruning to encourage small, compact needles. Likes acid soils.

Pinus contorta 'Latifolia' (Lodgepole pine)

Zone 7. Protect when really cold. Protect from desiccating winds in the spring, especially if the soil is frozen, the tree has been repotted, or a warm spell preceded the hostile weather. Use mycorrhiza in the soil. Leave old needles on during tree development. Reduce candles to one-third their length once they are 1 inch (2 to 3 cm) long. Do heavy pruning in the spring at repotting time when new buds are about to burst. Never remove all leaves. Wire in the spring or early summer. Provide full sun. Water normally during the growing season; avoid waterlogging as it causes excess needle growth. Needs more than average amounts of low-nitrogen feed starting in February/March with low dose or foliar feed. Likes acid soils.

Pinus densiflora (Japanese red pine)

Zones 5 to 7. Protect from cold in a hoop tunnel or cold greenhouse. Keep soil a little drier over the winter but never dry out. Protect from desiccating winds in the spring, especially if the soil is frozen, the tree has been repotted, or a warm spell preceded the hostile weather. Use mycorrhiza in the soil. Leave old needles on during tree development. Reduce candles to one-third their length when they are 1 inch (2 to 3 cm) long. Do heavy pruning in the spring at repotting time when new buds are about to burst. Never remove all leaves. Wire in the spring or early summer. Remove all wires before winter. Provide full sun. Water sparingly to normal during the growing season; avoid waterlogging as it causes excess needle growth. Needs more than average amounts of low-nitrogen feed starting February/March with low dose or foliar feed. Delicate pine needing careful winter protection.

Pinus mugo (Mountain pine)

Zones 2 to 3. Hardy on benches. Very winter hardy. Protect from desiccating winds in the spring, especially if the soil is frozen, the tree has been repotted, or a warm spell preceded the hostile weather. Use mycorrhiza in soil. Mildly prone to woolly aphis (adelgids); treat with liquid malathion. Leave old needles on during tree development. Reduce candles to one-third their length when they are 1 inch (2 to 3 cm) long. Every three years, do not needle-prune in the spring, but remove old shoots in September to encourage smaller new-shoot growth. Do heavy pruning in the spring at repotting time when new buds are about to burst. Never remove all leaves. Wire in the spring or early summer. Provide full sun. Water normally during the growing season; avoid waterlogging as it causes excess needle growth. Less than average amounts of low-nitrogen feed starting April. Lime tolerant.

Pinus nigra (Austrian pine)

Zones 4 to 5. Hardy on benches. Protect from desiccating winds in the spring, especially if the soil is frozen, the tree has been repotted, or a warm spell preceded the hostile weather. Use mycorrhiza in the soil. Leave old needles on during tree development. Reduce candles to one-third their length when they are 1 inch (2 to 3 cm) long. Do heavy pruning in the spring at repotting time when new buds are about to burst. Never remove all leaves. Wire in the spring or early summer. Provide full sun. Water normally during the growing season; avoid waterlogging as it causes excess needle growth. Needs more than average amounts of low-nitrogen feed starting February/March with low dose or foliar feed.

Pinus parviflora (Japanese white pine)

Zone 5. Protect from cold in a hoop tunnel or cold greenhouse. Protect from desiccating winds in the spring, especially if the soil is frozen, the tree has been repotted, or a warm spell preceded the hostile weather. Use mycorrhiza in soil. Very prone to woolly aphis (adelgids); low nitrogen reduces severity of such attacks. Needle cast is rare but affected pines should be sprayed with zineb as soon as needle discoloration is observed. Foliar and liquid feed to regain vigor. Leave old needles on during tree development. Reduce candles to one-third their length when they are 1 inch (2 to 3 cm) long, but do not remove new shoots entirely. No mid- and late-season pruning as growth ceases early in the summer. Leave old needles on during tree development. Do heavy pruning in the spring at repotting time when new buds are about to burst. Never remove all leaves. Wire in the spring or early summer. Provide full sun. Water normally to dryish during growing season; avoid waterlogging as it causes excess needle growth. Needs more than average amounts of low-nitrogen feed starting in February/March with low dose or foliar feed. Only one growth period per year.

Pinus pumila (Dwarf Siberian pine)

Zone 5. Hardy on benches. Winter hardy. Protect from desiccating winds in the spring, especially if the soil is frozen, the tree has been repotted, or a warm spell preceded the hostile weather. Use mycorrhiza in soil. Leave old needles on during tree development. Reduce candles to one-third their length when they are 1 inch (2 to 3 cm) long. Do heavy pruning in the spring at repotting time when new buds are about to burst. Never remove all leaves. Wire in the spring or early summer. Remove fine, young branch wires before winter. Provide sun with a little shade. Water normally during the growing season; avoid waterlogging as it causes excess needle growth. Apply sequestered iron February/March. Needs more than average amounts of low-nitrogen feed starting in February/March with low dose of foliar feed. Use acid soil and no hard water to keep tree healthy.

Pinus sylvestris (Scotch pine)

Zone 2. Hardy on benches. Very winter hardy. Protect from desiccating winds in the spring, especially if the soil is frozen, the tree has been repotted, or a warm spell preceded the hostile weather. Use mycorrhiza in soil. Very prone to woolly aphis (adelgids); treat with liquid malathion; low nitrogen reduces severity of such attacks. Needle cast is rare but affected pines should be sprayed with zineb as soon as needle discoloration is observed. Foliar and liquid feed to regain vigor. Leave old needles on during tree development. Reduce candles to one-third their length when they

Pinus sylvestris (Scotch pine)

are 1 inch (2 to 3 cm) long. Do heavy pruning in the spring at repotting time when new buds are about to burst. Never remove all leaves. Wire in the spring or early summer. Provide full sun. Water normally during the growing season; avoid waterlogging as it causes excess needle growth. Needs more than average amounts of low-nitrogen feed starting in February/March with low dose or foliar feed. Excellent bonsai subject.

Pinus thunbergii (Japanese black pine)

Zones 5 to 6. Protect from cold in a hoop tunnel or cold greenhouse. Keep soil a little drier over winter but never dry out. Keep good light levels to avoid lower/under branch dieback. Protect from desic-cating winds in the spring, especially if the soil is frozen, the tree has been repotted, or a warm spell preceded the hostile weather. Use mycorrhiza in soil. Very prone to woolly aphis (adelgids); low nitrogen reduces severity of such attacks. Needle cast is rare but affected pines should be sprayed with zineb as soon as needle discoloration is observed. Foliar and liquid feed to regain vigor. Leave old needles on during tree development. Reduce can-dles to one-third their length when they are 1 inch (2 to 3 cm) long. Every three years, do not needle-

prune in the spring, but remove old shoots in September to encourage smaller new-shoot growth. Do heavy pruning in the spring at repotting time when new buds are about to burst. Never remove all leaves. Wire in the spring or early summer. Provide sun. New growth can be delayed for several weeks or months in excessive heat early or late in the season. Provide full sun in the summer to avoid lower/under branch dieback. Keep in an open, well-lit area. Water normally during the growing season; avoid waterlogging as it causes excess needle growth. Needs more than average amounts of low-nitrogen feed starting in February/March with low dose or foliar feed. Superb bonsai subject needing adequate light, winter protection, and late-season pruning to encourage small, compact needles.

Pinus thumbergii (Japanese black pine)

Populus alba (White aspen)

Zone 4. Hardy on benches. Keep soil a little drier over the winter, but never dry out. Pollution tolerant. Remove canker-affected shoots, seal, and burn. Spray with bordeaux mixture or copper fungicide from August to October and at the following bud burst. Prune long shoots back to one-third. Remove suckers mid- and late season if not required in the design or for trunk thickening. Do heavy pruning in the spring at repotting time when new buds are about to burst. Total leaf removal is done every 3–4 years to help reduce leaf size. Wire in the spring or early summer. Provide sun. Water well during the growing season and keep moist. Beautiful foliage especially in late summer. Needs well-drained soil. Lime tolerant.

Populus deltoides (Cottonwood)

Zones 2 to 3. Hardy on benches. Winter hardy. Remove canker-affected shoots, seal, and burn. Spray with bordeaux mixture or copper fungicide from August to October and at the following bud burst. Prune long shoots back to one-third. Do heavy pruning in the spring at repotting time when new buds are about to burst. Total leaf removal is done every 3–4 years to help reduce leaf size. Wire in the spring or early summer. Provide sun. Water well during growing season and keep moist. Needs well drained soil.

Populus tremuloides (Quaking aspen)

Zone 1. Hardy on benches. Very winter hardy. Remove canker-affected shoots, seal, and burn. Spray with bordeaux mixture or copper fungicide from August to October and at the following bud burst. Prune long shoots back to one-third. Remove suckers mid- and late season if not required in the design or for trunk thickening. Do heavy pruning in the spring at repotting time when new buds are about to burst. Total leaf removal is done every 3–4 years to help reduce leaf size. Wire in the spring or early summer. Provide sun. Water well during growing season and keep moist. Needs well drained soil.

Prunus genus

Needs cold winters below 45°F (7°C) to produce a successful burst but some need winter protection from extreme cold as detailed below. Prunus plants are affected by canker, rust, mildew, peach leaf curl, and silverleaf. Water during the growing season.

Prunus avium (Gean or Bird cherry)

Zone 4. Hardy on benches. Protect from frost and rain during flowering. Prunus plants are affected by canker, rust, mildew, peach leaf curl, and silverleaf. Trim back to one-third after flowering and remove untidy old wood. Do not prune in winter. Do heavy pruning in the spring at repotting time when new buds are about to burst; seal all wounds carefully to avoid fungal attack; mid- to late-season pruning is done during the second week of July. Total leaf removal is done every 2–3 years to reduce leaf size. Most shaping is by pruning. Wire in the spring after flowering. Remove fine, young branch wires before winter. Provide sun. Water moderately to well during the growing season and keep tree moist; this helps pevent attacks of rust. Feed well. Lovely autumn colors. Protect bonsai from finches by using netting from December onward; they can strip buds.

Prunus domestica (plum)

Hardy on benches. Keep soil a little drier over the winter but never dry out. Protect from frost and rain during flowering. Prunus plants are affected by canker, rust, mildew, peach leaf curl, and silverleaf. Trim back to one-third after flowering and remove untidy old wood. Do not prune in winter. Do heavy pruning in the spring at repotting time when new buds are about to burst; seal all wounds carefully to avoid fungal attack; mid- to late-season pruning is done during the second week of July. Total leaf removal is done every 2–3 years to reduce leaf size. Most shaping is by pruning. Wire in the spring after flowering. Remove fine, young branch wires before winter. Provide sun. Water moderately to well during the growing season and keep tree moist; this helps prevent attacks of rust. Feed well. Protect bonsai from finches by using netting from December onward; they can strip buds.

Prunus mume (Japanese apricot)

Zone 6. Protect from cold in a hoop tunnel or cold greenhouse. Keep soil a little drier over winter but never dry out. Protect from frost and rain during flowering. Prunus plants are affected by canker, rust, mildew, peach leaf curl, and silverleaf. Trim back to one-third after flowering and remove untidy old wood. Do not prune in the winter. Do heavy pruning in the spring at repotting time when new buds are about to burst; seal all wounds carefully to avoid fungal attack; mid- to late-season pruning is done during the second week of July. Most shaping is by pruning. Wire in spring after flowering. Protect bark. Remove fine, young branch wires before winter. Provide sun. Water moderately to well during the growing season and keep moist; this helps prevent attacks of rust. Feed well. Almond scented pink flowers. Protect bonsai from finches by using netting from December onward; they can strip buds.

Prunus cerasifera 'Pissardi' (Purple-leaf plum)

Zone 5. Protect when really cold. Protect from frost and rain during flowering. Prunus plants are affected by canker, rust, mildew, peach leaf curl, and silverleaf. Trim back to one-third after flowering and remove untidy old wood. Do not prune in the winter. Do heavy pruning in the spring at repotting time when new buds are about to burst; seal all wounds carefully to avoid fungal attack; mid- to late-season pruning is done during the second week of July. Most shaping is by pruning. Wire in the spring after flowering. Protect bark. Remove fine, young branch wires before winter. Provide sun. Water moderately to well during the growing season and keep moist; this helps prevent attacks of rust. Feed well. Lovely pink flowers on trees from five years old onward. Protect bonsai from finches by using netting from December onward; they can strip buds.

Prunus spinosa (Sloe)

Zone 5. Hardy on benches. Protect from frost and rain during flowering. Very pollution resistant species. Prunus plants are affected by canker, rust, mildew, peach leaf curl, and silverleaf. Trim back to one-third after flowering and remove untidy old wood. Do not prune in the winter. Do heavy pruning in the spring at repotting time when new buds are about to burst; seal all wounds carefully to avoid fungal attack; mid- to late-season pruning is done during the second week of July. Most shaping is by pruning. Wire in the spring after flowering. Provide sun. Water moderately to well during the growing season and keep moist; this helps prevent attacks of rust. Feed well. Protect bonsai from finches by using netting from December onward; they can strip buds.

Prunus triloba (Flowering almond)

Protect when really cold. Protect from frost and rain during flowering. Prunus plants are affected by canker, rust, mildew, peach leaf curl, and silverleaf. Trim back to one-third after flowering and remove untidy old wood. Do not prune in the winter. Do heavy pruning in the spring at repotting time when new buds are about to burst; seal all wounds carefully to avoid fungal attack; mid- to late-season pruning is done during the second week of July. Most shaping is by pruning. Wire in the spring after flowering. Protect bark. Remove fine, young branch wires before winter. Provide sun. Water moderately to well during the growing season and keep moist; this helps prevent attacks of rust. Feed well. Lovely double pink blooms in March. Protect bonsai from finches by using netting from December onward; they can strip buds. Try training as a weeping style.

Pseudotsuga menziesii (Oregon Douglas fir)

Zone 6. Protect when really cold. Prone to woolly aphis (adelgid) attack. Treat early (e.g., with liquid malathion; heavy-spray to wash off) and keep tree in good light to help reduce severity of attack. Prone to root rot and needle cast. Do heavy pruning in the spring at repotting time when new buds are about to burst. Never remove all leaves. Wire early in the summer. Provide sun and good light levels. Water normally during the growing season. Dislikes lime soil.

Pseudotsuga menziesii 'Glauca' (Blue Douglas/Rocky Mountain/Colorado Douglas fir)

Zone 5. Protect when really cold. Prone to woolly aphis (adelgid) attack. Treat early (e.g., with liquid malathion; heavy-spray to wash off) and keep tree in good light to help reduce severity of attack. Prone to root rot and needle cast. Do heavy pruning in the spring at repotting time when new buds are about to burst. Never remove all leaves. Wiring early in the summer. Provide sun and good light levels. Water normally during growing season. Dislikes lime soil.

Pterocarya fraxinifolia (Caucasian wing-nut)

Zone 6. Protect from cold in a hoop tunnel or cold greenhouse. Protect emerging shoots from air frost and cold winds to avoid burning new shoots. When repotting, avoid windburn or sun scorch during spring or early summer. Must have a deep pot. Shorten back to one-third as new shoots emerge. Remove suckers mid- and late season if not required for trunk thickening. Do heavy pruning in the spring at repotting time when new buds are about to burst. Total leaf removal is done every 2–3 years to reduce leaf size. Shoots tend to grow long and vertical and must be wired early in the first year before they lignify. Remove all wires before winter. Water well during the growing season. New shoots are prone to frost damage if not protected; tree does recover and reshoot if so affected.

Pyracantha 'Beauty of Bath'

Zones 6 to 9. Protect from cold in a hoop tunnel or cold greenhouse. Protect from frost and rain during flowering. Pollution tolerant. Prone to fireblight and scab. Scab can occur on pyracantha fruit; emerging leaves can be sprayed with copper fungicide; repeat sprays as required in the growing season. Remove sacrificial branches and any unwanted old wood but retain short shoots. Trim back to one-third selectively after flowering. Do heavy pruning in the spring at repotting time when new buds are about to burst. Never remove all leaves. Wire shoots while young; older shoots are too set to be wired. Wire in the late spring and early summer. Full sun. Water very well during the growing season. Feed well but stop during flowering until fruits are half size.

Pyracantha 'Beauty of Bath'

Quercus genus (Oak)

Remove all garden soil over several repots to discourage root rot. Oaks host many insects and are very prone to fungal attacks. Try to prevent mildew by avoiding still air, shade, and by not watering leaves. Remove all fungus-affected material back to healthy wood; seal and burn affected material. Water during the growing season.

Quercus cerris (Turkey oak)

Zone 6. Protect from cold in a hoop tunnel or cold greenhouse. Keep soil a little drier over winter but never dry out. Repot infrequently and remove no more than 20 percent of root. Oaks host many insects

and are very prone to fungal attacks. Try to prevent mildew by avoiding still air, shade, and by not watering leaves. Remove all fungus-affected material back to healthy wood; seal and burn affected material. Preseason, reduce shoots to one-third length. Do heavy pruning in the spring at repotting time before new buds are about to burst. Heavy root pruning must be well sealed; use pure grit beneath as oaks are prone to fungal attack. Total leaf removal is done every 2–3 years to reduce leaf size. Most shaping is by pruning. Wire early in the summer. Remove fine, young branch wires before winter. Provide full sun. Water normally during the growing season. Use low-nitrogen feeds. Avoid waterlogged soil. Loves lime soil.

Quercus coccinea (Scarlet oak)

Zone 5. Protect when really cold. Repot infrequently and remove no more than 20 percent of root. Oaks host many insects and are very prone to fungal attacks. Try to prevent mildew by avoiding still air, shade, and by not watering leaves. Remove all fungus-affected material back to healthy wood; seal and burn affected material. Do heavy pruning in the spring at repotting time before new buds are about to burst. Heavy root pruning must be well sealed; use pure grit beneath as oaks are prone to fungal attack. Total leaf removal is done every 2–3 years to reduce leaf size. Wire in the spring and early summer. Provide full sun. Water normally during growing season. Use low-nitrogen feeds. A very slow growing oak. Avoid waterlogged soil. Leaves are rather large but are lovely deep-autumn reds. Dislikes lime.

Quercus ilex (Holm oak)

Zones 7 to 8. Protect from cold in a hoop tunnel or cold greenhouse. Keep soil a little drier over the winter but never dry out. Repot infrequently and remove no more than 20 percent of root. Oaks host many insects and are very prone to fungal attacks. Try to prevent mildew by avoiding still air, shade, and by not watering leaves. Remove all fungus-affected material back to healthy wood; seal and burn affected material. Do heavy pruning in the spring at repotting time before new buds are about to burst. Heavy root pruning must be well sealed; use pure grit beneath as oaks are prone to fungal attack. Never remove all leaves. Most shaping is by pruning. Wire early in the summer. Remove fine, young branch wires before winter. Provide full sun. Water normally during the growing season. Use low-nitrogen feeds. Avoid waterlogged soil. Loves lime soil.

Quercus robur (Common oak)

Zones 5 to 6. Protect from cold in a hoop tunnel or cold greenhouse. Keep soil a little drier over the winter but never dry out. Repot infrequently and remove no more than 20 percent of root. Oaks host many insects and are very prone to fungal attacks. Try to prevent mildew by avoiding still air, shade, and by not watering leaves. Remove all fungus-affected material back to healthy wood; seal and burn affected material. Do heavy pruning in the spring at repotting time before new buds are about to burst. Heavy root pruning must be well sealed; use pure grit beneath as oaks are prone to fungal attack. Total leaf removal is done every 2–3 years to reduce leaf size. Wire in the spring and early summer. Provide full sun. Water normally during the growing season. Use low-nitrogen feeds. Avoid waterlogged soil. Loves lime soil.

Quercus rubra (Red oak)

Zone 5. Protect when really cold. Repot infrequently and remove no more than 20 percent of root. Prone to root rot. Oaks host many insects and are very prone to fungal attacks. Try to prevent mildew by avoiding still air, shade, and by not watering leaves. Remove all fungus-affected material back to healthy wood; seal and burn affected material. Preseason, prune away all long new shoots and reduce others to two leaves. Do heavy pruning in the spring at repotting before new buds are about to burst. Heavy root pruning must be well sealed; use pure grit beneath as oaks are prone to fungal attack. Total leaf removal is done every 1–2 years to reduce leaf size. Wire in the spring and early summer. Provide full sun. Water normally during the growing season. Use low-nitrogen feeds. A large tree. Avoid waterlogged soil. Leaves are rather large but lovely, fast trunk growth and autumn colors make this a challenge worth taking on.

Robinia pseudoacacia (False acacia)

Zone 4. Protect from cold in a hoop tunnel or cold greenhouse to avoid branch dieback. Tolerates pollution. Do heavy pruning in the spring at repotting time when new buds are about to burst. Brittle branches can only be wired when young. Remove all wires before winter. Provide sun. Needs good light levels to avoid branch dieback. Water normally during the growing season.

Salix genus (Willow)

Remove all garden soil over several repots to discourage root rot. Prone to scale insect attacks, treat with tar oil spray (e.g., liquid malathion) in January or during the growing season. Prone to aphid attack, mildew, and honey fungus. Water duing the growing season.

Salix alba (White willow)

Zone 3. Hardy on benches. Winter hardy. Loses vigor once root bound; use a deep pot. Prone to scale insect attacks, treat with tar oil spray (e.g., liquid malathion) in January or during the growing season. Prone to aphid attack, mildew, and honey fungus. Preseason, trim back untidy growth from the previous season. Leave most new shoots to grow, wiring in place and shortening some to add variety to the design. Do heavy pruning in the spring at repotting time when new buds are about to burst. Wire new growth in position through growing season. Provide partial shade. Water very well during the growing season.

Salix babylonica (Weeping willow)

Zone 6. Protect when really cold. Keep soil a little drier over the winter but never dry out. Repot before pot-bound as it loses vigor; use a deep pot. Prone to scale insect attacks, treat with tar oil spray (e.g., liquid malathion) in January or during the growing season. Prone to aphid attack, mildew, and honey fungus. Anthracnose disfigures and kills new S. babylonica leaves in wet springs after first showing as brown spots on the leaf surface. Burn affected leaves and shoots (which can become cankerous) and spray with copper fungicide as leaves emerge and occasionally through the season. Preseason, trim back untidy growth from the previous season. Leave most new shoots to grow, wiring in place and shortening some to add variety to the design. Do heavy pruning in the spring at repotting time when new buds are about to burst. Wire new growth into position through the growing season. Remove fine, young branch wires before winter. Partial shade. Water very well during the growing season.

Sambucus nigra (European elder)

Zone 6. Hardy on benches. Very winter hardy. Relatively insect free, spray aphids early. Prune back long shoots to an appropriate dormant bud just prior to bud burst annually. Remove any leggy new shoots. Prune as required during the season and remove unwanted suckers. Do heavy pruning in the spring at repotting time when new buds are about to burst. Total leaf removal is done every 2–3 years. Annually, remove basal suckers if not used to fatten trunk base. Wire through the growing season to lower and shape the typically straight, vertical new growth. Provide full sun. Water well during the growing season; keep soil moist during the growing season. Not an easy or common bonsai subject but by persistently wiring new straight shoots downward and removing excess new growth, a rewarding result is possible. Likes lime.

Sequoiadendron giganteum (Wellingtonia/Giant redwood)

Zone 7. Protect from cold in a hoop tunnel or cold greenhouse. Protect from cold spring winds. Fairly disease free but any branches attacked by a gray mold should be pruned off back to healthy wood, sealed, and affected material burned; then spray tree with mancozeb. Reduce new growth to one-third as growth occurs. Do heavy pruning in the spring at repotting time when new buds are about to burst. Never remove all leaves. Wire new shoots downward in typical pendulous style. Remove fine, young branch wires before winter. Provide partial shade. Water well during the growing season.

Sorbus genus

Prone to aphis, canker, mildew, and fireblight. Incinerate rust-affected shoots, prune back to healthy wood, and seal; then spray early with zineb or maneb or as per Chapter 2. Quarantine affected trees as some rusts are common to other bonsai species. Seal all wounds well mid- to late season. Water during the growing season.

Sorbus alnifolia (Whitebeam)

Zone 6. Protect when really cold. Pollution tolerant. Incinerate rust-affected shoots, prune back to healthy wood, and seal; then spray early with zineb or maneb or as per Chapter 2. Quarantine affected trees as some rusts are common to other bonsai species. Shorten new shoots to two leaves. Seal all wounds well mid- to late season. Do heavy pruning in the spring at repotting time when new buds are about to burst. Total leaf removal is done every 2–3 years. Annually, remove basal suckers if not used to fatten trunk base. Wire in the spring or early summer after flowering. Provide partial shade as tree can suffer from heat stress. Water sparingly to normal during the growing season but do not dry out. Water soil not leaves to avoid mildew. Avoid still air and shady places. Tolerates lime. Nice autumn colors.

Sorbus aucuparia (Rowan)

Zone 3. Hardy on benches. Winter hardy. Incinerate rust-affected shoots, prune back to healthy wood, and seal then spray early with zineb or maneb or as per Chapter 2. Quarantine affected trees as some rusts are common to other bonsai species. Shorten new shoots to two leaves. Seal all wounds well mid- to late season. Do heavy pruning in the spring at repotting time when new buds are about to burst. Total leaf removal is done every 2–3 years. Annually, remove basal suckers if not used to fatten trunk base. Wire in the spring or early summer after flowering. Provide sun. Water during the growing season. Water soil, not leaves, to avoid mildew. Avoid still air and shady places. Tolerates highly acid soils.

Sorbus hupehensis (Hupeh rowan)

Zone 6. Hardy on benches. Winter hardy. Pollution tolerant. Incinerate rust-affected shoots, prune back to healthy wood, and seal then spray early with zineb or maneb or as per Chapter 2. Quarantine affected trees as some rusts are common to other bonsai species. Shorten new shoots to two leaves. Seal all wounds well mid- to late season. Do heavy pruning in the spring at repotting time when new buds are about to burst. Total leaf removal is done every 2–3 years. Annually, remove basal suckers if not used to fatten trunk base. Wire in the spring or early summer after flowering. Provide sun. Water normally during the growing season. Drought tolerant. Water soil not leaves to avoid mildew. Avoid still air and shady places. Birds are not as attracted to *Hupehensis* berries as they are to most *Sorbus*.

Stewartia pseudocamellia and *Stewartia monodelpha* (Japanese Stewartia)

Zone 6. Protect from cold in a hoop tunnel or cold greenhouse. Keep soil a little drier over the winter but never dry out. Avoid really fine soil or old garden soil and add extra gravel drainage. When repotting, avoid windburn or sun scorch during spring or early summer. Dislikes repotting, hence, only repot if necessary. Vigorous fine root growth will demand repotting every 2–3 years. Trim shoot tips back to dormant buds in August but not in the spring. Shorten new shoots to two or three leaves every three or four years only. Prune April to August as required. Do heavy pruning in the spring at repotting time when new buds are about to burst. Total leaf removal is done every 2–3 years to reduce leaf size, in May or June. Wire through the growing season taking care not to damage bark. Remove fine, young branch wires before winter. Provide sun early and late in the growing season except for a few weeks after repotting. In the summer, provide sun with some shade only when young branches are wired or weather is very hot. Water copiously during the growing season using non-lime bearing water if possible. Apply sequestered iron in February/March. Keep soil moist. Feed more than normal late summer, use a low/no lime release fertilizer such as Miracid. A vigorous tree needing lime-free soil.

Tamarix juniperina (Tamarisk)

Zones 4 to 7. Protect from cold in a hoop tunnel or cold greenhouse. Prune back well in February before bud break. Leave most new shoots to grow, wiring in place and shortening some to add variety to the design. May be pruned at the end of the season in September. Do heavy pruning in the spring at repotting time when new buds are about to burst. Wire new shoots downward carefully in summer in typical weeping style. Remove fine, young branch wires before winter. Provide sun or partial shade. Water well during the growing season and keep moist. Feed less than normal. Dislikes lime.

Taxodium distichum (Swamp cypress/Bald cypress)

Zone 5. Protect when really cold. Protect fine branches in winter. Do heavy pruning in the spring at repotting time when new buds are about to burst. Wire early in the summer. Remove fine, young branch wires before winter. Provide sun or partial shade. Water very well during the growing season; keep moist, and use a deep pot.

Taxus baccata (Common yew)

Zone 6. Protect from cold in a hoop tunnel or cold greenhouse. Keep soil dryish in winter but avoid drying out. Protect from frost and rain during flowering. Use deep pots and repot before tree becomes pot-bound. Pollution resistant. Prune new shoots back to one-third. It is possible to encourage compact second growth in selective areas by removing a portion (20 percent maximum) of old leaves, leaving the narrow base of the leaf in place. Pluck in May as per Chapter 10. Do heavy pruning in the spring at repotting time when new buds are about to burst. Use a deep pot and well draining soil to avoid waterlogging. Never remove all leaves. Wire new young shoots but take care as base joint is very fragile. Wire may be left on over the winter. Provide sun or partial shade. Water

Taxus baccata (Common yew)

normally during the growing season; avoid waterlogging. Tree requires winter protection. Be careful about moving trees from a period of shade into full sun; this can kill the tree. Wide acid/alkaline soil tolerance but prefers alkaline soil.

Taxus cuspidata (Japanese yew)

Zones 4 to 5. Protect from cold in a hoop tunnel or cold greenhouse. Keep soil dryish in winter but avoid drying out. Protect from frost and rain during flowering. Use deep pots and repot before pot-bound. Yew scale insect strikes around mid-summer and must be treated early to avoid the honeydew stage. Jet spraying with liquid malathion at the white egg stage every two weeks is very effective. Few fungal diseases unless soil is waterlogged. Prune new shoots back to one-third. It is possible to encourage compact second growth in selective areas by removing a portion (20 percent maximum) of old leaves, leaving the narrow base of the leaf in place. Pluck in May as per Chapter 10. Do heavy pruning in the spring at repotting time when new buds are about to burst. Use a deep pot and well draining soil to avoid waterlogging. Never remove all leaves. Wire new young shoots late spring after flowering but take care as base joint is very fragile. Remove fine, young branch wires before winter. Provide sun or partial shade, but not full sun. Water normally during growing season; avoid waterlogging. Tree requires winter protection. Be careful about moving trees from a period of shade into full sun; this can kill the tree. Wide acid/alkaline soil tolerance.

Taxus cuspidata 'Media' (Hybrid of Japanese yew)

Zones 4 to 5. Protect from cold in a hoop tunnel or cold greenhouse. Keep soil dryish in winter but avoid drying out. Protect from frost and rain during flowering. Use deep pots and repot before pot-bound. Yew scale insect strikes around mid-summer and must be treated early to avoid the honeydew stage. Jet spraying with liquid malathion at the white egg stage every two weeks is very effective. Few fungal diseases unless soil is waterlogged. Prune new shoots back to one-third. It is possible to encourage compact second growth in selective areas by removing a portion (20 percent maximum) of old leaves, leaving the narrow base of the leaf in place. Pluck in May as per Chapter 10. Do heavy pruning in the spring at repotting time when new buds

are about to burst. Use a deep pot and well draining soil to avoid waterlogging. Never remove all leaves. Wire new young shoots late spring after flowering but take care as base joint is very fragile. Remove fine, young branch wires before winter. Provide sun or partial shade, but not full sun. Water normally during growing season; avoid waterlogging. Tree requires winter protection. Be careful about moving trees from a period of shade into full sun; this can kill the tree. Wide acid/alkaline soil tolerance.

Thuja plicata (Western red cedar)

Zones 6 to 7. Protect when really cold. Protect from drying spring winds. Red spider mite infestations are common in warm weather. Blight affected shoots (brown) must be removed back to healthy wood, sealed, and all infected material burned. Prune back new shoots to one-third. Do heavy pruning in the spring at repotting time when new buds are about to burst. Never remove all leaves. Wire early in the summer. Remove fine, young branch wires before winter. Provide sun. Water very well during growing season using non-lime bearing water. Apply sequestered iron in February/March. Keep soil moist. Feed sparingly. Use a low/no lime release fertilizer. Likes low-nitrogen feed. Prefers slightly acid, moist, lime free soil.

Tilia cordata (Small-leaf lime)

Zone 4. Hardy on benches. Avoid water on leaves as sun can then burn them. Repot before pot-bound. Pollution tolerant. Prone to leaf hopper infestations. Aphid attacks will produce the dreaded honeydew unless sprayed early. Prone to fungal attack. Remove long, straight, uninteresting first shoots and reduce others to two buds. Use mainly more compact second shoots. Do heavy pruning in the spring at repotting time when new buds are about to burst. Total leaf removal is done every 3–4 years. Wire new young shoots but take care as base joint is very fragile. Provide partial shade. Water very well during growing season and use a deep pot. Do not dry out. Medium- to high-nitrogen feed in spring and to mid-summer. Ideal leaf size and well suited to bonsai; should be grown more. Keep up moisture levels. Avoid drought or heat stress, which droops the leaves for the rest of the season.

Tilia cordata (Small-leaf lime)

Tilia europaea (Common lime/linden)

Zone 4. Hardy on benches. Avoid water on leaves as sun can then burn them. Repot before pot-bound. Pollution tolerant. Prone to leaf hopper infestations. Aphid attacks will produce the dreaded honeydew unless sprayed early. Remove long, straight, uninteresting first shoots and reduce others to two buds. Use mainly more compact second shoots. Do heavy pruning in the spring at repotting time when new buds are about to burst. Total leaf removal is done every 3–4 years. Wire new young shoots but take care as base joint is very fragile. Provide partial shade. Water very well during growing season and use a deep pot. Do not dry out. Medium to high-nitrogen feed in spring and to mid-summer. Keep up moisture levels. Avoid drought or heat stress, which droops the leaves for the rest of the season.

Tsuga canadensis (Eastern hemlock)

Zone 5. Protect when really cold. Very disease resistant. Prune back new shoots to one-third. Do heavy pruning in the spring at repotting time when new buds are about to burst. Never remove all leaves. Wire new shoots in the spring. Provide partial shade. Water sparingly during the growing season. Lime tolerant. Remove galls and burn; they are caused by mite infection but are not harmful.

Tsuga heterophylla (Western hemlock)

Zone 6. Protect from cold in a hoop tunnel or cold greenhouse. Very disease resistant. Prune back new shoots to one-third. Do heavy pruning in the spring at repotting time when new buds are about to burst. Never remove all leaves. Wire new shoots in the spring. Remove fine, young branch wires before winter. Provide partial shade. Water sparingly during the growing season. Dislikes lime.

Ulmus elegantissima 'Jacqueline Hillier' (Jacqueline Hillier elm)

Protect when really cold. Fairly winter hardy. Repot before pot-bound. Aphid and mite attacks should be treated early. Thin out new growth which is rather dense. Prune as required through the season. Remove suckers as they occur. Do heavy pruning in the spring at repotting time when new buds are about to burst. Total leaf removal is done every 2–3 years to reduce leaf size. Wire young shoots into shape; they become rigid in later life. Provide sun. Water very well during the growing season. Remove and burn any galls. Rapid trunk and branch growth plus small leaves make this a good subject.

Ulmus glabra (Wych elm)

Zone 5. Hardy on benches. Hardiest of all the elms. Pollution resistant. Aphid and mite attacks should be treated early. Prune back new shoots to one-third. Not prone to suckers. Do heavy pruning in the spring at repotting time when new buds are about to burst. Total leaf removal is done every 2–3 years to reduce leaf size of this large leaved elm. Wire young shoots into shape early in the season. Provide sun. Water very well during the growing season. Remove and burn any galls.

Ulmus procera (English elm)

Zones 5 to 6. Protect when really cold. Fairly winter hardy. Dislikes pollution. Aphid and mite attacks should be treated early. Prune back new shoots to one-third. Prone to suckers, which should be removed unless required for trunk thickening. Do heavy pruning in the spring at repotting time when new buds are about to burst. Total leaf removal is done every 2–3 years to reduce leaf size markedly. Wire young shoots into shape early in the season. Provide sun. Water very well during the growing season. Remove and burn any galls. Very suitable for bonsai; it has smallish leaves and lovely bark.

Ulmus parvifolia (Chinese elm)

Zones 5 to 6. Protect from cold in a hoop tunnel or cold greenhouse. Keep soil a little drier over winter but never dry out. Avoid really fine soil or old garden soil and add extra gravel drainage. Wean from shade to avoid sun scorch. When repotting, avoid windburn or sun scorch during spring or early summer. Remove all garden soil over several repots to discourage root rot. Aphid and mite attacks should be treated early. Remove and burn any galls. Prune back long shoots to an appropriate dormant bud just prior to bud burst annually. Prune back long new shoots to two or three leaves during the growing season. Do heavy pruning in the spring at repotting time when new buds are about to burst. Wire young shoots into shape early in the season. Provide sun or partial shade if hot. Water normally, keep moist during the growing season. Lovely bonsai material having rough, deeply fissured bark on some varieties, fine twigs, and very small leaves. Keep spring light levels high to avoid long (etiolated) new shoots which grow like watercress. If they appear, they can be totally removed.

Viburnum opulus (Guelder rose)

Zone 4. Hardy on benches. Wean from shade to sun to avoid leaf scorch in spring and early summer. When repotting, avoid sun scorch during spring or early summer; repot before pot-bound. Aphid attacks including blackfly should be treated early. Treat crown gall by removing affected shoots; seal wounds, then burn infected materials. Spray with copper fungicide. Prune back long shoots to an appropriate dormant bud just prior to bud burst annually. Most long first

Ulmus parvifolia (Chinese elm)

Viburnum opulus (Guelder rose)

shoots need removing mid-May, or wiring if they grow straight and upright. Remove suckers unless used for trunk thickening. Do heavy pruning in the spring at repotting time when new buds are about to burst. Total leaf removal is done every 2–3 years to reduce leaf size and improve autumn color; complete before mid-May. Wire through the growing season after flowering to lower and shape the typically straight, vertical new growth. Provide sun but partial shade in hot spells. Water well during the growing season; do not let the soil dry out as it loves moist soil. Has lovely summer and autumn leaf color, fully hardy and deserves to be grown more. Excellent bonsai subject.

Wisteria floribunda 'Macrobotrys' (Japanese wisteria)

Zones 5 to 9. Protect from cold in a hoop tunnel or cold greenhouse. Keep soil dryish over winter but do not dry out. Protect from air frost and rain during flowering. Wean from shade to sun to avoid sun scorch. When repotting, avoid windburn or sun scorch during spring or early summer. Magnesium and/or manganese deficiencies are indicated by yellowing of leaflets between veins normally induced by acid soil. Correct soil and feeding regime. Flowers on old short shoots; remove remainder of sacrificial branches in February or early March. Prune new shoots back to two or three leaves immediately after flowering and retain some long sacrificial shoots. Mid- and late-season pruning of sacrificial branches grown through the summer aids production of other shorter shoots. Reduce sacrificial shoots back by one-third in late summer. Do heavy pruning in the spring at repotting time when new buds are about to burst. New and old shoots and swelling buds are very brittle, so take great care to wire new shoots during early summer. Remove all wires before winter. Provide sun. Water very well during growing season. Never drought. Feed well after flowering in the growing season with low-nitrogen feed every 7 to 10 days. Root-bound plants flower better.

Wisteria floribunda 'Premature' (Japanese wisteria)

Zones 5 to 9. Protect from cold in a hoop tunnel or cold greenhouse. Keep soil dryish over winter but do not dry out. Protect from air frost and rain during flowering. Wean from shade to sun to avoid sun

Wisteria floribunda 'Macrobotrys' (Japanese wisteria)

scorch. When repotting, avoid windburn or sun scorch during spring or early summer. Magnesium and/or manganese deficiencies are indicated by yellowing of leaflets between veins normally induced by acid soil. Correct soil and feeding regime. Flowers on old short shoots; remove remainder of sacrificial branches in February or early March. Prune new shoots back to two or three leaves immediately after flowering and retain some long sacrificial shoots. Mid- and late-season pruning of sacrificial branches grown through the summer aids production of other shorter shoots. Reduce sacrificial shoots back by one-third in late summer. Do heavy pruning in the spring at repotting time when new buds are about to burst. New and old shoots and swelling buds are very brittle, so take great care to wire new shoots during early summer. Remove all wires before winter. Provide sun. Water very well during growing season. Never dry out. Feed well after flowering in summer with low-nitrogen feed. Root-bound plants flower better.

Wisteria sinensis (Chinese wisteria)

Zones 5 to 9. Protect from cold in a hoop tunnel or cold greenhouse. Keep soil dryish over winter but do not dry out. Protect from air frost and rain during flowering. Wean from shade to sun to avoid sun scorch. When repotting, avoid windburn or sun scorch during spring or early summer. Magnesium and/or Manganese deficiencies are indicated by yellowing of leaflets between veins normally induced by acid soil. Correct soil and feeding regime. Flowers on old short shoots; remove remainder of sacrificial branches in February or early March. Prune new shoots back to two or three leaves immediately after flowering and retain some long sacrificial shoots. Mid- and late-season pruning of sacrificial branches grown through the summer aids production of other shorter shoots. Reduce sacrificial shoots back by one-third late in the summer. Do heavy pruning in the spring at repotting time when new buds are about to burst. New and old shoots and swelling buds are very brittle, so take great care to wire new shoots during early summer. Remove all wires before winter. Provide sun. Water very well during the growing season. Never dry out. Feed well after flowering in the summer with low-nitrogen feed. Root-bound plants flower better.

Zelkova serrata (Japanese gray bark elm)

Zones 5 to 6. Protect from cold in a hoop tunnel or cold greenhouse. Wean from shade to sun to avoid leaf scorch in spring and early summer. Avoid water on leaves as sun can burn them. When repotting, avoid windburn or sun scorch during the spring or early summer. Repot before pot-bound. Prone to red spider mite and aphids. Prune back long shoots to an appropriate dormant bud just prior to bud burst annually. Prune new shoots back to two or three leaves. Remove suckers at the base of branches to avoid weakening branches. Do heavy pruning in the spring at repotting time when new buds are about to burst. Total leaf removal is done every 2–3 years to reduce leaf size. Wire new shoots into position, prune remaining unwanted shoots. Wire spring and early summer; bark is delicate. Remove fine, young branch wires before winter. Provide summer shade, especially when young branches are wired. Water well during the growing season. Keep soil moist and avoid drying out, otherwise leaves will droop for the remainder of the summer. Feed well using a low-nitrogen feed. Winter-protect and keep spring light levels high to avoid etiolated new shoots. Wean carefully from shade to sun to avoid new leaf scorch. One session of heat stress or drought causes leaf droop all that season. Needs regular repotting.

Zelkova serrata (Japanese gray bark elm)

Appendix 2

Table of Soil Mixes

Base #1

7 parts sterilized loam

3 parts peat

2 parts sand or grit

Fertilizer: 4 ounces in 8 gallons (3 grams in 1 liter)

Lime or chalk: ¾ ounce in 8 gallons (0.5 grams in 1 liter)

Base #2

This is the same as Base #1, but you will double the fertilizer and the chalk.

Base #3

This is the same as Base #1, but you will triple the fertilizer and the chalk.

Seed compost

The fresher the sterilization, the better the germination.

2 parts sterilized loam

1 part moss peat

1 part sharp sand

Put the loam and peat through a ⅜ inch (9 mm) sieve.

To each bushel or 8 gallons (36 liter), add

1–2 ounce (42 gram) superphosphate

½ ounce potassium nitrate

4–6 ounces (21 gram) ground limestone

Ericaceous Mix

Use the base but leave out the lime.

Soilless

3 parts peat

1 part sand

Potting Compost

7 parts sterilized loam

3 parts moss peat

2 parts sharp sand

Put the loam and the peat through a ⅜ inch (9 mm) sieve.

To each bushel or 8 gallons (36 liter), add:

¾ ounce (21 gram) ground limestone

4 ounces (110 gram) 14:14:14: Osmocote

Japanese and European larch in a group.

Index

Note: Page numbers in *italics* indicate references to Appendix 1 or 2.